CW01395421

LFC
STORIES

LFC
STORIES

DAN KAY

Reach Sport
www.reachsport.com

Reach Sport

www.reachsport.com

1

Published in Great Britain and Ireland in 2025 by Reach Sport.

www.reachsport.com
@Reach_Sport

Reach Sport is a part of Reach PLC.

Hardback ISBN: 9781916811331
eBook ISBN: 9781916811324

Photographic acknowledgements:
Alamy, Reach Plc.

Cover Design: Chris Collins
Editing and production: Roy Gilfoyle, Sam Carroll

Every effort has been made to trace copyright.
Any oversight will be rectified in future editions.

Printed and bound by CPI Group (UK) Ltd,
Croydon, CR0 4YY.

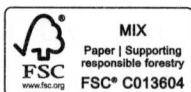

MIX
Paper | Supporting
responsible forestry
FSC
www.fsc.org   FSC® C013604

CONTENTS

FOREWORD

By Sir Kenny Dalglish

WHEN Liverpool supporters stood together to applaud the life of Dan Kay during the seventh minute of the match against Aston Villa in 2023, it showed just how much Dan meant to them.

I'm told that after his tragic passing, Dan's family, friends and colleagues were inundated with messages about Dan and, in particular, his prolific volunteering. He would deliver food hampers to those less fortunate, feed the homeless on Christmas Day, and donate his time to charities around Liverpool. Those closest to Dan have channelled their grief into The Dan Kay Foundation.

But it was Dan's dedication to the Hillsborough families, to support their fight for justice, where he will be most fondly remembered, as he used his platform as a journalist to show how much he cared. Like everyone connected to Liverpool Football Club and Hillsborough, the families come first and Dan had the families in mind at every turn. I am aware of the formidable impact Dan had on the long fight for justice.

Hillsborough left an indelible mark on both Liverpool

Football Club and the city as a whole. I will never be able to imagine or comprehend what the families of the 97 have been through. Thanks to Dan, each family was given a voice in the media.

As Anfield stood to applaud Dan's life, I was told the seventh minute was chosen in honour of the shirt number I wore during my playing days, and that I was Dan's first Liverpool hero. The truth is, Dan Kay will always be remembered as a hero in his own right by so many.

You'll Never Walk Alone,
Kenny

INTRODUCTION

DAN Kay was a celebrated Liverpool ECHO journalist for more than two decades, joining the newsroom in 2003 and working across news, sport and digital teams.

Dan was central to the wide-ranging coverage relating to the campaign for justice of the 1989 Hillsborough tragedy, leading to the inquests where a jury determined the 97 innocent men, women and children who lost their lives were unlawfully killed.

In his personal life, Dan was a passionate Liverpool supporter, travelling the globe to follow his beloved Reds. During his final years at the ECHO, he penned thoroughly captivating player profiles of some of the biggest characters in Liverpool Football Club history.

This book is a loving collection of those profiles, capturing the good, the bad, the ugly and the legendary – as well as the inside story of The Transfer That Never Was, featuring Steven Gerrard, Jose Mourinho and John Terry!

The book also contains a poignant tribute to those who passed away at Hillsborough, written the same week Liverpool lifted their first ever Premier League title in 2020.

Dan was passionate about helping others, collaborating

with numerous charities across the North West, including youth centres, foodbanks and mental health initiatives. Each Christmas, Dan would deliver hampers to vulnerable families, before volunteering at homeless shelters and soup kitchens on Christmas Day.

After his tragic passing, Dan's family, friends and Liverpool ECHO colleagues set-up The Dan Kay Foundation in 2024 to continue his incredible legacy of helping others. A portion of proceeds from this collection will be donated to The Dan Kay Foundation.

CRAIG JOHNSTON

The Adidas Inventor

First published: June 2021

"YOU are the worst player I've ever seen in my whole life. Now f*** off."

The game of football is, of course, littered with tales of players who overcame setbacks and challenges before going on to enjoy successful careers despite doubts over size, mental resilience and ability having been levelled against them.

But when such a scathing assessment is delivered to a 15-year-old who has travelled halfway across the world to pursue his dream, and by a football legend and World Cup winner no less, it's clear that serious strength of character will be required to bounce back from it.

Liverpool over the years have been blessed to have numerous players who have demonstrated that in spades, as well as plenty who have displayed above-average intelligence, both on and off the field, but not too many have had as much of both as Craig Johnston.

We've become used to seeing a plethora of players from overseas in the modern game but, while Anfield has been home to the occasional foreign player since the 1930s when South Africans Berry 'Nivvy' Nieuwenhuys and Arthur Riley plied their trade in front of the Kop, they were very much a minority during the 1970s and 80s and in some circles treated with a certain degree of suspicion.

That would certainly go some way to explaining the task facing the South Africa-born Australian, who would go on to be affectionately nicknamed 'Skippy' by the Anfield faithful – after a beloved kangaroo who starred on television – when he first arrived in the industrial wastelands of Middlesbrough from Newcastle, New South Wales, in 1975.

The fact a teenage Johnston was even able to consider a career in 'soccer' is further testament to his capacity to overcome adversity.

Keen to follow in the footsteps of his father, Colin, who also loved and played soccer having had trials in the UK for Preston North End and Dundee United, young Craig faced the horrific possibility of losing a leg when he was only a child.

As a result of sustaining an injury during a fight, Johnston developed a form of polio – osteomyelitis – which rotted the bone and at the time was thought to be incurable. Doctors thought they would have to amputate and his mum even signed the consent form agreeing to it before a specialist visiting from America managed to save the limb.

Years later, having seen a touring Middlesbrough side beat his local team, he displayed the initiative he would become famed for and wrote to the Teesside club asking for a trial.

Despite receiving only a lukewarm reply informing him he would have to pay for his own travel and accommodation, his family downsized their home to raise the funds and a 15-year-old Johnston travelled 10,000 miles across the world to pursue his dream of making it in English football.

"The day before, I was on Nobby's Beach back home, which is a beautiful sandy beach with aqua blue water and palm trees.

"Forty-eight hours later, I'm on Hutton Road in Middlesbrough. It was December, it was snowing and it was muddy."

Plunged straight into his trial match which was attended by the then-Middlesbrough manager Jack Charlton, the teenager received a rude awakening as to the hard road facing him if his ambitions were to be fulfilled.

With Boro three goals down at half-time, the England 1966 World Cup hero marched into the dressing room and began laying into his players. Upon reaching Johnston, he asked where the youngster hailed from and when he was told – with the traditional 'mate' added on for good measure – Charlton's infamous temper exploded with the withering assessment of the young Australian's abilities and the big Geordie's suggested course of action being mercilessly delivered, leaving the youngster in tears.

Unable to face playing the second half, Johnston grabbed his bag and headed to where he was told the trialists' digs would be, only to find his nightmare first day in English football was about to get worse.

"There was a lady called Nina Postgate who ran it," Johnston recalled. "In my tears, I explained to Nina that I'd been told to hop it.

"She said: 'I'm sorry, you can't stay here. This is the official digs for the trialists and people who make it. I might lose my job'."

Taking pity on the crestfallen teenager, she made him beans on toast and a cup of tea, and having considered his predicament offered Johnston some alternative, if not overly appealing, accommodation.

"There's an old coal shed out the back but it's been cleaned out," she said. "It's got a radiator and you can stay there overnight but don't say anything."

Johnston's pride and self-belief meant he could and would not let himself throw the towel in but he knew, however harsh the manager's assessment had been, it was not without some truth, years later admitting: "The truth of my story was that Jack Charlton was 100% right. I couldn't control the ball, I couldn't pass, I couldn't shoot. I just couldn't play.

"I had that realisation in the next couple of days and I was fortunate that Nina was hiding me from everybody. She gave me valuable time to think about how I was going to solve the problem.

"I ended up staying for at least two or three weeks in the coal shed. Maybe it was a month. My parents weren't very wealthy and it was a one-way trip. So I couldn't go home either."

Johnston figured the only way he could prove Charlton wrong was to work on and improve his ability and that is what he set about doing, devising a series of drills to improve his basic skills based on four of the main tenets of the game: control, pass, dribble and shoot, which would decades later become a cornerstone of a soccer skills programme he designed to roll out to youngsters across the world.

Hour after hour over a period of months, Johnston trained on his own in the Middlesbrough car park, dribbling in and out of a line of rubbish cans to slowly but surely hone his abilities.

Little by little Johnston built up a skill base to go alongside his relentless energy and enthusiasm and, after returning to

Australia briefly to play for Sydney City, demonstrated enough to Middlesbrough to earn a contract in 1977 shortly after Jack Charlton left the club, and he made his first-team debut in the January of the following year in a 3-2 FA Cup win at Everton shortly after his 17th birthday.

He gradually established himself in the Boro first team and showed he was capable of performing in the top flight, scoring 16 goals in 64 games over the following three seasons, which persuaded Bob Paisley to pay £650,000 to bring Johnston to Anfield in April 1981.

He received a warmer initial welcome on Merseyside than he did on Teesside, with no less a figure than Kenny Dalglish making a point of picking him up outside his hotel on only his second day in the city and taking him house hunting. However, a lingering knee injury and the attractions of a big city like Liverpool meant Johnston's dream move was in danger of being cut short before it really got started.

He recalled in his autobiography 'Walk On': "Later, when I had really paid my dues at Liverpool, I perceived how critical it was for new players to adopt a low profile when entering the Anfield portals.

"Being a brash young man, I wasn't astute enough to understand that people were trying to help and guide me.

"The situation would have been better if I'd been fully fit. In fact, I had a serious knee injury. After a few games in the reserves I reported the problem to Bob Paisley and it would only be a matter of time before it went altogether. It was another legacy of the car park wear and tear. The outcome was that I wouldn't play again for the rest of the season.

"The boss had always prided himself on being able to pick an injury a mile away. And he must have been furious with himself – and especially me – when it was revealed that

Liverpool had paid a fortune for a player carrying a serious knee problem.

"No doubt, he had been made abundantly aware that his expensive and injured signing was carving out a bigger reputation on the party and night club circuit than on the training field. At Anfield they miss very little.

"In his grandfatherly fashion, the boss called me into his office for a long overdue chat. He said that now the management had had a chance to see me at close quarters, they were of the opinion that the deal hadn't worked as sweetly as they would have wished. Manchester United were about to sign Bryan Robson from West Brom and the Midlands club was eager to part with some of the proceeds to secure a suitable midfield replacement.

"Liverpool, said Bob Paisley, would agree to let me go. I was rocked to the soles of my feet. Could they be serious? Would they really show me the door before I'd had a whiff of first-team action?"

It was Graeme Souness who soothed the troubled waters in Johnston's mind and helped set him on the right track again when the Aussie sought his advice.

"I wouldn't be surprised if it's a shock tactic," the Scot – who would soon take over the Liverpool captaincy from Phil Thompson – told the worried young Aussie.

"They either want you to knuckle down and get on with the job, or p*** off."

It was all Johnston needed to know.

He said: "The injury meant there was nothing I could do about my playing form, but I could do something about the party circuit. I knocked it on the head.

"In that introductory period at Liverpool I stayed out too late, had too many drinks and believed too many people when they told me what a good bloke they thought I was. What I should have been doing was putting my head down and preparing for the day when Liverpool would want some return on their £650,000."

Having worked hard to get himself fit for the start of the 1981/82 season, Johnston was handed the number 12 shirt (back in the days when there was only one substitute) for the Reds' opening match at Wolves but still had to bide his time for a further few months and make do with fleeting appearances off the bench.

A crucial extra-time goal which broke the deadlock, however, in a League Cup fourth-round replay at home to Arsenal in December convinced Paisley his young Antipodean signing was finally ready for first-team action and later that week he was handed his first Liverpool start in the exotic surroundings of Tokyo's national stadium as the European champions took on Brazilian side Flamengo in the club's first attempt to win the World Club Championship.

This was very much a Liverpool side in transition with a Boxing Day home defeat by Manchester City – Johnston's first Anfield start – leaving the Reds an unheard-of 12th in the First Division table and some media pundits speculating the era of Anfield dominance was at an end.

They had not reckoned with young talents like Ian Rush, Ronnie Whelan, Bruce Grobbelaar and Mark Lawrenson growing into Paisley's side and by March, Johnston had become a key part of the team which was coming up on the rails to close in on yet another – but far more unexpected – league title.

The Aussie bagged his first league goal for the club in a 3-1 Merseyside derby win at Goodison Park and followed it up barely a week later with the only goal in a win over Manchester United at Old Trafford, adding further important strikes against Manchester City and Stoke along with a brace against Nottingham Forest.

He was back on the bench by the time Liverpool clinched the club's 12th championship by fighting back from a goal down at half-time to beat FA Cup holders Tottenham at Anfield on the final Saturday of the league season, but had now proved that he belonged in such exalted company.

After scoring seven times in 23 appearances in his breakthrough season, Johnston struck ten times in 46 games the following campaign as Paisley's side cruised to another championship during the canny north-easterner's final season at the Anfield helm, with the departing boss making it clear it was Johnston's attitude as much as his ability which enabled him to make his mark at the club.

"He is a highly committed young man, and his commitment to the club is obvious in his play," Paisley said.

"You would think he had grown up on the Kop judging by the effort and eagerness that spills out of him every Saturday afternoon.

"He is a fellow who prides himself on his level of fitness. I think he tells himself that he wouldn't be where he is in the game today unless he had such energy, and motivates himself by that thought.

"His other great asset as a forward is that he's a bit of an individualist. I used to say to him, 'I'm sure your parents kept you locked in your own back yard at home when you were a boy'. He played the game as if he had never been in a team with other players, as if he was only used to chasing the ball around on his own. When we bought him from Middlesbrough in 1981, it was his team work that was in need of improvement.

"Football tends to reflect national traits. Craig may be a man of many nations, but first and foremost he is an Australian. The Aussies don't lack self-confidence as a rule, and Craig is no exception to that rule. But neither do they hold back when somebody offers them an opportunity to get on in life. Our Anfield Aussie has had a crack at just about everything. He's an avid photographer, he takes guitar lessons, he's learning an extra language, he's written a song and directed a video to go with it; I'm half expecting him to come into training one morning and tell me he's just come back from the moon!"

Life at Anfield would get harder for Johnston under Paisley's successor in the manager's office, Joe Fagan, but not initially, with the Aussie playing 52 matches in all competitions as Liverpool won the club's first Treble in 1984, with the third league title and League Cup in successive years being augmented with a fourth European Cup in seven years.

The confidence provided by the Reds' outstanding performances away from home in that year's competition proved vital when their opponents in the Rome final turned out to be none other than Italian champions AS Roma. Before the game, Johnston was among those Liverpool players who stunned their opponents by showing how relaxed they were in the tunnel by belting out the song which had been the soundtrack of their run to the final and demonstrating they were in no mood to be intimidated by their surroundings.

"Having been in Middlesbrough I knew about Chris Rea," he said years later in Tony Evans's book, 'I Don't What It Is But I Love It', which was named after the track in question.

"It had become one of the team's anthems; one of us would sing a verse and the rest would come in on the chorus clapping and chanting. As we're going down the tunnel, David Hodgson broke into a solo version of the verse. One or two joined in and by the time we were outside the Roma dressing room every one of us was singing."

The arrival of John Wark in March 1984 had put Johnston's future at Anfield in doubt, however. The Scot had been ineligible for the European Cup so the Aussie kept his place in the side in the run-up to Rome, but the following campaign, which became one of comparative struggle at Anfield following the departure of Graeme Souness to Sampdoria, saw Wark regularly preferred with Johnston making only 17 appearances in all competitions.

The disgruntled Aussie expressed his frustration at the situation through the media which led to an escalating feud with the manager and the player considering a future away from Anfield – but the appointment of Kenny Dalglish as player-manager in the summer of 1985 improved Johnston's fortunes.

The Scot recognised Johnston's single-minded desire to succeed – he even had a key cut for Liverpool's training ground at Melwood so he could 'break in' and do extra training – could become all-consuming at times and realised even at this formative stage of his own managerial career that psychological support was just as important as technical and tactical help.

"Craig was his own worst enemy," Dalglish said.

"He just didn't believe in his footballing abilities, and I could see that, when his form deserted him, Craig became depressed and the dark cycle continued. Several times during the season I had to beat away this black dog of depression chasing Craig."

It paid off for the new Reds boss in spades. Johnston was part of all but two of the 63 matches Liverpool played in all competitions as the club became only the third team that century to win the hallowed League and FA Cup Double, reaching double figures again by notching ten times with his final strike of the campaign without question being the most important.

Having won at Chelsea on the final Saturday of the league season to take the title back across Stanley Park, a week later at Wembley Liverpool were a goal behind to Howard Kendall's Everton at half-time in the first all-Merseyside FA Cup final, with their Double dreams hanging by a thread.

But after Ian Rush equalised 12 minutes into the second half (with Johnston sliding in to make sure and only just failing to get a touch before it crossed the line), the Australian was in the right place at the right time six minutes later to convert Jan Molby's cross at the far post to put Liverpool in front. It was the crowning glory of his career and vindication for all those years of self-doubt and hard work.

"At half-time I'd barely had a kick and I feared the biggest game of my life was passing me by," Johnston recalled.

"Then halfway through the second half this ball just popped up magically, the goalkeeper just off his line, just at the edge of the six yard box, and I thought, 'look, it can't be that easy just to connect my foot with the ball', and it was like that slow motion sweet spot that everybody talks about when your life stands still for a moment.

"Then the colour, the light, the noise, the rush, just came over me and everybody started jumping all over me and I just kept saying, 'I've done it! I've done it! I've done it!' and Ian Rush, Ronnie Whelan and those guys were saying, 'alright, alright, you've scored, you've scored'.

"But I didn't mean 'I've done it, I've scored', it meant 'I've done it, I'd got through the polio and hospitalisation, I'd took my parents' sacrifice and come from Australia, fought the odds and made it work, I'd took Jack Charlton's dismissal on the chin and figured out how to get out of the coal shed'.

"I got to be in the best team in the world on that Saturday afternoon. I could've honestly died on that spot that afternoon and I'd have died a happy man."

Having become a father earlier in cup final week, 1986 should have been the happiest year of Johnston's life but it was to end in a tragedy which would have far-reaching consequences for his football career.

That December, his younger sister Faye became critically ill following a gas leak caused by a faulty heater in a hotel room she was staying in while on holiday in Morocco, which left her in a coma and permanently brain-damaged.

Johnston was at Liverpool's Christmas party when he heard the devastating news and immediately flew to Morocco to be by his sister's side and arranged for her to be initially brought back to England and cared for in London.

The situation was kept out of the public domain with only Dalglish being aware Johnston was spending hours travelling up and down the country to see his sister, who it was becoming clear would need lifelong care.

He still managed to perform for Liverpool, making 37 appearances in 1986/87 and 35 the following campaign as he played his part in another memorable league title win, but Johnston had already made the typically-selfless decision to retire from football at the end of that season and return to Australia to help his family care for Faye.

A tabloid newspaper broke an agreement and ran the story of his shock retirement on the morning of his final Liverpool match, the 1988 FA Cup final against Wimbledon, much to Johnston's distress.

"Nobody really knew about the situation but somebody got a sniff of it and said they wanted to do a story.

"I trusted this journalist, and I said, 'well on the absolute strict prerequisite that the story is done after the cup final'. We shook on it, we did a deal and I did the story.

"Then the night before the cup final, the editor of the paper phoned me and said, 'we're running the story', and I said, 'you can't run the story; you've made a promise'. He said, 'the story's too big, we're running with it'.

"I had to then phone Kenny and say 'here's what's happened' and it was really, really unfortunate but I got totally turned over and the journalist himself has never forgiven himself for taking the story but it was because of the decision of the paper.

"It was one of those things that was not consciously done because the thing about Liverpool was team spirit and teamwork and respect for your mates, the club and the manager. I would never have done that knowing what an unscrupulous editor of a paper would do."

Johnston's innate humanity came shining through again less than 12 months later when 96 Liverpool supporters were unlawfully killed at Hillsborough. He immediately flew back to Merseyside to attend the memorial service and stayed for a number of weeks to both support survivors in hospital and help counsel the bereaved families, before returning home to Australia and raising tens of thousands of pounds for the disaster fund with the Liverpool Supporters Club in Sydney.

He recalled: "I was up at Palm Beach in 1989 surfing on a Malibu board that was decorated in Liverpool's colours when someone called me back to the shore and told me something awful had happened.

"I had to get the next plane I could back to England. There was this surreal scene at Anfield. The players' lounge, previously such a sacrosanct place, had been turned into a bereavement centre for the victims and their families to talk to (then

Liverpool manager) Kenny Dalglish, players, clergymen, counsellors, whoever.

"Then I went to the hospital in Sheffield, where lots of the victims remained in a coma from being crushed and losing oxygen: exactly what my sister had gone through three years before, where the brain is starved of oxygen.

"I knew the process of sitting by Faye's bed, talking to her to try to lift her from the coma.

"I used to bring her baby daughter in and pinch her so Faye could hear the sound of her girl crying. So with the Hillsborough victims, I tried to find out their favourite player and have a tape made up by that player to play on the ward.

"I was trying to help where I could in the background. You can play for that club for nine years as I did but have no idea what it really means to people.

"After a few weeks I felt like I'd done what I could, so I went in to see Kenny Dalglish. He reached into his drawer and told me that in all the rush to leave the year before, I'd left behind my league championship winners' medal.

"All my other memorabilia I'd already asked my wife to give to the Liverpool Supporters Club in Sydney, who auctioned it. They made around $100,000 for the Hillsborough appeal.

"There was one guy who bought that surfboard I'd been on when I heard the news and he sent it to Liverpool, where it's now on the roof of the trophy room. Those fans in Sydney subsequently had a surfboard made for me themselves.

"I still think about it, so I know the pain will still be with the victims and their families."

Dalglish reportedly offered Johnston a new deal in 1989 and he continued to receive offers to resume his football career but he'd made it clear Liverpool (or "Liverpool reserves!", he said) was the only team he could ever play for again and his horizons had already broadened into different and innovative career paths, the most famous of which saw him design the world's best-selling football boot.

The idea came about while he was pursuing one of his other passions, coaching football to youngsters, which would later become a less-successful business venture.

"I'd had the idea while coaching kids in Australia when I was trying to teach them how to bend the ball by really feeling it," he said.

"It was pouring with rain and one of the kids said, 'I can't feel the ball, my boots are made of leather not table tennis bats.' It was a funny thing to say, but something went ping in my head. I went home, ripped the front off a table tennis bat, attached it by rubber band to my boots and it worked.

"I spent a lot of time and a lot of money patenting and experimenting. I took my prototypes to Nike, Reebok, Puma, they all knocked me back. So I went to see some players I thought Adidas would respect – Beckenbauer, Rummenigge, Breitner – and videoed them trying out my prototypes. They said a whole load of stuff in German I couldn't understand. I went to Adidas, showed them the film, and they went, 'oh my gosh, don't leave the room, we have to do a deal'.

"I still don't know what they said, the players. But the deal they gave me was so good that later, when the company was taken over, the new owners were told by their accountants that the first thing they had to do was get out of their contract with Johnston. They offered to buy me out.

"I took the money. Since then, they've sold millions of boots, at over a hundred quid a pair. And I was on two per cent of the action, so you can do the maths."

After also inventing a minibar security system that enabled hotels to keep track of what guests had actually used (devised after years spent in hotels as a footballer he admitted), Johnston used his Adidas pay-off to develop a football coaching system for children called SoccerSkills which gained official FIFA approval but the Football Association dragged their heels on whether to license the system which left him penniless and bankrupt, also losing his marriage in the process.

Never one to take adversity lying down – he has also survived a number of bouts of skin cancer – Johnston picked himself up and poured himself into making his lifelong hobby of photography a viable career.

"Photography was my first love," he admitted. "I even had a studio in Liverpool. You see, I was never made to be a footballer mentally. I preferred to hang around with the press photographers after the games. They would use my darkroom and I would study their techniques.

"Years later I'd been declared bankrupt and dealing with administrators, lawyers, stuff you don't want to do, I was extremely depressed.

"I broke up with my wife, the kids had gone back to Australia, I had no house, no car, nothing. It would have been easy to hit the bottle. But I had my old camera. I went for a walk, it was pouring with rain, and for me photography is like meditation.

"I suddenly saw this mannequin, beautifully dressed in beautiful light in a window. Just then this nasty tramp was coming along the road, swearing at me. And I saw him in the window, and I thought how interesting, the haves and have nots in the same picture. I got his reflection in the window, with this lovely model, it was a great moment. Mate, it really lifted my spirits. It took me to a different place."

His photography skills also got him into television production where he worked Down Under for both Kerry Packer and Rupert Murdoch, while his artistic talents were further evidenced by him writing the Anfield Rap during his final season at Anfield, and he also co-wrote World in Motion with New Order for England's World Cup song in 1990.

"I've never been able to sit still and thankfully my brain is still incredibly active and creative," explained Johnston, who has taken on an ambassadorial role during Liverpool's pre-season trips to Australia.

He's been a man of many talents and given pleasure to thousands of Liverpool fans over the years, something he should remember before modestly asserting: "You have no idea how crap I was. Even when I was playing for Liverpool, I was the worst player in the best team in the world."

JIM
BEGLIN

From Kop To Commentator

First published: November 2021

SHOWING some fight is often the minimum requirement football supporters want and expect to see from their team, particularly in times of adversity. Usually in a metaphorical sense and meaning putting a proper shift in, running and tackling hard no matter how badly things are going and essentially not throwing in the towel, even when it seems all is lost.

On the rare occasions that spills over into actual fighting between team-mates, a certain satisfaction can even be gleaned from the knowledge that the players are hurting like their fans are, as evidenced by the bust-up between Jamie Carragher and Alvaro Arbeloa at West Brom the day after Liverpool's 2009 Premier League title dream finally bit the dust.

And every so often it can act as a turning point leading to

greater things, which was very much the case during Liverpool's unforgettable 1986 FA Cup final victory over perennial rivals Everton when, with the Reds a goal behind and teetering on the brink of conceding a second, goalkeeper Bruce Grobbelaar and left-back Jim Beglin were involved in a furious on-pitch row after a defensive mix-up.

"I wish I had a quid for every time a Liverpool fan over the years has said to me, 'That woke us up, that got us going again'. If that's true, I'm delighted it happened," the Irishman would later say when reflecting on a day which arguably proved to be the highlight of an eventful but regrettably brief career with the team he had joined only three years earlier.

Beglin had crossed the Irish Sea in May 1983 for a modest fee of £20,000 much to the delight of his father, who had played in the League of Ireland for Waterford and Sligo, and was a Liverpool fan.

"My older brother was a Man United fan. My younger brother was an Everton fan. And I was a Chelsea fan. So we all got on awfully," Beglin quipped of his sport-mad family. Having tried his hand at hurling, Gaelic football, squash and tennis, the County Waterford-youngster's talents were spotted by Shamrock Rovers after impressing in schoolboy football in his native city and three years with the Hoops saw him play under former Leeds and Eire legend Johnny Giles and compete in Europe.

"I remember thinking 'this is it'," he recalled. "It's either stay at Rovers, get a job, or go back to Waterford. And I never wanted to go back to Waterford because I didn't want to be deemed a failure. You go back to your own town and everyone says 'ah, he didn't make it'. I'm not having that.

"Having arrived at Anfield, I was very apprehensive, because I'm going into a completely different world – this is the best club in Europe. At the time, I remember thinking, 'this is a hell of a jump'. I played a couple of reserve games in the first ten days, which went really well for me, and out of the blue one day I was offered a permanent deal.

"It was tremendous for me. My dad passed away that summer – he didn't get to see me play for Liverpool but at least he got to see me sign for them. He was always a Liverpool fan and would regularly make trips across to Anfield. He came over that particular weekend and we watched Liverpool lift the league trophy. I think they'd played Aston Villa, and we sat in the stands. I was there thinking 'oh my God, I now have a chance of a crack at this'. I was determined not to waste the opportunity."

He would have to wait a while for that opportunity though. First-choice left-back Alan Kennedy was firmly established as one of new manager Joe Fagan's senior players and would conclude Beglin's first season at Anfield by scoring the decisive goal in the European Cup final for the second time in four seasons. Although he had been training with the first team and featuring on the bench in some of the Reds' European ties, Beglin was sent to Japan to play in a youth tournament while Fagan's men conquered AS Roma on their own turf and it would be November 1984 before an injury to Kennedy finally enabled him to make his senior bow in Liverpool colours in a 1-1 draw at home to Southampton.

"I felt I was ready for it but the team was so settled, it was difficult. We didn't exactly have a rotation policy back then," he remembered. "Joe Fagan pulled me aside on the pavilion at Melwood and said, 'You're playing tomorrow'. The emotions were incredible. From utter joy, to nervousness, and then desperation for three o'clock."

Kennedy was back in the side the following week but a

serious ankle injury picked up in a home defeat to Manchester United at the end of March ruled the north-east defender out for the rest of the campaign and thrust the 21-year-old Irishman firmly into the spotlight. Liverpool were suffering their worst league campaign in years following the departure of captain Graeme Souness to Sampdoria and had been mired in the relegation zone in late October. Although they would eventually recover to finish a distant second to Howard Kendall's resurgent Everton, hopes of salvaging a difficult campaign rested on progress in the cup competitions and in only his fourth game for the club, Beglin helped put the Reds on the brink of a second successive European Cup final by helping keep a clean sheet and scoring his first senior goal to put the seal on a 4-0 rout of Greek champions Panathinaikos in the first leg of the semi-final at Anfield.

"That was lovely because we went through it on the training ground," he said. "They were very good, the Liverpool coaching staff, at spotting little details. I was at other clubs as well and you'd never get that attention to detail. They'd picked out the fact that the Greek lads would just follow the runners – they weren't that bothered about the ball, sometimes they'd just get drawn. I had to make out I was uninterested and just kind of loitering outside the box. Everybody would make the run to the front post, hopefully drag the whole Panathinaikos team with them. And then it was my job to suddenly sprout into life and get into the back.

"I always remember, little Sammy Lee ran over. Kenny was on free-kick duty and just got the perfect depth, because at the last minute one of them realised that they'd fallen for it. He tried to kind of back-pedal and get there, but Kenny had played it absolutely inch-perfect for me. Luckily, I was able to come on to it and get a good strong header behind it. It was a moment

I'll cherish forever because it was my only goal at the Kop end. That was very special, to do that on a European night.

"The following night, I went into my local chippy. The guy behind the counter, an Italian bloke, was refusing to serve me. He had 100 quid on 3-0. I had popped up and got the fourth with five minutes remaining."

Defeat after a Maine Road replay to Manchester United in the FA Cup semi-final scotched dreams of a cup double but Panathinaikos were duly despatched 1-0 in the second leg in Greece to set up a showdown with Italian giants Juventus in Brussels as Anfield hopes turned to what would be a fifth European Cup triumph in only eight years. Although Kennedy was battling desperately to prove his fitness, Beglin's assured performances in the 14 games he had deputised in – which included another goal in a win at West Ham – meant Fagan had few concerns over naming him in the starting line-up at the Heysel Stadium. What should have been one of the greatest nights of his career, however, turned into a nightmare when crowd trouble before the game saw the collapse of a wall inside the dilapidated stadium and the ensuing deaths of 39 Juventus supporters.

"It was the biggest game of my life, only my 15th in the first team," Beglin wrote in the Independent ahead of the 20th anniversary of the disaster in 2005. "When we were on the coach to the ground, the rival supporters appeared to be mixing well. After we arrived there was a kids game on the pitch so we strolled over to the terrace where many of our fans were massed. A plastic ball was thrown from the crowd; Sammy Lee and Bruce Grobbelaar volleyed it back.

"The atmosphere was positive. Our crowd were separated from the Juventus fans by some flimsy fencing. As we passed the Italians we had bits of bricks hurled at us. But we were able to step out of the way and they landed harmlessly on the track. We laughed it off.

"We started to hear that there was serious violence as we were putting the finishing touches to our preparations in the changing room. I was eventually told there might be three deaths, but not until just before we finally went out. During the delay, which lasted for an hour and a half, the coaching staff were telling us to relax and start our whole routine again in order to be ready for a rescheduled kick-off time. I was young and apprehensive; I didn't want to let anybody down, so I wanted no distractions. I knew something bad was going on but had no idea of the scale. We were being told to stay focused. It's possible the management and my more experienced colleagues shielded me from things.

"Some of the lads have said they felt low-key during the match. They must have been more aware of what had happened. I saw a Liverpool side striving to win. Everybody. We didn't know any other way to play. Yet when we heard so many lives were lost, no-one cared about the result.

"The enormity of Heysel hit me like a train after the game. Dejection over losing the match quickly gave way to disbelief when I learned that 39 people had died. I walked with my Liverpool team-mates to where the wall had crumbled and the Italian fans were crushed. The remnants of people's lives – handbags and shoes, scarves and spectacles – were strewn among the rubble. Back home, I'd set my video for the great occasion. The tape ran out before the game ended. Graeme Souness and Terry Venables did a little analysis before it was off to the BBC newsroom. There was a warning about 'disturbing images' from Brussels. I sat there in silence, aghast."

Kenny Dalglish took over from Joe Fagan that summer initially as player-manager and, with one of the new manager's first moves being to jettison Liverpool's ageing full-backs with Alan Kennedy sold to Sunderland and Phil Neal joining Bolton Wanderers, Beglin now found himself as first-choice left-back and would go on to play 53 out of the 63 matches in the Reds' marathon 1985-86 campaign. With the eyes of the football world on Liverpool after the harrowing events of the previous May, it could have been a daunting prospect for the inexperienced young Irishman but Beglin admitted it was made easier by the calibre of defenders he was playing alongside.

"It was so well-drilled. Alan Hansen and Mark Lawrenson were good talkers and that's a big help. I've played with a lot of centre-backs who, if they're in trouble, just give it to the full-back, even if somebody's two yards away from you. But every time it was on for Jocky to do that, he'd just drop the shoulder, turn inside someone and create the space for himself. To come into a back four like that was a hell of a lot easier."

Although an early-season victory over the reigning champions Everton at Goodison Park had served notice Liverpool were determined to regain their league crown, Manchester United's blistering start which saw Ron Atkinson's side win their first ten league matches and a poor spell from Dalglish's side over Christmas and New Year meant it was Easter Monday before the Reds would top the First Division that campaign, and even then Howard Kendall's Toffees had games in hand which meant they were in control of the destiny of the title.

After losing the return derby at Anfield in mid-February to fall eight points behind their neighbours, Dalglish's side looked out of the running but, with the player-manager restoring himself to the starting line-up after an injury to Paul Walsh, embarked on a remarkable winning run to whittle away at the Blues' lead, securing three points in all of their remaining league fixtures bar a draw at Sheffield Wednesday. As the season entered its final week, however, they still needed help from elsewhere with Everton having a game in hand.

On the Wednesday night before the last Saturday of the season, the Reds travelled to face Leicester City while the Blues were at the Manor Ground taking on relegation-threatened Oxford United. With Liverpool's game kicking off 15 minutes later and Dalglish's men two up early on through goals from Ian Rush and Ronnie Whelan, the away end at Filbert Street broke out into scenes of jubilant celebrations as news filtered through of Les Phillips' late winner for Oxford which meant the league championship trophy would return to Anfield if Dalglish's men won their final match away to Chelsea. Although they had won an FA Cup fourth-round tie there three months earlier, Liverpool hadn't won a league fixture at Stamford Bridge since 1974, but a sublime volley – fittingly from the player-manager himself – was enough for the three points required with Beglin providing the deft assist for Dalglish's strike.

"It was one of the best days of my life," Beglin said. "The following we had during that run-in was phenomenal. We must have had 12,000 fans at Stamford Bridge that day. I had gone up for a corner and had an effort cleared off the line. I hung around the penalty box and when the ball dropped to me I knew that Kenny was on my right. I just helped it on its way, Kenny took it on his chest and volleyed into the corner. We got the goal, shut up shop and won the league which was incredible."

The joy at winning back the league championship from their closest rivals across Stanley Park was tempered by the knowledge the job was only half-done. Victories over Norwich, Chelsea, York City, Watford and Southampton had taken Liverpool to their first FA Cup final in 12 years where their opponents, inevitably, were Everton, who had won through to their third successive final.

Desperate to make amends having lost their championship crown and salvage something from their own impressive season, the Toffees edged the opening stages at Wembley and took the lead shortly before the half hour mark with double Footballer of the Year Gary Lineker's 40th goal of his one and only season at Goodison Park.

An out-of-sorts Liverpool were initially unable to gain control even after a half-time dressing room talking to from Dalglish and his coaches and Everton looked likely to extend their lead in the opening stages of the second period, with Kevin Sheedy flashing a cross-shot inches wide and Mark Lawrenson having to clear off the line after Bruce Grobbelaar dropped a cross before the now-infamous bust-up between the Reds goalkeeper and Beglin which ultimately proved to be the spark which helped Liverpool turn the game around.

"People have said that was the turning point, it made us realise we were 1-0 down and in danger of blowing it," Beglin recalled. "The ball was running along the line and Bruce was shouting for me to let it run, but I was thinking, if I let it run, Trevor Steven's going to get on it. Bruce timed his jump thinking I was going to do as he said, but in the meantime I'd put my foot on it and I had to shield it before he got back. He got a bit panicked about it all and once he'd got the ball, he called me something unrepeatable. I told him where to go and he hit me. I thought I've got to hit him back, then you realise the occasion and everything flashes through your mind. I'm thinking the whole world is watching, the stadium is jam-packed, I need to hold it together and of course Bruce was a jungle fighter so it was probably best to leave it. Thankfully I did and he rolled the ball to me, I tapped it back to him, and from that moment it was over."

Within minutes Ian Rush had equalised after a move begun by Beglin and the Irishman had a hand in the further goals by Craig Johnston and Rush again which secured a 3-1 victory and only the third League and FA Cup double that century. It was a moment of supreme triumph to conclude one of the most difficult years in Liverpool's history with the images beamed all around the world of tens of thousands of Reds and Blues travelling and watching the match together being just what the city's image needed.

"I always like to think that that's the biggest derby ever," Beglin said. "I remember the fans risking their lives trying to get into the stadium. You see the footage of Wembley at the time and it's absolutely mad. I had guests that ended up sitting round the track, because it was so crowded. But that was a very special time, because either Liverpool or Everton were winning the league once you got to the mid-80s. So Merseyside was the place to be, it was as good as it got. I think there were two very good sides fighting it out. And credit to the Evertonians that day too, they were still very proud of their team and what Merseyside was achieving at the time. They did themselves proud that day too."

Liverpool would reach the League Cup final the following season but by then Beglin's season – and sadly his Liverpool career – was all but over after a horrific broken leg picked up earlier in the same competition. With the Merseyside rivals again locked in another fierce battle at the top of the First Division, they were drawn together at Goodison in the quarter-final of what was then known as the Littlewoods Cup and with the game goalless midway through the first half, the Irishman and Gary Stevens contested a stray ball midway inside the visitors' half after a loose touch from the Everton right-back which left the Liverpool man prone and in agony with part of his leg facing the wrong way, as a furious Kenny Dalglish followed Ronnie Moran and Roy Evans on to the pitch to remonstrate with referee Neville Ashley who did not even award a free-kick.

"I knew it was bad," said Beglin. "It was a derby occasion, you didn't shirk a tackle and I was always happy to get stuck in. The play seemed to carry on for an eternity for me, but it was probably just a few seconds. I looked down and I couldn't believe where my foot was, but I knew it was where it shouldn't be, adjacent to my shin. The pain was a nightmare and the break was fairly horrific; it was car crash material."

He was rushed to hospital with Bob Paisley – who had returned to the Reds' dug-out as an advisor to Dalglish in the Scot's early years as player-boss – with the man who had brought Beglin to Anfield four years earlier quoted as saying: "The injury he suffered was as ill-timed, as it was painful. It was painful to look at, never mind to experience. I've seen one or two broken legs in going on 50 years in the game and none made me really wince, but Jim's did."

"A mile high and an hour late," was the verdict of Liverpool captain Alan Hansen and the anger within the dressing room was still evident when Beglin was visited in hospital by Dalglish soon afterwards.

"Word came to me that Gary Stevens wanted to come and see me," Beglin told Off The Ball. "Kenny Dalglish came to visit me in the hospital and said to me, 'Don't do it'. I said to him, 'Gaffer, if I had done that to somebody, I would want to go and tell them that I didn't mean to do that... maybe he wants to do that to me.' He said: 'I'm telling you now, all he wants to do is put himself in a better light and move on. It is going to be a PR thing for him if he does it.' I ignored that advice and immediately regretted him coming to see me, because I'm all drugged up and in a lot of pain. He came in and he just sat there.

"Clive Tyldesley, who was at Radio City in Liverpool at the time, came as a mutual friend. Not to be part of anything, or to report on anything. He sat on the chair beside my bed, and Clive sat in the corner. He said nothing. I'm sitting there thinking: 'What's the point?' I said to him, 'Did you know you had broken it?' and he said, 'No, I didn't – I went into the tackle, got up and got on with it.' I just immediately switched off. It was very abrupt after that; very short. I hadn't taken Kenny's advice and I was wrong. He went straight to Matt D'Arcy, an Evertonian who was working at, I believe, the Daily Star at the time. The back page headline the next morning was: 'I Don't Blame Gary'. I had fallen into the trap that was set – that Kenny had alerted me to and I ignored."

Surgery and a long period of rehabilitation followed with Beglin suffering the further blow of a serious knee cartilage injury when attempting a comeback in the Reds' reserves in October 1988. With Gary Ablett and David Burrows having now emerged as replacements in the left-back position, he left Anfield to join Leeds United the following June but suffered further injury problems and was only able to make 19 appearances for the Yorkshire side before brief spells with Plymouth Argyle and Blackburn Rovers and premature retirement from football at the age of only 27 in 1991.

"There was a lot of self-pity – 'why me?' – and I went through every emotion in the book," he admitted. "I hated myself. I got terribly down and lost my confidence, not just as a footballer but as a person. Football was my life. Football gave me my confidence. And all of a sudden, it was gone. I ended up training and playing in pain, stupidly, and went on probably for a year or 18 months too long when I should have retired.

But back then, it was all about being a man, about not quitting. I just kind of got wrapped up in that whole world and stupidly, I kept going, hoping that things might improve injury-wise. But that was never going to happen. It's all mental health these days and I probably suffered at that time, but the whole culture at the time was: be a man, shut up, get on with it and behave. I bottled it all up. I thought it was something that I had dealt with well, but – looking back – I didn't and I could have done with some assistance.

"It was my knee that retired me in the end, and I've now ended up with an osteoarthritic knee. But it's not the worst thing in the world.

"Of course, the one thing I would change in my career is going in for that tackle at Goodison. But what I will say is I won the ball. The guy who caught me didn't. And that's what obviously ended what could have been a great run. I'd like to think I could have gone on to win a lot more with a club like Liverpool. My attitude was never going to change. What the injury did, unknowingly, was start my media career. I had no designs on chasing a media career. I wasn't leaning that way. All of a sudden, I was asked to do bits and bobs, so I had little bits of experience of it. I was thinking about coaching and staying in the game but then the phone started ringing and thank God, it's still ringing."

A regular presence in the broadcast and print football media for many years now, Beglin's enduring love for the game and Liverpool in particular always comes shining through and was never better highlighted than when he penned an emotional poem which he shared with the Liverpool ECHO in tribute to Jurgen Klopp's side ending the Reds' 30-year wait for a 19th league title in 2020. Titled 'Thanks to Shanks', it read:

Thanks to Shanks by Jim Beglin©
The mighty ambition of Shanks
Strengthened LFC ranks
He brought the thirst
To finish first
And will always merit great thanks
The next in line was Sir Bob
Who concocted a thoroughbred mob
Three European Cups
Plus many more ups
And a wholly magnificent job
The succession meant genial Joe
A treble to increase the flow
A streamlined team
All set to gleam
Then Heysel, a harrowing low
And so a call for the king
A double to start with a fling
But Hillsborough came
It was never the same
96 etched forever that spring
A return to the club for Souness
With designs on a spell of excess
But too much change
Reduced the range
And slowed the run of success
Evo stepped up to the plate
With knowledge of how to be great
Spice boy nous
Filled the house
LFC found a healthier state
A Frenchman entered the fray

Gerard Houllier planned to make hay
A different style
A trophy pile
He did it all his way
Now Rafa could script a good tale
Of a team that just wouldn't fail
Istanbul heaven
From the wrong starting eleven
A historic fifth holy grail
Roy found it tough from the start
A struggle with LFC art
Inspiration was lacking
The fans chanted sacking
There were better fits for the part
Sir Kenny was back in the seat
With the hope of a little more heat
From a hasty assembly
There were three trips to Wembley
A standard Dalglish feat
Brendan had licence to thrill
SAS and their sumptuous skill
Times were exciting
The exception was biting
Two points from climbing the hill
Then Jurgen came through the door
Heavy metal was brought to the fore
A few years of yearning
Completed the learning
The Liver Bird ready to soar
Big ears was back in the mix
Madrid after Kiev, the fix
It triggered a spark

That set a new mark
The count had moved onto six
A Premier League now the aim
The spark has turned into flame
A thirty-year search
To get back on the perch
Time to uncork the champagne.
Hats off to Bill on his throne
He set the club's standards in stone
Navigating a storm
Is a Liverpool norm
You'll Never Walk Alone.

MILAN BAROS

The Hidden Hero Of Istanbul

First published: December 2021

ONE of the most enduringly fascinating aspects of Liverpool's miraculous 2005 Champions League triumph in Istanbul is how many unsung heroes it produced.

The Reds' astonishing fightback from three goals down to ensure the European Cup was coming back to Anfield for keeps will of course be forever associated in the minds of many with captain Steven Gerrard's inspirational leadership, goalkeeper Jerzy Dudek's match-winning saves that defied the disbelieving Italians, and manager Rafa Benitez's tactical reshuffles that helped turn humiliating defeat into unforgettable victory.

It can be argued that every individual who featured in the most jaw-droppingly astonishing triumph in Liverpool's storied history deserves their place in the Anfield pantheon of greatness, but there are certain names who will always come to the fore. Jamie Carragher summoned every last vestige of energy in extra-time and battled through crippling bouts of cramp to keep Milan's attacks at bay; Dietmar Hamann shrugged off the disappointment of being dropped from the starting line-up to change the game as a half-time substitute and score a penalty in the shoot-out with a broken foot; Djimi Traore battled back from his horror Burnley own goal earlier in the season and escaped his aborted half-time substitution to make a crucial goal-line clearance after the Reds had drawn level; even the likes of Neil Mellor, Igor Biscan and Antonio Nunez, who made vital contributions on the way to the final but never made it on the pitch in the Turkish capital.

Vladimir Smicer famously scored the final goal of his Reds career to really bolster belief – two minutes after Gerrard's header – that an unlikely comeback was possible after being surprisingly introduced from the bench.

And that heady night on the border between Europe and Asia was also the last time one of Smicer's Czech Republic team-mates wore the red shirt of Liverpool, having made his own valuable contributions, particularly towards the conclusion of a campaign he had played an important part in.

The news of Milan Baros's transfer to Liverpool was overshadowed a little initially after being announced at the same time as Nicolas Anelka's loan move from Paris Saint Germain in late December 2001.

It meant that the £3.2m acquisition of an unheard-of 20-year-old Czech forward from Banik Ostrava was always likely to pass under the radar initially, although caretaker manager Phil Thompson spoke at the time of Baros's unveiling at his excitement over the young striker's potential.

"Gerard and our European scout, Alex Miller, first saw him

three years ago in a youth tournament when the Czech side was outstanding," Thompson said. "We've wanted him since then, and in the same way as Gregory Vignal and the two French boys from Le Havre, Milan is a signing who makes the future of the club very bright.

"I would describe him as a strong, fast player. He is a goal poacher with a lot of pace."

It was a dream come true for Baros himself, who had grown up in the Czech Republic following the Reds because of his dad who was a Liverpool fan.

"I was so happy that my first experience in England was with such a huge club like Liverpool," he told This Is Anfield years later. "My father was a Red and we'd always watch the matches on TV. Liverpool became my favourite team.

"Tottenham were also quite popular in the Czech Republic back then, but Liverpool were the team for us."

Delays over his work permit, however, meant a difficult beginning to life on Merseyside for the young Czech, who admitted virtually everything about his new country – the lifestyle, the food, the pace of the game – came as a culture shock to him.

It was clear Baros had been bought with an eye on the future and he would only make one first-team appearance in that first half-season at Anfield, but the venue and context of if perhaps highlighted just how high Liverpool's hopes for him were.

The Champions League introduced a short-lived second group phase before the quarter-finals between 1999/2000 and 2002/03 and, after successfully negotiating the first one in their maiden appearance in the competition by topping a group containing Borussia Dortmund, Dynamo Kyiv and Boavista, Liverpool began the second with a harsh reality check when losing 3-1 at home to Barcelona.

A series of draws at AS Roma as well as home and away to Galatasaray meant the Reds travelled to the Camp Nou for the penultimate group fixture knowing defeat would likely be fatal to their chances of qualifying for the last eight.

Houllier's men had secured a crucial goalless draw in the Catalan capital only 11 months earlier in the first leg of their UEFA Cup semi-final and were closing in on grinding out another valuable stalemate that would likely mean victory in the final match at home to Roma would be enough to qualify when, with just over a quarter of an hour remaining, Baros was introduced as a substitute for his Liverpool debut in place of Emile Heskey.

It raised a few eyebrows among the travelling Liverpudlians high up in the stands who soon got a snapshot of the Czech's vivid but raw talent when he picked up the ball on the left-hand touchline near the halfway line and embarked on a diagonal run right into the heart of the Barcelona penalty area – seemingly without once ever lifting his head up – before eventually getting crowded out by defenders.

Baros's inclusion wasn't just a surprise to those watching but also to the man himself given the difficulties of his settling-in period but his mentality in those early months had not gone unnoticed by Houllier, who would return to the dug-out the following week for that crucial decider against Roma after life-saving heart surgery.

"Milan's attitude was right from when he arrived, he just needed time," Houllier said. "He was a young boy who had come from a small club in the Czech Republic, with all respect to Banik Ostrava, to a big club and a big environment in Liverpool.

"It is something special and takes some getting used to. The boy had a good 'pre pre-season' if you could call it that."

Baros made his first appearance for Liverpool on British soil by coming off the bench again for Heskey in the second half of Charity Shield defeat to Arsenal in Cardiff's Millennium Stadium the following August and a month later was given his full Premier League debut as the Reds – aiming to go one better after the previous campaign's second-place finish – looked to return to winning ways at Bolton Wanderers after three successive draws following wins in the opening two matches against Aston Villa and Southampton.

Michael Owen had been left on the bench but Baros rose to the occasion magnificently to play a big part in a 3-2 victory that raised the Reds to third in the league table. He opened the scoring on the stroke of half-time, receiving a Hamann pass following a smart dummy by Bruno Cheyrou on the edge of the penalty area, spinning away from his marker and rocketing a right-foot shot high beyond Jussi Jääskeläinen.

He added a second on 71 minutes, producing a deft outside-of-the-boot volleyed finish from Gerrard's left-footed right-wing cross to put Liverpool back in front, and reflecting on those two opening salvos of his Anfield career Baros said: "The Barcelona game when Phil Thompson was in charge, I was on the bench but wasn't nervous because I never expected to be involved.

"It was a big surprise to get 15 minutes and it was great to play in front of 75,000 people in one of the world's best stadiums, but my bigger memory is the Bolton game. I knew I was going to start three or four days before the match and could prepare myself. It made the experience more emotional for me.

"I was so happy with how it went. I managed to score two goals and almost got a hat-trick because I hit the post too. It's a moment that will stand out in my mind forever.

"It was my first start for Liverpool and I got the two goals, amazing."

Owen was back in the team for what would be a chastening defeat in Valencia's Estadio Mestalla but Baros started and scored in Liverpool's next two matches, at home to West Brom in the Premier League and Basel in the Champions League, fostering real hope that Houllier's side now boasted the kind of strength in depth which would be required for a sustained assault on the top prizes.

The Reds went top and stayed there for the best part of a month after victory at Leeds United in mid-October but the wheels came off their season – and ultimately Houllier's reign overall – when a first league defeat of the season at Middlesbrough in early November was followed three days later by elimination from the Champions League at the first group stage following a 3-3 draw in Basel, leading to an 11-game run without a league win that stretched into January.

A campaign which had begun with so much hope and promise ended in disappointment when defeat at Chelsea on the final day meant failure to qualify for the following season's Champions League, although Baros did finish with a respectable tally for his maiden campaign of 12 goals in 22 starts (42 appearances overall), which put him joint-second in the club standings.

He also gained the first medal of his career by playing a brief – but at the time somewhat unsatisfactory – role in Liverpool's League Cup final victory over Manchester United in Cardiff, replacing Heskey on the hour mark but then himself being substituted for his Czech mate Smicer in the 89th minute.

"At the time I was unhappy," he admitted. "You don't want to go off as a substituted substitute, but it's especially disappointing in a cup final against massive rivals.

"We had just gone 2-0 up and the game was won. I was stunned because I had only come on for Heskey with half an hour left. I was young, so I was disappointed but you have to think of what's best for the team. That's the most important thing. We won the trophy and that was what mattered.

"I let it get to me in the celebrations because I felt a bit embarrassed. I should have savoured the moment more. It's many years ago now and I only look back with pride. It was the first major honour of my career, so I have a very different view of it now."

Further frustration was to follow in the fifth game of the following season as Baros suffered a broken leg at Blackburn which ruled him out of action for five months.

Baros was back on the scoresheet with a stunning equaliser at Leeds within a week of his return to first-team action the following February and soon afterwards scored the opener in Liverpool's UEFA Cup quarter-final first leg against Olympique Marseille but, with Houllier trying to salvage Champions League qualification from another disappointing campaign as his Anfield era drew to a close, the manager largely went with his tried-and-trusted Owen and Heskey partnership until the end of the season.

Fourth place was eventually secured before Liverpool called time on Houllier's reign as manager and the lack of recent game time for Baros did not seem to do him much harm when that summer he was top goalscorer at Euro 2004, notching five goals in five games for the Czech Republic.

During the tournament, Baros's frustration at how life at Anfield had been going reared its head when he accused Houllier of destroying his confidence and claimed he would have been looking to leave the club if the French manager had not already done so.

"I had lost my motivation at Liverpool and it was only when I met up with my national team-mates that I lost weight, gained some mental belief and got my motivation back," he said. "I have heard people say I play differently for my country but that's simply not true. I play exactly the same at Liverpool.

"Houllier knocked the confidence out of me. I wasn't being picked and I thought it would be best to leave Liverpool in the summer. I was very hurt at not being in the side. I was fit and felt it was an injustice.

"But a new coach has come in now and the situation has changed. Every player will start next season from the same point under Rafael Benitez."

The departure of Owen to Real Madrid that summer was offset by the arrival of £14m French forward Djibril Cisse and meant Baros's hopes of playing more lay in the balance but Benitez began the season with the two of them up front. The Czech scored the first Anfield goal of the Spaniard's reign in a comeback victory against Manchester City and also scored in the Champions League group stage opener against AS Monaco, which set Liverpool officially on the road to Istanbul.

It would prove to be the most productive period of Baros's Anfield career, with the Czech bagging 11 goals by mid-December of the new campaign including the only hat-trick of his Liverpool days in a 3-2 win over Crystal Palace at Anfield, sealed with a last-minute Kop-end penalty.

The Reds' wildly inconsistent league form inevitably meant Benitez had to find a solution to make his side more resolute leading to fewer and fewer occasions when two forwards were picked and, with experienced Spanish striker Fernando Morientes arriving from Real Madrid in the January, Baros's opportunities became more limited.

Morientes's protracted transfer, however, meant he was cup-tied for Europe and, with Cisse having suffered a broken leg at Blackburn earlier in the campaign which would rule him out until its final weeks, Baros became Benitez's go-to guy as Liverpool's unexpected and exhilarating Champions League campaign built to its incredible crescendo. The Czech started every one of the knockout ties against Bayer Leverkusen, Juventus and Chelsea as well as the final against AC Milan – and while he might only have scored in one of them (the final goal in the ultimately comfortable 6-2 aggregate triumph over Leverkusen), he played a big part in two of the most significant moments at the business end.

After having the visitors' best chance of the goalless first leg of the semi-final against Chelsea at Stamford Bridge when his header from Gerrard's cross was brilliantly denied by his compatriot Petr Cech, it was Baros's quick thinking and burst of pace beyond Ricardo Carvalho from Gerrard's cute dink four minutes into the Anfield second leg that caused the Chelsea keeper to race out and clatter him with Luis Garcia following in to score the eternally-disputed and forever-treasured 'ghost goal' that took Liverpool to the final.

"I always say that was the noisiest game I've ever played in," Baros later admitted. "It was powerful before the kick-off and during the game, but after that final whistle it was unbelievable.

"I can remember how crazy it was for Luis Garcia's goal. I tried to get to the ball and got brought down by Petr Cech. I looked back at the referee expecting a penalty but then Anfield just exploded!

"I don't care what is said about it being over the line. We scored. It was better than getting the penalty, you can always miss that. It gave us the lead and we fought with everything to make sure we held onto it."

Cisse's remarkable return to fitness for the final six weeks of the season from his compound leg fracture at Blackburn the previous October bolstered Benitez's striking options ahead of the final and, with Liverpool already being linked with new forwards ahead of the summer transfer window, there were suggestions Baros could be on his way with the Czech admitting before the trip to Turkey that it was a possibility.

"I have had several offers from other clubs and it is now the job of my agent to talk to them," Baros told the Daily Mirror. "Maybe I'll leave Anfield, maybe I'll stay. We'll listen to what is offered.

"I am calm about my future and I can concentrate fully on the Champions League final. But my main aim at the moment is that I can keep my place ahead of Cisse for the final against Milan, and I will do my best to make that happen."

Cisse had started and scored twice in Liverpool's final Premier League game of the season against Aston Villa at Anfield but, while Benitez would spring a surprise in his Istanbul team selection by dropping defensive midfield linchpin Hamann in favour of Harry Kewell, Baros was named in the starting line-up to face AC Milan, much to his relief.

"To be honest, I was surprised that I started," he said. "Djibril had scored twice in the last league game before we flew out for the final. I was expecting him to play. Rafa chose me and I was also surprised Harry Kewell was in the side as he had been injured a lot. But that's the manager's job. He picks the side and has his idea for the match."

Benitez's initial idea for the match was in tatters by half-time when the Italians were 3-0 up and Liverpool stared down the barrel of humiliation on the global stage.

But as no Liverpudlian old enough to remember it will ever forget, everything changed within six logic-defying minutes early in the second half. Gerrard's 54th-minute header from John Arne Riise's left-wing cross induced the first tentative spark of hope before two minutes later Smicer – surprisingly introduced in his final match for the club as the Reds' first substitute – slammed home the second to further reduce the deficit. Baros smartly took evasive action on the edge of the box so as not to block his compatriot's strike as it whistled past him.

"Whenever I speak with Vladi about the game, I always wind him up and tell him it is my goal!" he later joked. "I tell him, 'it just brushed me, a very slight touch but it counts!' I'm only joking of course.

"He hit it really well and I could tell it was going on target. I just got myself out of the way. Thankfully it went in and it gave us massive belief."

Barely 120 seconds later, the Reds unbelievably had the chance to draw level from the penalty spot after a slick move featuring undoubtedly the most important touch of Baros's career.

With confidence suddenly surging through Liverpool veins again, Carragher surged forward over the halfway line before playing a slide-rule pass into the direction of the penalty-box run the Czech was making in the inside-right channel. Spotting Gerrard charging into the box behind him, Baros deftly nudged a backheel into the skipper's path, which he latched onto before being brought down by Genaro Gattuso, giving Spanish referee Manuel Mejuto González no option but to point to the spot.

Gerrard was full of praise for Baros's heaven-sent touch in his autobiography, saying: "I was running in behind. I hoped to God that Baros saw me. If he did, I was in on goal. Baros heard my prayers, and found me with a spot-on touch. During his time at Liverpool, Baros was slated for being selfish, but he showed unbelievable awareness that night in Istanbul."

After a nerve-wracking, interminable delay while the referee dealt with the shell-shocked and panicking Italian protests,

Xabi Alonso slammed home the rebound after Brazilian goal-keeper Dida saved his initial effort from 12 yards. A delirious Baros was the first of his ecstatic team-mates to reach Alonso as he celebrated and nearly throttled the scorer through excitement.

Recalling his part in one of the most important moments in Liverpool history, Baros later said: "Stevie shouted to me that he wanted the one-two. I had my back to goal and tried to touch it into his path. He got in front of his man and it was 100 per cent a penalty.

"Rafa had picked Xabi to take it before the match and I was so relieved he got to that rebound! I was first to celebrate with him but accidentally hooked him over by his neck! It was an amazing fightback."

The Czech's on-field involvement would end when he was substituted for Cisse with five minutes of normal time remaining and, after no further goals in extra-time, he watched on from the halfway line as his team-mates won the penalty shoot-out 3-2 to seal the greatest and most miraculous fightback in European football history and spark celebrations so wild he later couldn't fully recall them.

"There's ten seconds or so there where I can't remember anything," Baros said. "Sometimes I watch the highlights of the penalties and I see us all running like mad men towards Jerzy. I can't remember that run. It was crazy, you can't describe it. The emotion and the euphoria, just wow. When you go in at half-time to the dressing room and you are 3-0 down, you probably think that winning the game is something impossible. We were sitting in the dressing room and we were really very sad. We were thinking about how to score at least one goal for our fans, who had travelled a long way to Istanbul.

"But we scored very early in the second half and after a few minutes the score was 3-3. Then we were lucky in extra-time and we came to penalties. Jerzy Dudek made great saves and he won the trophy for us. He was a big part of our success. It was something which may only happen once in a hundred years."

As the dust began to settle, Liverpool's new status as European champions added a new dimension to their summer recruitment plans. Baros's future at Anfield became shrouded in doubt and, after being told by Benitez he would likely only have a bit-part role to play, he signed for Aston Villa for £6.5m in August 2005, a decision he later came to regret.

"Rafa came to me and told me he wanted to bring in Peter Crouch. It meant I would be second or third choice," said Baros. "It seemed an easy decision at the time, but if I could go back to that moment now, I would choose to stay.

"There are a lot of games in a season and I'd have got my chance again. Now I know it was a bad decision. I wish I had stayed and been patient."

After scoring 14 goals in 51 appearances over 18 months at Villa Park, he hooked up again with Houllier at French side Olympique Lyonnais in January 2007, a somewhat surprising move considering Baros's comments following the French coach's Anfield departure three years earlier.

He said: "The media made more of it than there was. We never really had a problem. Sometimes the player and the manager will have different views on things. We had that but I always respected him.

"He is one of the biggest influences on my career. He took me from the Czech league to England and I always have to thank him for that. There wasn't a major issue, so when he looked to sign me again for Lyon, I was grateful for a new opportunity to play for another successful club."

Baros would win a Ligue 1 championship medal in France

and, after returning to the Premier League for a loan spell with Portsmouth where he won an FA Cup winners medal in 2008, spent five years in Turkey with Galatasaray picking up a Super Lig title winners medal in 2012. He finished his career back home in the Czech Republic with former club Banik Ostrava, Mlada Boleslav and Slovan Liberec.

His short but eventful time at Anfield remains precious to him. "We won the Champions League and playing in England for the team I had watched on TV with my father was amazing," he said.

"2004 to 2005 was a special period for me with Euro 2004 and then that run in Europe. I still watch every Liverpool game now."

ANDY CARROLL

Calamitous Carroll

First published: January 2021

THERE are few things that hurt football supporters more than the departure of a star striker.

Goals, after all, are the lifeblood of the game itself, the moments of sheer unadulterated joy which make us leap into the air, scream ourselves hoarse and hug strangers with abandon.

When your club smashes its transfer record to bring in a new goal-getter, the excitement levels generally go through the roof, with fans rushing to get new shirts with their new hero's name on the back, devouring every word from press conferences and interviews, and figuring out new songs to serenade their new star.

So on the face of it, when Liverpool paid £35million back in

2011 for Newcastle United's 22-year-old 6ft 4in striker Andy Carroll, it should have ticked every box.

The big Geordie had enjoyed the most significant spell of his career to date, scoring 26 goals in the previous calendar year and earning his first senior full international England caps.

Even more pertinently, Reds fans had only the previous month seen the full scale of his capabilities with Carroll playing a key role in a 3-1 Newcastle win over Liverpool at St James' Park, sealing the victory over Roy Hodgson's hapless side himself with a thunderous long-range strike.

If a week can be a long time in politics, then a month can be a lifetime in football and the Liverpool FC of late-January 2011 suddenly seemed a far cry from the basket case club of the previous autumn.

After teetering on the brink of administration, the near-catastrophic ownership of Tom Hicks and George Gillett finally came to an end when the £300m takeover by John W. Henry and Fenway Sports Group (then known as New England Sports Ventures) was confirmed in mid-October 2010 after a dramatic week of legal manoeuvrings at the High Court in London and in the United States.

That feeling of a much-needed fresh start at Anfield evolved further a week into the new year when Hodgson was relieved of his duties as team manager after another dispiriting defeat at Blackburn, Liverpool's ninth in 20 Premier League matches so far that campaign, which left them 12th and only four points clear of the relegation places.

He was replaced, on a caretaker basis initially, by arguably the club's greatest icon – Kenny Dalglish – who jetted back from a cruise in the Middle East to take charge of the Reds 24 hours later in an FA Cup third round tie at Manchester United.

Although the team's fortunes were to see no instant improvement with referee Howard Webb awarding the Old Trafford side a penalty after just 33 seconds which Ryan Giggs converted for the game's only goal and Steven Gerrard being red-carded after half an hour, the sight of Dalglish's double clenched-fist salute to the 9,000 travelling Liverpudlians as he walked down the touchline before kick-off seemed hugely symbolic for the new era beginning at Anfield.

With the promise of more stability in the boardroom and in the manager's office, along with the new owners' assertions that they were 'here to win' and would back that up when appropriate in the transfer market, thoughts began to turn to that month's window and how Liverpool might be able to salvage a floundering season.

Dalglish – back in charge of a football team for the first time in over a decade – initially had little time to focus on who he might bring in with a re-arranged Premier League game at Blackpool in the midweek after Old Trafford, and a Merseyside derby at Anfield to come.

By the time of the following weekend's league fixture, a 3-0 win at Wolves on 22 January, the transfer window was nearing its final week with the only movement at Anfield so far being the exit of Ryan Babel and the departure on loan of young striker David Amoo.

Dalglish delighted supporters following the win at Molineux when, in response to hectoring transfer questions from Sky's Andy Burton that fans 'had a right to know what's happening', he replied: "It's a bit sad when you spin it onto the fans.

"We know more about our fans than what yourselves do, so we know how they want to be treated – and they know what we want.

"They want us to treat them with respect. And they want us to treat them the way Liverpool fans have always been treated by the club. If we've got business to do we'll do it behind closed doors.

"I know what's going on, but it doesn't mean I've got to tell you."

King Kenny was back, and hopes were high that the final week of the window would see some serious business at Anfield.

And it did – although probably not in the way many fans were expecting.

Persistent rumours of a move for Ajax's 24-year-old striker Luis Suarez had increasingly gained in substance as the month wore on and with reports suggesting Liverpool were closing in on a deal, Kopites allowed themselves to start dreaming of a new dynamic strike partner for Fernando Torres, with the Uruguayan forward having already showed the full extent of his unique repertoire of skills when helping his country to the quarter-finals of the previous summer's World Cup.

It was a link-up which sounded perfect on paper but would never be seen in practice because on 29 January, just two days before the window was due to shut, Torres dropped a bombshell by handing in a formal transfer request.

The star Spanish striker's demeanour and body language, particularly during that tortuous first half of the 2010/11 campaign, portrayed his frustration at the decline in the club's fortunes since his arrival in 2007 but many assumed the introduction of Dalglish – on the back of the FSG takeover – would soothe his concerns.

By the time deadline day itself on the 31st came around, everything was still up in the air and fans, journalists and interested observers settled in for what promised to be a long day and potentially long night.

While there had been nothing to suggest any last-minute hitches with the Suarez deal, the fact it had yet to be confirmed

– along with the angst caused by the Torres transfer request – meant there was still a fear Liverpool could end deadline day actually weaker than when they started.

Just after 11am, a bolt from the blue arrived with the news Liverpool had reportedly made a £30m offer for Newcastle United striker Carroll.

This was the first time Carroll's name had been mentioned in conjunction with Liverpool and reports circulated that Newcastle had turned down the offer but Reds were likely to return with an improved bid.

Sure enough, by early afternoon rumours emerged that a second bid for Carroll – now worth £35m – had been tabled by Liverpool and this time the early noises were that it had matched Newcastle's valuation and that the player himself was keen on the move.

The truth, according to Carroll himself, was somewhat different.

Toon boss Alan Pardew had repeatedly stated the player was not for sale as Carroll's stock had begun to rise and it emerged soon after that the big striker felt he was forced out by the Newcastle ownership.

Text messages he reportedly sent to his friend Steve Wraith, editor of the Toon Talk fanzine, were published in the Daily Star and remain online today illustrating Carroll's apparent disquiet at being effectively sold against his will:

Text One: They have kind of said we don't want u but want me to say I wanna go. And I said I don't wanna go.

Text Two: I don't know mate. Gutted tho. (In reply to question: what's happening?)

Text Three: They said they wanted the money.

Text Four: Gutted to be leaving but I was kind of pushed out the door.

Text Five: Just what I've just said really. Gutted to be leaving my home club but I was practically told to go. Don't want to leave. That's why I signed 5 year deal.

Speaking about that tumultuous day after his return to St James Park in 2019, Carroll himself even revealed that he secretly hoped he would fail his medical at Liverpool so he wouldn't have to leave the club he loved, having only signed a new five-year deal the previous October.

The rapid pace of events that Monday afternoon meant he had to fly down to Liverpool via helicopter to complete the move before the 11pm deadline and Carroll recalled: "I was injured at the time, and all I'm thinking is, 'Please, just fail the medical'.

"The minute I got on that helicopter I wanted to come back.

"I remember leaving Newcastle's training ground in Kevin Nolan's car because loads of people were outside. We went to his house and watched it on TV. I was like, 'I'm not going'. I'd just bought a house, and a cat the day before!

"But then I was told, 'You're going', and that was that.

"Derek Llambias, Newcastle's managing director, asked me to hand in a transfer request, so I was pushed into a corner and had no choice.

"I wasn't wanted by them and they made it clear they wanted the money.

"I'd had a season ticket, it was my club and it was a shock to move. I was 22. I could never get a grip at Liverpool.

"When I was in the helicopter down to Liverpool, I was like, 'I know Stevie G, I know Carragher. Who else?'

"I'd never watch football, I never knew any players. I would work at the training ground and knew my tactics, but until we had a meeting I didn't know who we were playing unless I asked someone.

"I was signing and I didn't know who my team-mates would be! I had to go on Google to find out."

Alan Pardew would subsequently deny Carroll's claims he was forced out, insisting the player decided to leave after asking for a new deal which the club were not prepared to offer having only given him a new one the previous autumn.

"We didn't force anybody to leave," Pardew said.

"He had a contract here for five years, and at some point it would get renewed, but for him to sign in October and it be renewed in January – where would it stop?"

While all this was happening behind the scenes, the afternoon drew on with minutes and hours ticking by as fans and journalists alike nervously checked phones and refreshed web pages, with further rumours shortly before 5pm suggesting Newcastle had also turned down Liverpool's second bid for Carroll.

Events were starting to develop apace and within half an hour, at 5.26pm and with some reports now saying Suarez had agreed terms at Anfield and passed his medical, Liverpool announced they had agreed a club record fee with Newcastle for Carroll and the player was on his way to Melwood for a medical and to discuss personal terms.

A reported ten million people rushed to the official club website to check the latest news, causing it to crash, showing just how much this deadline day saga had captured the imagination.

Now the wheels were in motion and barely an hour later at 6.35pm reports emerged that Liverpool and Chelsea had agreed a fee for Fernando Torres and the Spaniard was on his way to Stamford Bridge to tie up the formalities of his Anfield departure, news that Liverpool confirmed an hour later at 7.37pm.

Shortly after 8pm, Carroll was pictured arriving at Melwood

for his medical, pictures of which nearly caused the Liverpool ECHO website to crash, and at 8.47pm – finally – a Liverpool done deal: Luis Suarez had completed his move from Ajax for a fee of £23m.

The tales and rumours kept flying thick and fast, with news dribbling through that the Torres fee was a whopping £50m as Chelsea chairman Bruce Buck was pictured arriving at Stamford Bridge at 9.48pm.

But as the final hour of the window drew on there was still no confirmation on the Torres and Carroll deals which increasingly seemed to be interlinked.

At 10.56pm – four minutes before the official close of the window – Liverpool announced the signing of Andy Carroll for a club record fee of £35m on a five-year deal, the Reds confirming the departure of Torres to Chelsea for £50m shortly after the deadline closed, at 11.21pm.

It was the final act of a transfer deadline day we are unlikely to see anything similar to ever again.

In the immediate aftermath, John Henry described the Carroll acquisition as 'a hell of a deal' and confirmed the fee paid to Newcastle was entirely dependent on how much the Reds would receive from Chelsea for Torres.

"The negotiation for us was simply the difference in prices paid by Chelsea and to Newcastle," Henry said.

"Those prices could have been £35 million [for Torres] and £20 million [for Carroll], 40 and 25 or 50 and 35.

"It was ultimately up to Newcastle how much this was all going to cost.

"They [Newcastle] made a hell of a deal. We felt the same way."

Liverpool's then director of football strategy, Damien Comolli, revealed the club knew they were paying over the odds for Carroll but had been backed into a corner by Torres' sudden wish to leave Anfield.

Speaking to The Athletic's The Ornstein and Chapman Podcast, he said: "We were stuck at the time because Fernando was going and we didn't know who to replace him with.

"The night before deadline day, I had a call from someone who had nothing to do with transfers saying they'd heard from Newcastle's chairman that he would entertain the sale of Andy Carroll.

"I kind of agreed a deal with Newcastle that night, and the next day they read in the paper how much we were getting for Torres so they changed the deal and increased it by £5 million which absolutely drove me crazy.

"We decided to do it. I emailed the owners and said I need a conference call with you. The owners, Kenny [Dalglish], the chief executive himself, and I said this is the deal and this is the risk.

"We voted and we knew we were paying over the odds for Andy but he was young, he was English and at the time I told them if it doesn't work out, we'll sell him for £20 million.

"The scenario I had in my mind at the time was either he's a massive hit and success, or he was not but there was some money still to be made. We knew we were overpaying but we were also getting incredible money for Torres and Chelsea were grossly overpaying as well.

"I think it got to about 5pm and we got together and voted, and then I got on the phone to the agent of Andy and he started saying he wants this and that. He said this is not right, if you pay £35 million I want more money.

"I said look, this is going to be very simple. It's 5pm now and the window shuts in six hours so you take it or leave it. He called me back and it was all agreed."

Liverpool's recruitment has evolved drastically over the past decade away from such a reactive approach with a clear strategy emerging which has been held up as a model for others to follow.

It's clear that FSG's first experience of a transfer window proved to be very much a learning curve for the new owners.

DJIMI
TRAORE

Red Redemption

First published: March 2022

THERE are a myriad of reasons Liverpool's extraordinary fifth European Cup triumph will be remembered and celebrated by supporters for as long as the club exists.

The miraculous fightback from three goals down at half-time against a star-studded AC Milan side, the Reds regaining their crown as Kings of Europe after a 21-year wait, and Rafa Benitez's side blunting the taunts of Everton fans cock-a-hoop at their side finishing above Liverpool and qualifying for the Champions League play-offs to name but three.

That redemptive aspect also applies to a fair few of the Liverpool players who wrote themselves into immortality on that heady night in the Turkish capital. Nobody could ever credibly claim the Reds' 2005 vintage was among the club's greatest when it came to ability, but that such a relatively limited outfit managed to defy the odds and overcome a clearly superior outfit of proven winners only adds extra lustre in the eyes of many.

As does the fact several of the squad who engineered the Reds to glory had long been written off as duds. That includes one much-maligned defender who only months earlier had become a figure of ridicule after a high-profile, hall-of-fame own goal, but was picked up off the floor by an inspiring pep talk from a team-mate who knew only too well how it feels when your name becomes a punch-line.

Djimi Traore was only 18 when he arrived at Anfield in February 1999 as one of Gerard Houllier's first signings as Liverpool manager.

Although Traore had only made a handful of appearances after breaking through at his local club, Stade Lavallois, the teenager – able to operate both at centre-half and left-back – had already drawn interest from Paris St Germain, AC Milan, Parma and Lazio, and Houllier wasted no time in tying up a £550,000 deal to bring him to Merseyside as one for the future, declaring to the Liverpool public via the press: "You'll thank me for signing him."

It would be the start of the following campaign before the manager felt he was ready for a first-team bow and, although the young defender started both legs of the Reds' League Cup second-round tie with Hull City, they would be his only appearances until almost another year later and the opening day of the 2000-01 season when he began the first five Premier League matches at left-back.

It was the campaign which truly began Houllier's reign in earnest with his side winning an unprecedented cup treble but Traore's youthful naivety was evident from those early-season games, inadvertently setting up Southampton's Marian Pahars for the stoppage-time equaliser which earned the Saints a point after they had been three goals behind on Liverpool's last-ever visit to the Dell. Soon after, he clumsily conceded a penalty to Alf Inge Haaland which enabled Manchester City to draw level from two goals down at Anfield before a late Dietmar Hamann winner snatched victory. The young Frenchman would make 12 appearances in total that campaign but none after late November and the following summer returned to France on a season-long loan with Lens.

"Before I joined Liverpool I had only played five games as a professional and that was in the second division in France," Traore admitted. "I wasn't well known and didn't have much experience as a professional. Liverpool was my learning process and it was a high level, so it was not easy. I had to play a year-and-a-half in the reserves, where we won the championship and I was named captain. At first I was a bit apprehensive about coming to Liverpool but fortunately I knew there were some players like Rigobert Song and Jean-Michel Ferri who could take me under their wing and the fact the manager and his coaches are French influenced my choice. There were no regrets.

"I started off as an attacking midfielder at Laval and did quite well because I scored pretty regularly and got forward very often. But after a while I was pulled back into a defensive role because I kept hold of the ball too much. Well, that's what people told me.

"You see, my game was based too much on the football I used to play when I was with my friends in Paris, where we wouldn't run back after we lost the ball. I prefer to play in the middle of the defence as that's where I learnt my trade but I've noticed that in France and in England too that people tend to have more confidence in a youngster who plays left-back rather than central defence."

On his return to Anfield for the 2002/03 season, Traore was thrust straight into the first team, an early season injury to Stephane Henchoz giving the young Frenchman a run in his preferred position of centre-back. But it proved to be the campaign when Gerard Houllier's reign started to decline after such promising beginnings.

The decision not to make former Arsenal striker Nicolas Anelka's loan a permanent move, and instead sign Traore's former Lens team-mate El-Hadji Diouf – along with two more acquisitions from the French league, Salif Diao and Bruno Cheyrou – highlighted how Houllier's golden touch had begun to desert him since his illness and although the Reds began the season well, leading and remaining unbeaten in the Premier League until early November, a defeat at Middlesbrough sparked an 11-game winless run from which the campaign – and in truth the Frenchman's time as manager – never recovered.

Three days later, Liverpool crashed out of the Champions League in the group stages after drawing a game at Swiss minnows FC Basel they had to win and, although the League Cup was won the following March after victory in Cardiff over Manchester United (a match Traore was left on the bench for), defeat at Chelsea on the final day confirmed failure to even qualify for the following season's Champions League.

Traore would score his first Liverpool goal the following season – a superb strike in a rain-sodden UEFA Cup draw at Steaua Bucharest – but that was one of only 14 appearances he made in all competitions as he seemed to fall completely out of favour. It was another campaign of depressing decline with Liverpool never close to being even on the fringes of a

title shout while suffering domestic cup exits to lower division
Bolton Wanderers and Crystal Palace and being knocked out
of Europe by Marseille in the quarter-finals. The Reds did at
least manage to finish fourth and qualify for the following
season's Champions League, but nobody was surprised when
Houllier's five-and-a-half year spell in charge was brought to
a close with Traore admitting he had lost trust in his former
mentor and would have left had he stayed in charge.

He said: "He was much appreciated by the Englishmen and
I can see why. But a lot of the French players didn't have a
chance to play and express themselves. We had to work twice
as hard to play. I mainly played left-back but left-back was
not my position; centre-back was. And when I played centre-
back it was on the right because I was mainly next to Sami
Hyypia and Sami didn't like playing on the right. For a left-
footed player that is also not easy. In the end, I didn't trust him
anymore. I was upset. So many times I knocked on his door
saying I wanted to leave the club. It was frustrating because I
didn't play."

Houllier's replacement was Spanish coach Rafa Benitez who
had briefly challenged the dominance of Real Madrid and
Barcelona in La Liga by leading Valencia to two league titles as
well as lifting the previous season's UEFA Cup and, although
he would swiftly install Jamie Carragher as Hyypia's centre-
back partner, Traore was very much back in the fold – despite
almost signing for Everton during the summer – and figured in
42 of the 60 matches Liverpool played in what was a season of
startling contrasts. A slow start in the league saw the Reds win
only once away from home before January and fail to claim a
Champions League qualifying spot.

Benitez's side would go all the way to Cardiff in the League
Cup but were not able to hold on to the early lead provided by

John Arne Riise's volley. Chelsea fought back to win 3-2 after extra-time.

The Reds had already exited the FA Cup at the first hurdle due to a moment which could have ended up cruelly defining Traore's career had he let it. Drawn away in the third round to mid-table Championship side Burnley, Benitez rang the changes with youngsters David Raven, Zak Whitbread, John Welsh and Darren Potter all given starts, but it was Traore – at nearly 25, one of the senior members of the team – who proved the inadvertent match-winner six minutes into the second half. With the game goalless and under minimal pressure, he attempted to silkily turn with the ball when dealing with Richard Chaplow's cross across the face of the six-yard box but only succeeding in clumsily dragging the ball into his own net. Such an embarrassing exit only heaped further pressure and scrutiny on Liverpool's season, with the previous weekend's home defeat to Manchester United leaving the Reds already 21 points behind runaway league leaders Chelsea.

"I'm not ashamed of the own goal against Burnley," Traore would later insist to the Guardian. "It is the story of my career – some highs, some lows. It was my fault and I take responsibility for it. I was trying to turn with the ball but it bounced on the wrong part of the field, hit my Achilles and went in. A big mistake and Rafa thought the same – that is why he subbed me soon afterwards. He also told me I had been too relaxed in the game and the own goal was my punishment for that. I agreed.

"The following day I was in the locker room at Melwood and Jamie Carragher came and sat next to me. He could tell I was not in a good place. We had a long discussion during which he said, 'Djimi, that's nothing, I once scored two own goals in one game, and it was against Manchester United. So don't worry'. That meant a lot and allowed me to move on."

That resilience of spirit would be very much required as Liverpool's rollercoaster campaign reached its astounding conclusion in the Champions League. The Reds had been on the brink of elimination from the group stages until Steven Gerrard's sublime volley against Olympiacos took them into the last 16 where, after comfortably seeing off Bayer Leverkusen, Benitez's side edged out Juventus in the clubs' first meeting since the Heysel tragedy 20 years earlier to set up a semi-final against champions-elect Chelsea.

After a goalless draw in the first leg at Stamford Bridge, the Londoners clinched their first league title in 50 years with victory at Bolton the weekend before the Anfield return and were strong favourites to reach the final, but Luis Garcia's early 'ghost goal' coupled with a herculean defensive rearguard and sheer force of will from the Liverpool players and crowd took the Reds to the final.

Traore started all but one of Liverpool's knockout ties, including both legs against Juventus and Chelsea during which only one goal was conceded, and spoke ahead of the final against Italian giants AC Milan – who had lifted the trophy only two years before – about how his decision to persevere on Merseyside through the tough times had been vindicated.

"When I left France at 18 years old for Liverpool, a lot of people said I made a mistake," he said. "But on Wednesday I will play the Champions League final! That is pride. Gerard Houllier signed me at Liverpool in 1999, when I was completely unknown. I owe him a lot. This season, Rafael Benitez has trusted me, and I play. That proves I don't need any string pulling to make a name for myself. When I came here, I felt some hesitation towards me. People said, 'he is a Frenchman like Houllier. So he will play'. I had to make twice as much effort as the other players just to be accepted. On an individual level, we are less strong than a lot of players of other teams. We don't have so many bombastic names other great European teams have either. But we are still here, despite everything. Because there is a soul at Liverpool. We are more closely-knit than all our adversaries. There is also a life between us away from the pitch."

Traore began at left-back in the Ataturk Olympic Stadium but suffered a first-half nightmare alongside his team-mates, conceding the final's first free-kick within 40 seconds which Andrea Pirlo swung in for Paolo Maldini to volley the Italians in front as Milan raced into a seemingly insurmountable 3-0 lead by half-time. It appeared the France-born defender – who had made his international debut for Mali the year before – was going to be put out of his misery when Benitez told him as he returned to the dressing room he was to be substituted, only for him to be handed a reprieve when it emerged right-back Steve Finnan would be unable to continue due to a thigh problem.

"With Rafa it was two ways," Traore recalled. "If he called me 'Djimi' I knew I was in his good books and if he called me 'Traore' I knew I was in trouble – at half-time he said 'Traore', so I knew I was done. The first half was a nightmare – we were losing 3-0 in the biggest game of our lives. I took off my kit and got into the shower, but I just stood there thinking about my performance because it had been poor and I felt as if I'd let down my team-mates. And then maybe 20 seconds later Rafa's assistant, Pako Ayestarán, came and said, 'Djimi, you're in again' – Steve Finnan was injured so he was coming off instead. I got out of the shower and refocused. This was a second chance for me to do well in a massive game and fortunately that is what happened with the clearance. It was redemption."

With Dietmar Hamann introduced to shore up the midfield

in place of the injured Finnan, Liverpool emerged from a chaotic dressing room to produce six minutes written inexorably into European Cup legend to draw level by the hour mark. The Reds withstood the shell-shocked Italians' attempts to regain their lead to take the final to penalties, where successful efforts from Hamann, Djibril Cisse and Smicer, coupled with two saves from goalkeeper Jerzy Dudek, secured Liverpool's fifth European Cup – but it may not have happened but for a vital goal-line clearance shortly after Alonso's equaliser from Traore to deny Andrei Shevchenko after Dudek had spilled a cross.

"I just tried to do my job and I was lucky to be in the right spot," Traore modestly said. "To be honest with you, everybody brought something to the team that night. You have to give a lot of credit to the 'Kaiser' (Hamann), he brought his experience and his confidence to the team in the second half. He gave us what we had been missing in the first half. We were also lucky to have one of the best keepers in the world that night. Jerzy Dudek was on fire. The save from Shevchenko was unbelievable. When you see your keeper do that kind of thing, we knew that when it went to penalties he would save some. It was when Stevie's header went in that I started to believe we could do it.

"I remembered the words of the coach. At half-time Rafa had said that if we could score one goal in the first 15 minutes of the second half we could come back. Only Stevie could have scored that kind of goal and lifted the team in that way. He brought back that spirit and desire. What we did in that second half showed that in sport anything can happen. Yes, it was a miracle. But for me it also showed the character of the group and the character of the manager. We did it for the fans and we did it for the city. I always loved playing in the Champions League for Liverpool because the fans were fantastic. European nights were special. You could feel that communication between the players and the fans. You could feel the spirit of Liverpool. We always played for them."

Traore was part of the squad which won the FA Cup the following season after another penalty shoot-out following a dramatic final drawn 3-3, but only made 24 appearances throughout the campaign with Benitez gradually compiling the squad he wanted and the 26-year-old joined Charlton Athletic for £2m in the summer of 2006 to bring his seven-and-a-half-year, 141-game Liverpool career to an end. He moved to Portsmouth a year later and, after loan spells at Rennes and Birmingham City, returned to France with Monaco and Marseille before finishing his playing days in the United States with Seattle Sounders, who he went on to coach. He later became head coach of the international Right to Dream academy, an organisation initially launched in Ghana over 20 years ago which provides youngsters with access to football training and educational opportunities and has produced more than 20 Ghana internationals.

Using his experience to help young players conquer obstacles – "I can say to them, 'you can score an own goal and then a few months later win the Champions League'" – is a role Traore admitted suits his personality. His considered outlook on the game and his own career was evident in the heartfelt tribute he paid to Gerard Houllier following the coach's passing at the age of 73 in December 2020.

He said: "It's a very sad day today. I'm devastated because we lost someone very important for the world of football and very important for my career as a player. He signed me for Liverpool when I was 18 and gave me the opportunity to play at Anfield and be part of club history. I had a relationship like father and son with Gerard. He was hard on me but at the end of the day, he wanted the best for me."

Outside Anfield, the name Djimi Traore still provokes tedious and cliched jibes over his comedy own goal at Burnley but his role, not just in the final but during the Reds' remarkable run to Istanbul, should never be forgotten and will forever be a source of immense pride to the man himself.

He said: "My Liverpool career was always like that – lots of ups and downs. But I always believed in myself. I always had trust from the manager and from my team-mates, and they helped me. I was always strong in my head and that helped me to put any bad times behind me. In difficult situations I stayed strong. What happened in Istanbul was reward for that. That was the greatest night of my career. To win the Champions League is the biggest achievement for any player and to win it with this football club made it extra special. It was the club's fifth European Cup so we got it for keeps. I'm very proud that I was a part of that.

"Whenever I meet Liverpool fans in America, Europe or Africa they all want to talk about that final. Everyone remembers where they were for that game. That's when you realise you touched people by being involved in something great. Overall I did my best and always fought to stay in the team. And in the end I played a lot of games for Liverpool, more games than a lot of players the club signed for big money. When you play for the Reds, you are a Red forever."

RAY KENNEDY

Shankly's Parting Gift

First published: November 2022

IT is sometimes said that the true measure of greatness in football managers is measured by legacy.

You only have to look at Nottingham Forest and Manchester United following the departures of Brian Clough and Alex Ferguson for two stark examples of how a lack of succession planning can undo much of the good work which went before.

Bill Shankly's position in the Liverpool pantheon was firmly established by virtue of the way he dragged a once-great club languishing in the doldrums of the Second Division into the modern era, revitalising the club on and off the field and establishing a culture of success which has persisted into the modern era.

But it was cemented by his parting gift when he bade Anfield farewell on 12 July 1974, the acquisition of his final Liverpool signing completed that very same day being initially massively overshadowed by the seismic shock of his resignation.

Ray Kennedy was already a player well familiar to Liverpool supporters.

After initially signing schoolboy forms with Port Vale after their manager, the legendary England winger Stanley Matthews, travelled to the family home in Northumberland to persuade him to put pen to paper, Kennedy made his name as a centre forward at Arsenal.

He was a key member of the Gunners side in 1970/71 which became only the second team that century to win the hallowed league championship and FA Cup double, scoring the goal away to north London rivals Tottenham which clinched the First Division title and five days later at Wembley playing his part against Shankly's Reds as Bertie Mee's side fought back from a goal behind in extra-time to win 2-1.

His fortunes, like Arsenal's, declined somewhat in the years after the Double triumph, so it was something of a surprise when he arrived at Anfield in the summer of 1974 for a then club record fee of £180,000.

His arrival inevitably went under the radar given the simultaneous announcement of Shankly's shock retirement but the Scot was clearly happy with his final bit of business at the Anfield helm.

"There is no doubt Kennedy will do a good job for Liverpool," Shankly declared. "He is big, brave and strong. His signing means that we now have the greatest strength in depth that we have ever had. Kennedy will cause plenty of trouble to defences.

"He fights all the way and he was at the top of my list of my wanted men. I've seen him in training and he looks good. He reminds me of Rocky Marciano.

"Maybe it will be said that one of the last things I did at this club was to sign a great new player."

Kennedy scored in each of his first three games for Bob Paisley's Liverpool but, like the new manager, took some time to truly acclimatise, finishing his first season at the club with the meagre tally of only five goals in 25 league matches.

There was speculation he may be off-loaded to Wolves but an injury to midfielder Peter Cormack early the following season prompted one of the most significant decisions of Paisley's management career, which would ultimately stand as indisputable proof of the canny north-easterner's own brand of managerial genius.

Drawing on his encyclopaedic memory for something he had been told years before, Paisley moved Kennedy to the left side of midfield for a match at Middlesbrough, later revealing, "One of my old friends told me that before Ray went to Arsenal he had played much deeper.

"I then knew I could back my instinct and see if he could recapture his spark."

His first crack in his new role was not overly auspicious, the Liverpool Daily Post commenting after the Reds' 1-0 win at Ayresome Park that "poor Kennedy looked a most temporary left-half" but he scored twice three days later in a 6-0 UEFA Cup win over Real Sociedad at Anfield and bagged two more in the next four games against Newcastle and Polish side Slask Wroclaw.

By the end of the season, it was becoming clear Paisley's hunch was turning into a masterstroke.

Kennedy proved to be a revelation in midfield, his new position allowing his vision and distribution to create chances for his team-mates while still allowing him to make late runs into the box to get on the scoresheet himself.

His rejuvenation mirrored that of Paisley's side as, with the middle of the park further bolstered by local lad and Ray's great mate Jimmy Case, Liverpool finished the season as league champions and UEFA Cup winners for the second time in four seasons, Kennedy scoring crucial goals in both the league decider at Wolves and the first leg of the European final against FC Bruges.

Another league and continental double followed the next season with the Reds becoming champions of Europe for the first time, Kennedy's influence again being evident in the iconic quarter-final comeback against Saint-Etienne when he struck at the Kop end to draw Liverpool level on aggregate before supplying the through ball for David Fairclough's famous late winner.

The European Cup was retained in 1978, Kennedy showing glimpses of his old centre-forward days with a forceful far-post header that started the semi-final second leg fightback against Borussia Moenchengladbach and in 1978/79 Liverpool recorded one of their most dominant title wins with the midfield four of Case-Souness-McDermott-Kennedy still being regarded by many as the club's finest ever.

Paisley was in no doubt of the importance of his repurposed left-sided midfielder and revealed that out of all the talented players he had at his disposal during his time as Liverpool manager, Kennedy was the one he received the most inquiries about from other clubs.

"He, out of them all, was the one that they were more concerned about than anybody in my time as manager. I had more people enquiring about Ray Kennedy than any of the others," Paisley admitted.

"His contribution to Liverpool's achievements was enormous and his consistency remarkable. So much so, in fact, that on the rare occasions he missed a match, his absence was felt deeply simply because he was a midfield powerhouse with tremendous vision and knowledge of the game. In my view he was one of Liverpool's greatest players and probably the most underrated."

One of Kennedy's finest moments in a Liverpool shirt came towards the end of his time at Anfield when a patched-up side travelled to Bayern Munich for the second leg of the 1981 European Cup semi-final following a goalless draw at Anfield.

Injuries meant Paisley was forced to name reserve team players Richard Money and Colin Irwin in the back four and the Reds' task was made harder when Kenny Dalglish was forced off after taking a heavy knock in the first ten minutes.

But with substitute Howard Gayle running the Germans ragged, Kennedy – captain on the night – pounced with a superbly-taken volley seven minutes from time, and while Bayern equalised late on it was not enough to stop Liverpool progressing to the Paris final on the away goals rule, where Kennedy supplied the throw-in for Alan Kennedy to score the late winner that sealed the Reds' third European Cup win in five seasons.

Sadly, though, it was the beginning of the end of Kennedy's time at Liverpool, as the first visible signs of Parkinson's disease, which would have such an impact on the second half of his life, began to reveal themselves.

He later revealed in his autobiography: "At Liverpool, I could never understand why I was the odd man out, particularly after a match.

"Usually the adrenaline is pumping and most of the lads would be talking about what happened on the pitch, grabbing a coke or chicken leg. They were always doing something, all except me.

"I used to slump hunched in my seat, too tired to move. I tried to kid myself I was more tired because I had worked harder than the others during a match, yet I knew it was not the case.

"The odd thing was I could always perform for the full 90 minutes and was rarely the one to be substituted."

Kennedy turned 30 in the summer of 1981 and the emergence of young Irish midfielder Ronnie Whelan led Ray to be sold to Swansea City in January 1982 to play under former team-mate John Toshack, where he received a sixth league championship medal that summer after playing enough games for Paisley's side before his departure.

Kennedy's time in south Wales became one of further struggle as he was stripped of the captaincy and accused of being lazy and overweight, with still no-one being aware of the medical difficulties he was suffering.

His playing days finished with similarly unsatisfactory spells back in the north east with Hartlepool United and Ashington as well as Cypriot club Pezoporikos before he was finally diagnosed with Parkinson's disease in November 1986.

He became a high profile ambassador to raise awareness for the disease and got to meet his childhood hero Muhammad Ali, who was also a sufferer.

Arsenal and Liverpool held a testimonial match for him at Highbury in May 1991 and in 2009 before a match at Anfield between the two sides, tributes were paid to Kennedy at both ends of the ground with his number at Liverpool, '5', being held up by fans with coloured cards on the Kop and his Gunners number '10' by those in the away end.

Afterwards he paid tribute to the Liverpool fans, led by Karl Coppack, who had set up the Ray of Hope appeal earlier that year to help him.

"It's tremendous," Kennedy said. "The Liverpool fans have always been very special and I always knew that, but I suppose I didn't realise just how special – now I do.

"I really appreciate how much they have done for me and it is hard for me to put into words just how much I appreciate it."

GINI WIJNALDUM

Social Media Storm

First published: November 2022

THE amount of column inches written about Liverpool's midfield in the latter days of Jurgen Klopp's reign could probably wallpaper the Taj Mahal a thousand times over.

Succession planning has largely been a major strength and carried out effectively at Anfield of late but refreshing Liverpool's midfield was never going to be as easy as some seem to think given the unique demands Klopp required from those in the middle of the park and the exalted level his team had been performing at on a regular basis. And it was made more difficult by the contentious departure in the summer of 2021 of a man whose versatility and tactical nous papered over many of the gaps within that area of the squad and who proved very difficult to replace.

Georginio Wijnaldum arrived on Merseyside in Klopp's first summer as Reds boss back in 2016 ostensibly as a playmaker in a £25m deal from Newcastle United, but his ability to shape-shift depending on what his coach required dates back to his formative years back in Holland. Starting out with Sparta in his home city of Rotterdam, young 'Gini' – largely brought up by his grandmother after his Surinam-born parents separated when he was six – began as a centre-half before becoming a right-back at under-11/12 level and then eventually a midfielder.

He moved to Rotterdam's biggest club, Feyenoord, in 2007 and soon afterwards became their youngest ever first-team player, making his debut against Groningen at the age of only 16 years and 148 days. His dribbling ability saw him moved out to the right wing in his third season at the De Kuip by new manager Gertjan Verbeek, a switch the affable youngster reluctantly went along with.

"I performed well there so they didn't want to move me out, but in my mind, I always believed I was better in midfield," he later admitted. "I was just happy to be playing, though, because I was young. When you're still developing, getting games is so important. I learnt a lot playing on the wing and now I understand what the guys in those positions want from me. But when I got older, I knew I wanted to be a midfielder. I've had to have discussions with my agent, managers, directors, chief executives to explain that I am a midfielder, especially at Feyenoord."

His final year with Feyenoord also saw him feature in the number 10 role before he moved to PSV Eindhoven for €5m in June 2011, where his ability to provide goals and assists from midfield rose to a new level, scoring 56 times in 154 appearances during four seasons with the 'Rood-witten', and captaining them to a first Eredivisie league title in eight years in 2014/15. It won him a move to the Premier League that summer where Newcastle United paid £14.5m and, although his 11 goals in 40 matches were not enough to save the Toon from relegation, his performances drew the attention of a number of clubs, including Liverpool.

Two months after Klopp took over from Brendan Rodgers in October 2015, Wijnaldum played a major role in the German's first away defeat as Reds boss, forcing Martin Skrtel into the 69th-minute own goal which broke the deadlock at St James' Park and then scoring the clinching second goal himself in stoppage time with the kind of calm finish at the end of a counter-attack Liverpool supporters would become used to from him. By the time of the Anfield return the following April, Rafa Benitez was in charge of Newcastle and Wijnaldum – left out of the starting line-up – came off the bench at half-time with the visitors two goals down and helped his side to a battling point in their bid for survival.

A player of Wijnaldum's calibre, already a well-established Dutch international having made his bow for the Oranje five years earlier, was never likely to be happy with second-tier football and in late July 2016, he became Klopp's seventh summer signing following the acquisitions of Sadio Mane, Joel Matip, Ragnar Klavan, Marko Grujic, Loris Karius and Alex Manninger.

"I'm really excited because Liverpool is a big club with a great history and it's always a dream to play for as big a club as Liverpool," he told the official LFC website. "Jurgen Klopp seems like a great man – from the outside – because I don't know how he works yet and I have to work with him. But I always love to watch him, his passion as a trainer, I like how he enjoys the game. He gives something back to the group with his passion so I look forward to working with him."

Klopp was equally delighted at securing the seventh and final signing of his summer spending spree.

"I think he can be a great player for us," the German predicted. "He has already shown some really good moments in his career but the most exciting and important thing for me and my staff is that there is still so much extra to come from him. When I talked to him I could tell that he knows we have to work together to get this level out of him to all be successful for the team. He has played a lot for his country already, been captain at a young age in Holland and also been involved in a tough Premier League season, so this experience gives him a good foundation for the challenge here, which everybody knows is huge. He can play a few positions for us and players that come through the Dutch system usually have a good tactical understanding and flexibility. That's really important. I can't wait to get him on the training pitch and for the fans to see him play in a Liverpool shirt."

The Dutchman was one of four debutants on the opening day of the season as Liverpool travelled to Arsenal – operating on the left side of a midfield three along with skipper Jordan Henderson and Adam Lallana – and played his part in an eventful 4-3 victory, producing a smart assist for Lallana to put the Reds in front shortly after half-time as four goals in an 18-minute blitz either side of the interval highlighted the raw potential of Klopp's rebuilt side.

That opening match ended up being something of a microcosm of Liverpool's rollercoaster season, with a 2-0 defeat at newly-promoted Burnley the following weekend – despite Klopp's men having 81 percent possession over the 90 minutes and registering 25 shots on goal as opposed to the hosts' two – illustrating how much work still lay ahead. The consistency in performances and results the manager and his staff were seeking did initially transpire, the Reds not being beaten again until early December at Bournemouth, having the previous month gone top of the Premier League for the first time since May 2014 with a 6-1 Anfield victory over Watford crowned by Wijnaldum scoring his first goal for his new club.

The Dutchman's second came on New Year's Eve, a thumping header which proved the difference as Pep Guardiola brought Manchester City to Anfield for the first time and opened up a four-point lead over the Etihad club for the second-placed Reds who were six behind leaders Chelsea, sending exuberant Kopites home with dreams of a possible title charge in the new year. Those ambitions were swiftly put into perspective as the talismanic Mane's departure on African Nations Cup duty prompted a slump which saw only one league win in the next two months to put even Champions League qualification in jeopardy.

Wijnaldum still showed his big-match temperament during that difficult period by poaching an equaliser against Chelsea and a late clincher in a 3-1 Anfield triumph over Arsenal at the start of March – running half the length of the field to sweep home in front of the Kop.

On the final day, Liverpool knew victory at home over already-relegated Middlesbrough would secure fourth place and the return to the Champions League, and it was Wijnaldum who settled Anfield's jangling nerves just before half-time, striding purposefully onto Roberto Firmino's pass and smashing the ball high into the net. Second-half efforts from Philippe Coutinho and Lallana secured an ultimately comfortable 3-0 victory and a successful first full campaign in charge for Klopp and debut season for Wijnaldum, who had featured in all but two of the Reds' league matches.

"When we scored the goal it looked like the weight just fell off our shoulders. That season we had already shown that we can handle big games. Against the top six we didn't lose a game that season but at that time we were not that consistent so that was a little bit difficult, but we knew that it would help us if we qualified for the Champions League, that we would develop more because you play against the best teams in Europe."

That proved to be very much the case as, after successfully negotiating the Champions League play-off against German side Hoffenheim and bolstered by the remarkable scoring feats of £36m Egyptian forward Mohamed Salah, who arrived during the summer from AS Roma, Liverpool produced a season which fully demonstrated the upward trajectory they were on under Klopp.

The eventual £75m arrival of his international team-mate Virgil van Dijk finally gave Klopp the defensive leader he was looking for and the Reds roared all the way into the Champions League final, Wijnaldum grabbing only his second goal of the campaign and his first away from Anfield since joining the club with what proved to be a crucial header in the second leg of the semi-final in Rome's Stadio Olimpico. The fates conspired against Klopp's men in the Kyiv final, Salah's extraordinary 44-goal debut campaign being brought to a premature conclusion by Sergio Ramos and Loris Karius's goalkeeping horror show as Real Madrid won 3-1 but the belief Liverpool were on the cusp of something special was inescapable.

With the defensive spine further bolstered with the summer signings of Brazilians Alisson Becker and Fabinho, seven straight victories at the start of 2018/19 – Wijnaldum grabbing his first league goal away from Anfield with a header in a 2-1 victory at Tottenham – set the tone and the Reds reached the turn of the year unbeaten in the Premier League and leading it by seven points from the previous season's 100-point champions, Manchester City. Narrow defeat days later at the Etihad – the only one in the league all campaign – kept Guardiola's men in the hunt and the Reds would suffer a relatively sticky late winter spell with draws against Leicester, West Ham, Manchester United and Everton allowing City to regain a slender, one-point initiative in the title race.

The evolution of Klopp's side from the 'heavy-metal' approach of the early years to a more composed outfit, able to control games better while still unleashing devastating attacking bursts, required real tactical intelligence and discipline throughout the side but particularly in midfield with Wijnaldum often doing a lot of the unsung 'donkey' work which enabled others to shine. He was still chipping in with the occasional goal, a sublime lob against Bournemouth in February 2019 highlighting the delicate touch he possessed, and his adaptation from goalscorer and creator to midfield link man was hugely valued within the dressing room. Along with compatriot Van Dijk, vice-captain James Milner and skipper Jordan Henderson, he was part of the squad's leadership committee.

"A lot of people see me differently, a lot didn't think I could play the way I am," the Dutch midfielder said. "They thought I was just an attack-minded player, the dribbler or the goalscorer without the discipline to defend and check on the movements of my team-mates. I think I've surprised many people because I'm showing I can still make the runs and get goals, but I'm regaining balls, keeping the rhythm in the passing, covering for those around me and getting assists."

"Gini can switch from one mindset to the other and that is pretty good for us," Klopp admitted, and it proved invaluable as one of the most outstanding seasons in Liverpool's long, decorated history reached a tumultuous conclusion. The Reds and Manchester City traded blow for blow in the highest-quality title race ever seen with Liverpool – just one point behind – praying for one slip-up to put them back in control of their own destiny which they gradually began to realise might never come.

Another run to the Champions League semi-finals had gone almost unnoticed such was the fixation with ending the long wait for the holy grail of a 19th league title but by the start of May, with only two league matches left and City still a point ahead, the prospect of a sixth European Cup suddenly loomed into view. Without the injured Firmino for the first leg of the semi-final against Barcelona in the Camp Nou cauldron, Wijnaldum – who had sometimes played as a second striker at Newcastle as well as attacking midfielder – was pressed into service by Klopp as the Brazilian's replacement in the middle of the front three.

The Dutchman didn't let anyone down as Klopp's men performed admirably but missed chances proved costly as they somehow found themselves on the wrong end of a cruel 3-0 scoreline to leave them on the brink of elimination, picking themselves up off the floor three days later to win their penultimate league fixture at Newcastle – but City responded to maintain their advantage going into the final weekend.

The following evening Liverpool's incredible campaign seemed set to come to a heartbreaking end with the slim chances of overturning Barcelona's three-goal first-leg advantage further harmed with Salah having joined Firmino and Naby Keita on the injured list for the Anfield return after picking up a head injury in the win at Newcastle. Wijnaldum's reward for having played out of position in the Camp Nou was to be left out of the starting line-up altogether but it inadvertently proved to be a Klopp masterstroke. With Divock

Origi's seventh-minute opener having reduced the deficit, the Dutchman was introduced into the fray at half-time in place of the injured Andy Robertson, with Milner moving to left-back, and within ten minutes Wijnaldum had scored twice to astonishingly draw Liverpool level on aggregate, sweeping Trent Alexander-Arnold's right-wing cross beyond goalkeeper Marc-Andre ter Stegen and, 90 whirlwind seconds later, arching his back to steer a precise header from Xherdan Shaqiri's centre into the top corner of the Kop end net as Anfield exploded in disbelieving joy.

Origi's assured 79th-minute side-foot finish from Alexander-Arnold's quickly-taken corner completed the most miraculous two-legged comeback Anfield had ever seen to send Liverpool to the Madrid final, with Wijnaldum producing one of the biggest cheers of the night during those agonising closing stages when a Barcelona goal would still have taken them through on away goals with a brilliant wriggle away from trouble when surrounded, and he admitted afterwards his performance had been motivated by the anger he felt at his rare omission from the team.

"It's unbelievable. Once again we showed that everything is possible in football. It's really emotional because I was really angry at the manager that he put me on the bench but I had to do something to help the team when I came on. I just tried to help the team and I'm happy that I could with two goals. After the game in Spain we were confident we could score four at home and win 4-0. I think the people from outside, they doubted us and thought we couldn't do it, but we won 4-0. We know it is possible at this club. We found a way to do it.

"Klopp probably spoke to me during half-time but I was so angry that I didn't listen to him. The only moment I listened to him was when the morning training stopped and he said,

'Gini, you have to be ready because I need you when you come on.' When I did come on, Pep Lijnders told me that when we built up I had to come into a back three to get the ball with the wing-backs higher. In my head, I was like, 'No, no, no. I'm not going to do that. I just try to play up front, try to score goals.' I was so angry that I wanted to do my own thing and, in the end, it helped."

Wolverhampton Wanderers were beaten at Anfield the following Sunday on the final day of the Premier League campaign to ensure Liverpool finished the domestic campaign with a club-record 97 points but City's win at Brighton meant they had agonisingly recorded one more and so retained their title. Three weeks later, Klopp's men – with Wijnaldum restored to the starting line-up – saw off Tottenham Hotspur in the Champions League final to at last win their first trophy under the German coach and ensure a season for the ages gained tangible and deserved reward.

As was the case following the Kyiv disappointment 12 months earlier, the hope was the Premier League title near-miss would inspire the Reds to go one better next time around and, filled with confidence having cast off their nearly-man tag, Liverpool simply steamrollered their way to the club's first championship in 30 long years by winning 26 and drawing one of their first 27 league fixtures, tying matters up with a record seven games to spare and gaining a club-record 99 points, while also lifting the UEFA Super Cup and, for the first time, the World Club Cup.

Wijnaldum figured in all but one of the Reds' Premier League matches, equalling his highest LFC goal tally from his debut season of six, and early on in the campaign Klopp paid glowing tribute, insisting his many attributes made him the perfect midfielder for what his team required.

"Gini's importance is just so obvious. It is both directions, small spaces, big spaces, it is hard challenges, fine football, pretty much all of that. Is he the perfect midfielder? From the skillset 100 per cent. He has all the things you need. There was his header against Barcelona too. He is not the tallest, but he is good in the air. He is a good jumper with good timing, all that stuff. It all makes him a pretty good footballer. That is how it should be. It is not my fault if he goes under the radar. You cannot ask me why he goes under the radar. I don't set the radar!"

Despite the high regard the manager clearly held for him, Wijnaldum began the season of Liverpool's title defence – played, as were the final delayed months of the title campaign, in front of empty stadiums due to the coronavirus pandemic – in the final year of his contract and with his future up in the air. Despite the likes of Salah, Mane, Milner, Matip, Origi, Firmino, Robertson and Alexander-Arnold having all received new deals, the Dutchman remained tethered to the same terms he had signed for in 2016 and speculation began to build that the midfielder – who turned 30 in November 2020 – could walk away for free, with Barcelona – now managed by the Dutchman's former international coach Ronald Koeman – mooted as a likely destination despite the player himself and Klopp insisting they both wanted him to stay.

"Just ask Liverpool those questions," Wijnaldum replied when probed over his future during the November international break. "Don't they answer?"

The issue rumbled on in the background of what was at times a tortuous season at Anfield where an unprecedented injury crisis meant the Reds were unable to defend their title.

They recovered to eventually finish third, which was secured with a final day 2-0 victory over Crystal Palace at Anfield in which Wijnaldum was named captain with it now clear he would not be signing a new contract and was set to leave the club.

"I'm fighting against tears right now," he admitted, having received a guard of honour from his team-mates after the match. "The people in Liverpool have shown me love during the five years. I will miss them. I hoped to have played many more years for the club but unfortunately things went differently. I have to start a new adventure. I didn't sign somewhere else."

"Gini Wijnaldum is an LFC legend – now and forever," Klopp wrote in his programme notes that day. "What this person – this wonderful, joyful, selfless person – has done for our team and club I cannot sum up in words, in truth, because my English is not good enough. He is an architect of our success. We have built this Liverpool on his legs, lungs, brain and his huge, beautiful heart."

Weeks later, Paris Saint-Germain confirmed they had secured the Dutchman's signature on a three-year deal and he admitted his decision to leave had been down to a sense of feeling under-appreciated by both the club's decision-makers and some Liverpool fans, particularly on social media.

"It was beautiful at the end at Liverpool and, for weeks after, I thought about it. Not every player who leaves has that. But there was a moment when I didn't feel loved and appreciated. Not my team-mates, not the people at Melwood. From them, I know... I can say they all love me and I love them. It was not from that side, more the other side.

"I have to say also there was social media. When it went bad, I was the player who they blamed – that I wanted to leave. Every day in training and in the games, I gave everything I had to bring it to a good end because, during the years, Liverpool meant so much to me and because of the way the fans in the stadium were treating me. My feeling was that the fans in the stadium and the fans on social media were two different kinds. The fans in the stadium always supported me. Even when they came back after the Covid lockout, already knowing that I was going to leave, they still supported me and, in the end, they gave me a great farewell.

"On social media, there was a moment when I was like, 'Wow. If they only knew what I was doing to stay fit and play every game.' Other players might have said 'Okay, I am not fit.' You get players in their last year who are like, 'I'm not playing because it is a risk.' I did the opposite. I didn't always play good but, after the game, I could look in the mirror and say, 'I gave it all. I trained hard to get better.' Even with the physios… I took the most possible treatment I could get. I cannot remember when I had a day off because I played so many games and basically it was too much for the body but I did everything to stay fit.

"There was a story that Liverpool made an offer, I didn't accept because I wanted more money and the fans made it like, 'Okay, he didn't get the offer, so he doesn't try his best to win games'. Then the results were not really good and everything looked like it was against me. Some moments, it was like, 'Wow, me again?' It's a collective. But my team-mates never gave me the feeling that I let them down or I was taking the p*** or something like that. With the team everything was fine. It was difficult to speak about football because every time, it was, 'What are you going to do?' Even my friends would read something and come to me and say, 'Is this true? Oh, you are going to do this?' I would say, 'You will see what is going to happen.' I just didn't want to talk about it because it was, 'My future this, my future that.' That was basically my last season at Liverpool – the future of Gini Wijnaldum, not beautiful things on the pitch."

Despite making 38 appearances as PSG cruised to another league title, Wijnaldum was unable to establish himself in the French capital like he had at Anfield. Whichever way his playing career concluded, the decision to allow him to leave Anfield when he did feels like one both parties may now look back on with a sense of regret.

IGOR
BISCAN

Croatian Cult Hero

First published: December 2022

WHENEVER Liverpool's miraculous Champions League triumph in Istanbul is recalled, chief among the aspects which have people shaking their heads in wonderment are the names of some of the players who made that heady night in the Turkish capital possible.

With the greatest of respect to them, Djimi Traore and Milan Baros – who both started against AC Milan at the Ataturk Olympic Stadium – along with the likes of Neil Mellor, Florent Sinama-Pongolle, Anthony Le Tallec and Antonio Nunez, who all made valuable contributions en route to the final, are unlikely to ever make anyone's all-time LFC XI.

Yet their names are written forever into Anfield folklore because of the cameo roles they played during Rafa Benitez's side's astonishing road to glory in 2004/05 – as is that of another unsung hero, who never saw a second of action in that season's Champions League final, but without whose efforts over the course of the campaign Liverpool may well not have even got out of the group stages.

Igor Biscan arrived at Anfield with a glowing reputation and made a hugely positive start before falling out of favour and becoming a figure of ridicule, after being pressed into service in an unfamiliar position.

The midfielder had already amassed an impressive amount of playing experience in his native Croatia before Gerard Houllier brought him to Anfield in December 2000. Having been talented enough to represent the national team at youth level, Biscan worked his way through the ranks at Dinamo Zagreb and, following a loan spell with NK Samovar, had established himself as a key figure in one of the the club's most successful sides, helping them to a fourth successive league title and impressive wins over FC Porto and Ajax in their first Champions League campaign in 1998/99. His progress saw him named captain and he led his team to another league title the following year, his powerful presence in midfield drawing further attention. His reputation was further bolstered by stellar showings in the European Under-21 Championships in the summer of 2000 and, with clubs such as Juventus, AC Milan, Ajax and Barcelona showing interest, the Liverpool manager swooped.

By the end of September, a £5.5m deal was agreed to bring him to Anfield once the Croatian season shut down for its winter break and he duly arrived in time for the hectic Christmas period with Houllier jubilant at having beaten off some of Europe's top clubs to secure the 22-year-old's signature.

"We are delighted to have him, especially as so many other

top European clubs were interested," the Frenchman said after securing the Reds' 19th overseas signing in just over two years. "He is an international player and a class player. We've been watching him for a long time. The price isn't low. We are aware of that, but we are living in an era of football where you have to buy the potential because the finished article is too expensive. We are trying to build a team and we now have a side that is starting to blossom. Igor will be part of that."

It was a huge opportunity for the young Croat and he admitted years later to the official Liverpool website that he didn't truly appreciate the scale of the challenge ahead of him. "I didn't know Liverpool were after me," he recalled.

"I was in talks with some other clubs; not me personally but Dinamo Zagreb. I went to Amsterdam to visit Ajax, they invited me to come there to get to know the club. There were rumours they would buy me but in the end, when Liverpool made an offer that was it."

The Reds were in the midst of a marathon season which would ultimately stretch to 63 games as Houllier's men – who had missed out on a first qualification for the Champions League on the final day of the previous campaign in the Frenchman's first term in sole charge – won an unprecedented cup treble and played every possible match available to them. With the squad already starting to show signs of wear and tear having played 25 games by the first week of December, Biscan was handed a first appearance just days after arriving on Merseyside, being thrown on as a second-half substitute against Ipswich Town at Anfield. The newly-promoted Tractor Boys had been the season's surprise package so far. That continued with a 1-0 victory, only their second triumph at Anfield, but the debutant showed enough to earn himself a start in the Reds' next league game away to Manchester United.

Danny Murphy's well-placed free-kick on the stroke of half-time in front of the Stretford End secured a precious three points and a first win over Alex Ferguson's side anywhere in five years and at Old Trafford in ten.

It was United's first home league defeat in almost three years and, while inevitably Houllier's men had to soak up a fair amount of pressure from the home team, the obdurate platform provided by Biscan alongside Steven Gerrard in the middle of the park ensured the result was no fluke, the BBC writing afterwards: "The central midfield partnership of Gerrard and Biscan were particularly impressive." While the Guardian were more even more effusive in their praise of the Reds' Croatian debutant, saying: "Gerrard enjoyed solid support from Igor Biscan, newly arrived from Dinamo Zagreb and justifying his inclusion at the expense of Gary McAllister with a display of unflustered tackling and passing that belied the passions that always accompany this fixture."

The following weekend the country's other leading side Arsenal pitched up at Anfield just two days before Christmas and Biscan, who kept his place in the team and again played the full 90 minutes, helped ensure it was a happy Yuletide for the Reds by producing another dominant showing in midfield as goals from Gerrard, Owen, Nick Barmby and Robbie Fowler saw a 4-0 win over the outplayed and out-fought Gunners who were now only two points ahead of Houllier's men. It was the perfect start for Biscan, whose ability to slot into the team at short notice and play his part in such significant results had Kopites dreaming of glory the following May as they tucked into their turkey.

"It was a special moment for me to make my debut against Ipswich so soon after signing," he recalled. "We lost that game, so the atmosphere in the dressing room after the game was not good, but I will remember that day forever. I then made my full debut at Old Trafford. Back then Man United was the team to beat and winning against our biggest rival at Old Trafford on my full league debut was great."

A third successive start for the Croat followed on Boxing Day at Middlesbrough but the winning streak came to an end as a Sander Westerveld error handed the Teessiders a 1-0 victory and, although a first Liverpool goal followed the following month when he raced through and finished calmly in front of the Kop as the Reds overturned a first-leg deficit to beat Crystal Palace 5-0 and reach the League Cup final, a red card against Rotherham United in the FA Cup third round had already signalled the settling-in problems he would endure.

"It was difficult from the start," he admitted. "But at the beginning, maybe because of the adrenaline and how big everything was and the games – suddenly you play against some of the top players in the world, against the top teams in the world, and you play with some great players, and the atmosphere and everything is just so big – you don't think about tiredness or fatigue. The first four or five games I was okay physically and mentally, but then I started to feel pain everywhere because the change of everything was just too big; the intensity, the physical demands were different to what I was used to in Croatia. I had some problems, if I can remember, especially my back was hurting a lot. Then I struggled a bit for the remainder of that season. But you cannot complain when you get a chance to play and that first season I arrived was unbelievable, we won almost everything and there was just no time to think about it because it was game after game in which you needed to win to progress and to give yourself a chance to win something. It was amazing."

Having already featured in Europe that season for Zagreb,

Biscan was cup-tied for Liverpool's UEFA Cup campaign but Houllier's insistence in utilising his squad to its full extent to preserve legs for the business end of the campaign still saw him feature regularly during the winter months, and Biscan won his first medal as a Liverpool player a little over two months after arriving when he started the League Cup final against Birmingham City in Cardiff, the Reds eventually triumphing on penalties. His appearances tailed off, however, and he played only four minutes of the last half-dozen Premier League games, not making the squad for either the FA Cup semi-final or the Owen-inspired victory over Arsenal in the Cardiff final.

"It was a rollercoaster season for everybody," he recalled, "But maybe for me even more because I was really young, and to come from this league and this type of football in this environment to something like that, in which every game is just so big and the atmosphere of the fans and the importance of the games was big. Of course, I wasn't playing all the time, but when you prepare for the game you are positive because your team is winning and everything around you is so positive, so it gets you through. In the end it was perfect, a perfect six months and season for us."

That was as good as it would get though for Biscan for quite some time. Although he came off the bench in both the Charity Shield and the UEFA Super Cup final early the following campaign, he started only seven Premier League games over the next two seasons. The consistent progress of the Houllier era may have initially continued with a second-place finish in 2002 despite the manager's life-threatening heart problem ruling him out for months, but the Croat's development stalled and forced him to consider his future even if he was brutally honest as to why he felt he had fallen out of favour.

"The main reason is that I wasn't good enough," he admitted.

"It took me some time to really adapt and understand and find my place in the team. It wasn't easy and I didn't play much. I just needed to change some things about the way I think about the game; then I did it and when I did it, when I changed some things, of course I still had to be patient and give myself a little bit of time. It was not easy, to be honest. I left home at a very young age, didn't speak the language very well, and on top of that I came there to play at a level that I had never played at before. The team was full of international players, as well as some of the best English players, and you soon realise that you are in for a bit of a tough time. I struggled a lot during those two seasons. I will put it simply – I just was not good enough to play more. At some point I wanted to leave because I wanted a fresh start and had some options abroad, but the manager convinced me to stay. In the end that proved to be the right decision."

Part of Houllier's reasoning in persuading him to stay was because he had earmarked Biscan for a significant positional change. Although Liverpool had started the 2002/03 campaign well and led the Premier League going into November, things tailed away badly to such an extent the Reds failed to even qualify for the Champions League with not even another League Cup final victory in Cardiff – this time over Manchester United – preventing the growing feeling they were beginning to go backwards. With Roman Abramovich's takeover of Chelsea during that summer of 2003 changing the financial landscape of English football, and Liverpool's first-choice centre-back pairing of Sami Hyypia and Stephane Henchoz nearing their 30s, Houllier identified Biscan as a credible option at the heart of his defence and spoke before the start of the new campaign as to why he felt that was where the Croat would play his best football.

"I like him in this position," the Frenchman said. "He is strong, powerful and quick, which are attributes I like. He could be good cover in that central defensive role. It will be his position in the future. In time he could be an awesome centre-back. Sometimes he loses the ball when he passes, but then who doesn't? I prefer players who try things."

Although Biscan would start the season opener against Chelsea, injuries to Henchoz and Jamie Carragher soon saw him pressed into service at centre-back and he would play 39 games in all competitions, the highest tally of his Liverpool career. But it was a campaign of toil for both the Reds, who never managed to recover from a poor start to even hint at any involvement in the title race, and the Croatian himself who never looked entirely comfortable in his new surroundings. Matters reached a head at Marseille in the second leg of Liverpool's UEFA Cup quarter-final – their last chance of silverware after dismal domestic cup defeats to Bolton Wanderers and Portsmouth – with the tie level at 1-1 after the Anfield first leg. Emile Heskey gave the visitors a 15th-minute lead in the Stade Velodrome but nine minutes before half-time Biscan, having been caught out of position, hauled back striker Steve Marlet as he ran through on goal and was shown a red card by Spanish referee Arturo Ibanez, who also awarded the home side a penalty despite the foul appearing to take place outside the penalty area.

Didier Drogba equalised from the spot and Abdoulaye Meite's second-half header sent the French side into the semi-finals with a furious Houllier claiming afterwards that Liverpool had not been beaten fairly.

"There was a pull but it was made some three or four yards outside the box," he fumed. "The referee let it go and played the advantage. If Marlet had scored, would he have disallowed it? You can either play advantage or not. It was dubious to say the very least."

Houllier's words were symptomatic of the woes which encircled the club during his final, dispiriting season in charge and perhaps masked the truth that the concerns over Biscan's unsuitability at centre-back, which others have feared were an accident waiting to happen, had finally come home to roost.

Houllier's men managed to at least salvage something from another desperately disappointing campaign by finishing fourth and qualifying for the Champions League, but the writing was on the wall for the manager, who departed by mutual consent shortly after the season's end and the expectation was that Biscan – who never even made the squad for the final six Premier League fixtures – would soon be following him through the exit door.

The arrival of Spanish coach Rafa Benitez, however, offered a fresh start. Although the former Valencia boss told Biscan – now into the final year of his Liverpool contract – prior to the campaign he was free to leave, once the Croat indicated his willingness to stay and fight for a place, Benitez's willingness to listen to where the player felt he could be most effective enabled a glorious swansong.

"When he first spoke to me, he asked me which position I preferred to play," Biscan recalled. "I told him I'd like to play as a central midfielder or defensive midfielder. Maybe that was the main thing for me, because I felt I could give my best in that position and it proved to be true. This season was really famous in the end; it was a special season, and for me personally as well because I would say that season was the only season out of the five I was there that I really, I believe, played the level at the top of my abilities. And I contributed the way I expected myself to contribute during the whole period I was there."

Biscan's appearances under Benitez were limited to brief outings from the bench initially, but he still managed to make his mark with a stunning last-minute finish to put the seal on a 4-2 win away to Fulham. His understated and somewhat bemused celebration as he was mobbed by his team-mates prompted chants of 'IGOOOR, IGOOOR' from the away end, which had not been heard since those early weeks of his Liverpool career when he'd broken into the team. A first start under Benitez followed soon afterwards in a League Cup win at Millwall and, a week later with Gerrard out injured, he was thrust into the side again as the Reds faced a make-or-break Champions League group game away to Deportivo La Coruna.

Only one point from the first nine available had placed hopes of qualifying for the knock-out stages in jeopardy but the Croatian produced a piece of midfield mastery midway through the first half which led to the game's only goal and secured a crucial victory. Biscan controlled the ball on the halfway line and spun away from his marker before evading three defenders and slipping in John Arne Riise down the left flank, whose cross was turned into his own net by defender Jorge Andrade. It got the Reds' European hopes back on track but illustrated too how being played in his correct position was key to getting the best from the reinvigorated midfielder.

'Where the Croatian midfielder was once painted as a figure of fun, his dozy expression befitting his rather ponderous and occasional displays in the first team, Biscan is a player reborn,' the Guardian wrote. While the Independent gushed: 'Biscan made the most of a rare opportunity to take the playmaking role normally held by Steven Gerrard or Xabi Alonso. His creativity and composure was complemented by tenacious tackling, helping Liverpool establish instant ascendancy.'

It was after Gerrard's late heroics against Olympiakos that

secured qualification from the group stages that Biscan truly came into his own. With the skipper suspended for the first leg of the last-16 clash at home to Bayer Leverkusen, Biscan started at Anfield against the Germans and set up the opening goal in Liverpool's 3-1 win, slaloming through a couple of tackles in the middle of the park before slipping a slide-rule pass through to Luis Garcia who slotted home. Biscan assisted Garcia again in the second leg as Benitez's men secured a handsome 6-2 aggregate victory to set up a quarter-final against Italian champions Juventus, where he again played a key role, having a hand in the build-up to Garcia's thumping 30-yarder which put the Reds two up within the first half hour of the tie, and then showing his tactical discipline and tackling ability as the Reds' secured a goalless draw against the odds to reach the last four.

Despite Alonso's return in Turin from a broken leg that had kept him out since January, Benitez now clearly recognised Biscan's calm and understated approach fitted perfectly into the tactical template of two holding midfielders, which was proving so effective in Europe, and the Croat was in from the start for both legs of the semi-final against Chelsea as Liverpool defied expectation to reach the club's first European Cup final in 20 years. He never made it off the bench in Istanbul against AC Milan as the Reds produced one of sport's greatest ever miracles, but his natural disappointment at not figuring in the Turkish capital never turned to resentment even when reflecting back years after the event.

He said: "It's normal that you're disappointed but the game was too big for any selfish thoughts. You want your team to win, your club to win because it's the final, probably the biggest game in club football. You just don't think in that way. Of course, you hope that you will play, but when you realise a few days before the game that you will not play, then you just keep working hard. You don't stop preparing. You're still happy anyway because you are in a final and preparing yourself to play a part if the team needs you.

"It was crazy. Once we managed to get from the group stage we just looked solid – very solid and tough. It looked like nobody would beat us. The celebrations in the stadium, after in the hotel and when we came back to the streets of the city, it's difficult to explain really. It's a blur, it's so emotional – really, really emotional. Unbelievable."

Scouse team-mate Jamie Carragher was in no doubt how important the Croatian had been to the Reds' Champions League heroics. "I felt a bit sorry for him really," the Bootle-born defender later said. "He was on the bench in the final so he's got a Champions League medal. He played as big a part as anybody."

Now out of contract, Biscan was not offered a new deal by Benitez and the Croatian signed for Greek side Panathinaikos, where he spent two seasons before returning home to Dinamo Zagreb. Despite a series of frustrating injuries, he led them to further silverware and ended his playing days in 2012 with eight Croatian top-flight titles as well as four Croatian Cups and a Croatian Super Cup to go alongside the medals acquired during his time on Merseyside. A career in management followed initially with Croatian second-tier side Rules, who he led to promotion in 2017, and he won the Slovenian league and cup double with Olimpia Ljubljana the following campaign before returning to Croatia for a brief spell at Rijeka and also went on to been in charge of Croatia's Under-21 side.

Despite the contrasting experiences he went through during his four and half years at Anfield, Biscan insisted, when featuring in LFC TV's 'Added Time' series, that his time on

Merseyside made him into the person he is and outlined how a lot of his coaching methods are implemented from what he learned at Liverpool under Houllier and Benitez, who he described as the biggest managers he worked under. His self-effacing nature, however, dismissed the notion he is a 'cult hero', which close to two decades after his departure would not be a view shared by the Liverpudlians who enjoyed his often slightly bewildered, just-got-of-bed demeanour and unveiled an iconic banner in honour of him in Istanbul which read 'Super Croat Igor Biscan Used To Be Atrocious'.

"I am thankful and really appreciate the fans' support but I do not consider myself a cult hero," he said. "There are so many other players who deserve that status before me. I know at times the fans didn't want to see me in the team. There were other players, and they were better than me. But I felt like I always had their support, they were loyal and are special fans. It's only when you are part of the club you realise how much.

"Liverpool is a place where I learned a lot and I owe a lot. You realise how big the club is and what qualities they teach you there; it stays with you for the rest of your life. I'm in coaching now and there are many things I learned there regarding work ethic, the way you treat everybody around you, the way you go about your job. Anfield is an iconic stadium. Every time you step on the pitch to play a game there, it is an unbelievable experience. I'll always be grateful and have so much respect for everything there – the club and the fans – because it's just something special. It was a happy ending. Having played so many games in that Champions League campaign, winning the competition not only made me very happy but also made me realise that the sacrifices I made and the things I had to do to remain at Liverpool all seem worthwhile."

JARI LITMANEN

The Bewitching Of Steven Gerrard

First published: May 2022

THERE are some footballers who just seem like they are born to play for certain clubs. Those who possess certain qualities – sometimes to do with their approach to the game, sometimes relating to their values or look, sometimes indefinable – which just feel the right fit.

The trick, of course, is getting them on board at mutually beneficial junctures for both player and club which is not always possible as Liverpool discovered when they were finally able to get Jari Litmanen to Merseyside.

The Finnish attacker had long been on the Anfield radar with his eventual arrival in 2001 a case of third time lucky after two previously unproductive attempts to bring him to the club.

It looked like a marriage made in heaven with Litmanen

widely known to have idolised Liverpool as a kid and main-taining an affinity to such an extent he reportedly irritated Ajax players with his constant references to the Reds during his time in Holland, but circumstances conspired against making his time in the red shirt the success all involved hoped and expected it to be.

The man who would go on to be regarded as Finland's greatest footballer began his professional career in his homeland with Reipas, making his top-flight debut at the age of only 16 in 1987. The son of parents who had both played international football, he would move to the country's biggest club, HJK Helsinki, four years later before a spell at MyPa 47 who he helped win the Finnish Cup. It was his goalscoring performance in the final against FF Jaro which alerted Ajax's scouting network.

A number of European clubs had expressed an interest in the 21-year-old but the Dutch side's long-established reputation as a breeding ground for young talent was enough to secure Litmanen's signature.

There was an acclimatisation period as the modest youngster found his feet both on and off the field, his first-team path initially blocked by Dennis Bergkamp who played in Lit-manen's preferred number 10 role just behind the strikers. But when the Dutch forward left to join Inter Milan in the summer of 1993, the Finn inherited the number 10 shirt as well as his place in the team and truly began to show what he was capable of.

It was the dawning of a golden age for the Amsterdam club with young homegrown talents Clarence Seedorf, Edgar Davids, Edwin van der Sar, the De Boer brothers and Patrick Kluivert emerging to blend effectively with shrewd buys like Litmanen, Marc Overmars, Nwankwo Kanu, Finidi George and the returning 80s legend Frank Rijkaard to take Ajax to three successive Eredivisie titles as well as putting them back on the European map they had graced in the 1970s.

Litmanen would finish as the league's top scorer with 26 goals during the 1993-94 campaign as Ajax won their first championship in four years, his overall tally of 36 in 39 appearances in all competitions also helping him win the Netherlands' Footballer of the Year award. But it was the following campaign when the Finn and his team-mates wrote themselves into history by embarking on a remarkable run which saw them go the best part of a season-and-a-half undefeated in both the Eredivisie (52 matches) and the Champions League (19).

Louis van Gaal's side easily retained their league title after becoming Holland's first 'Invincibles' but it was in Europe where they captured hearts and minds with their attacking, free-flowing style. After topping a group containing reigning champions AC Milan, they went on to set up another meeting with the Rossoneri in the Vienna final.

Patrick Kluivert's 85th-minute winner secured a victory which took the European Cup back to Amsterdam for the first time since 1973 and the following season, having again retained their Eredivisie title, they threatened to win back-to-back European titles but lost out to Juventus on penalties in the final.

Van Gaal would leave to manage Barcelona the following year and, although another Eredivisie title followed in 1997/98, the cream of the Champions League-winning side inevitably was being cherry-picked by Europe's moneyed elite with Litmanen among those being eyed. Roy Evans tried to entice him to Anfield without success during that unusual summer of 1998 when Gerard Houllier was installed alongside him as joint-manager and 12 months later the Frenchman, now in sole charge, tried again to bring the Finn to Merseyside but the financial package offered by Barcelona proved impossible to resist.

His propensity for picking up niggling injuries at Ajax had earned Litmanen the unwanted nickname 'The Man of Glass' and, now 28, his unavailability increased with him only able to make 32 appearances and score just four goals during his 18 months at the Camp Nou.

Van Gaal would be replaced as Barcelona coach by Lorenzo Serra Ferrer after a trophyless 1999-2000 campaign but there was no change in Litmanen's fortunes and, having lost his number 10 shirt to Brazilian star Rivaldo, the call of Anfield this time was just what he wanted to hear. Gerard Houllier's first season in sole charge had seen the Reds look certs to qualify for the Champions League for the first time before a barren run in the final five games of the campaign saw them fall just short and, having bolstered his squad with experienced internationals like Markus Babbel, Nick Barmby, Gary McAllister and Christian Ziege, the Frenchman was looking to similarly bolster his youthful frontline led by Michael Owen, Emile Heskey and Robbie Fowler.

After completing the mid-season free transfer of the 29-year-old Finn on a two-and-a-half year deal rumoured to be worth £55,000 a week, a delighted Houllier said, "We have signed a world-class player. He comes with a reputation which needs no improvement. He's one of the most exciting signings we have ever made. Jari knows all about Liverpool. He's a fan of the club and he wanted to play for us. He can play in a variety of positions in attack and will bring a different style of play than some of our other strikers. He is a player I'm aware this club has wanted for a long time and to get him on a free transfer is a snip."

For Litmanen, it was the fulfilment of a journey which began with his earliest memories of watching football and the Reds' all-conquering sides of the 1970s as a youngster back home in Finland.

"I grew up with Liverpool and still remember Kevin Keegan playing there. He left the club in '77 after winning the European Cup. Then Kenny Dalglish came. There was Ray Clemence, Phil Thompson, Phil Neal, Terry McDermott, Graeme Souness, I remember all those guys. I started to remember those early years of mine in the '70s when I started to follow football and I started to follow Liverpool. When I came to Liverpool it was a good moment to come. That team was growing and there were some young talented players coming through. We had a squad of 20 players who were all really good for the team and the club, and when I came we were just growing."

Liverpool's season so far had been something of a curate's egg with progress in the League and UEFA Cups offset by inconsistent Premier League performances, particularly away from Anfield, although consecutive victories just before Christmas against the country's dominant sides – Manchester United and Arsenal – were an indicator of the team's potential. Litmanen's debut came as a second-half substitute in the first leg of the League Cup semi-final away to second tier Crystal Palace where, despite asserting their superiority for much of proceedings and missing a host of chances, the Reds slipped to a 2-1 defeat which highlighted the distance they still had yet to travel, the Finn creating the goal for Vladimir Smicer which got Liverpool back in the tie after going two behind.

He was handed his first start the following weekend at Aston Villa, however, and produced a superb performance in a resounding 3-0 victory, his capacity to place the ball through the eye of a needle evident in the stand-out goal of the match (and one of the best of the 127 Liverpool scored that season) when he spotted Danny Murphy's break forward, the former Crewe man's first-time lay-off being crashed into the roof of the net by Steven Gerrard.

"In a 70-minute masterclass, Litmanen offered an exciting glimpse of why his signing could take Liverpool to an extra level," the ECHO's match report afterwards read. "This was the best passing performance the team has produced all season. The passing and movement in midfield was precise, fast, forward thinking and clinical. Many experienced judges suspect Litmanen could be the 'missing link man' Liverpool need. The Sheringham/Yorke/Bergkamp figure who has the vision and skill to think one yard ahead of the rest of the players on the pitch."

The Finn kept his place for the following weekend's goalless draw at home to Middlesbrough and four days later Anfield got a first real glimpse of his latent talent, Crystal Palace being swept aside 5-0 as Houllier's men easily overturned the first-leg deficit to reach their first cup final of the season with Litmanen producing an exquisite pass for Murphy to put the Reds in front on aggregate just moments after Vladimir Smicer's early opener.

The Finn's new team-mates were already in awe at what he was bringing to the team with Gerrard among those immediately impressed at his football brain and ability to bring others into play. "From the moment I saw Jari Litmanen at Melwood, I was bewitched," he wrote in his first autobiography. "He was like a chess grandmaster, always anticipating three or four moves ahead."

"It felt like a big statement to sign someone of his quality," Dietmar Hamann later told The Athletic. "I'm not sure Liverpool would have been able to attract him a few years before that. He was a very serious guy who tended to keep himself to himself. But he loved talking about football. He was so knowledgeable about the game. We already had another Finn in Sami Hyypia and they got on well. Jari was always one of the first ones at Melwood every day. He was always working out in the gym. He did his best to look after himself but the shame was that his body just didn't seem to be able to handle the demands. He suffered from a lot of niggling injuries. I remember him taping up his ankles before every session. He was always adamant that he had to do the strapping himself. He wasn't the quickest but he didn't need to be. His great strength was his vision and ability to pick the right pass. In terms of skill and technical ability, he's up there with the best if not the best I ever played with. In five-a-sides in training, some of the stuff he did in small spaces was just unbelievable. He had eyes in the back of his head. I always thought I had good vision, but then I watched him."

With Houllier now having four top-class forwards at his disposal, the Frenchman's rotation policy came into full effect and Litmanen would be in and out of the side in the coming weeks, scoring his first Liverpool goal from the penalty spot to earn a point at Sunderland after coming on as a substitute and notching at Anfield for the first time by grabbing the opener – again from the spot – to open the scoring in the 4-2 FA Cup fifth-round victory over Manchester City. A calf injury caused him to miss the League Cup final triumph over Birmingham City on penalties in Cardiff but he returned to come off the bench in the FA Cup and UEFA Cup quarter-final successes over Tranmere Rovers and FC Porto respectively to bolster Houllier's attacking options with the Reds' season continuing to build to an exciting climax.

With Wembley Stadium being developed, the fates would

have it that Finland's World Cup qualifier against England was to be played at Anfield but the dream scenario turned into something of a nightmare for Litmanen when he fell awkwardly following a challenge with Rio Ferdinand and, despite returning to the pitch in agony after treatment, later discovering his wrist was fractured in several places. The Finn was initially ruled out for Liverpool's upcoming European semi-finals against his former club Barcelona but hopes he might be able to be patched up to play some part in the run-in did not materialise and he was unable to feature at all for the rest of the season, having to watch on in frustration from the sidelines as Houllier's men added the FA and UEFA Cups to complete an unprecedented treble while also securing third place to confirm Champions League qualification.

Litmanen was fit enough to start the opening game of the following campaign back in his homeland as Liverpool cruised past FC Haka in the first leg of their Champions League qualifier and was also named in the side for the Premier League opener against West Ham at Anfield as a training ground row between Robbie Fowler and Phil Thompson overshadowed the Reds' start to the season. The Toxteth-born forward was soon back in the side but would be sold to Leeds United three months later and Litmanen would have to wait a month for another start, grasping the opportunity when it was presented by firing home a superb winner against Tottenham and four days later following it up with the only goal in Liverpool's first victory in the Champions League proper against Dynamo Kyiv. Remarkably though, they would be the only consecutive games the Finn would start all season. He found himself back on the bench the following weekend as the Reds travelled to Newcastle and it would be another five weeks before he started in the league again.

"There was lots of politics involved in me getting play time," Litmanen claimed. "When I joined Liverpool, Emile Heskey was considered too expensive an acquisition who didn't meet the expectations, Robbie Fowler wasn't in great shape, and Michael Owen suffered from constant injuries. In about three months, they were all in the England national team, often all three in the starting line-up. The competition setting was as hard as it gets: Owen was the club's own boy and European Footballer of the Year. Robbie Fowler was one of Liverpool's all-time top scorers, who had earned the nickname 'God' from the fans. Emile Heskey represented England in international football and was very physical, which the coaching team kept in high value. I, on the other hand, was a foreigner. Statistically, I should have played more but I was still on the bench."

It was an autumn of turmoil at Anfield with manager Houllier falling ill during the mid-October draw with Leeds United at Anfield, Phil Thompson taking over as caretaker. He kept Liverpool in contention for the top prizes at home and in Europe but Litmanen's chances of getting more game time were not helped when two more strikers – former Arsenal frontman Nicolas Anelka and Czech Republic youngster Milan Baros – arrived shortly before Christmas.

The Finn responded well to the new challenge, coming off the bench to score in the home defeat to Arsenal and then three days later scoring a bizarre opener in the Boxing Day win at Aston Villa, calmly rolling the ball into an empty net from 30 yards out after goalkeeper Peter Schmeichel's throw out had hit referee Andy D'Urso and rebounded into his path. But goals in successive games again weren't enough to prevent him being back on the bench for the following game at West Ham and it would be early March before he found the net again.

Liverpool were firmly in the title race in third place, only a point behind both Manchester United and Arsenal, and hopes of another exhilarating finale like the year before were boosted soon afterwards by Houllier's return to the dug-out on an emotional Anfield night against AS Roma. The Reds needed to beat the Italian champions by two goals to reach the quarter-finals and the Frenchman's appearance on the touchline just before kick off took an already-electric atmosphere up a notch, his side taking advantage early on when Litmanen – in for the injured Michael Owen – nervelessly converted a seventh-minute penalty. Emile Heskey's second-half header secured the necessary result and when Vladimir Smicer's 92nd-minute volley the following weekend beat Chelsea to put Liverpool top of the Premier League, the Reds were potentially 'ten games from greatness' as the manager would memorably phrase it.

They proved to be words which would sadly come back to haunt him as the Reds crashed out of the Champions League in the last eight to unfancied German side Bayer Leverkusen. Defending a one-goal lead from the Anfield first leg, Abel Xavier's headed equaliser after Michael Ballack's opener had put the Reds firmly in command with an away goal under their belt before, just after the hour mark, defensive midfield linchpin Dietmar Hamann was bizarrely replaced despite Houllier's side just needing to see the game out. Two quick-fire goals put the hosts ahead on aggregate but 12 minutes from time Litmanen struck with arguably the best (and last) of his nine goals for Liverpool, picking up the ball on the left side of the penalty area and shimmying past two challenges before curling a precise drive into the bottom corner. The Reds couldn't hold out and Brazilian defender Lucio's 84th-minute strike took the Germans through to the last four.

Litmanen would start the following game at Sunderland as Michael Owen's second-half winner kept the title dream alive but made only two more substitute appearances, the final of them being in the defeat at Tottenham – the Reds' first in the league since early January – which confirmed they would have to settle for runners-up spot.

Houllier's post-season decision not to make Nicolas Anelka's loan deal permanent and instead pay £10m for Senegal World Cup star El-Hadji Diouf proved ill-judged and, only weeks into the following campaign, Litmanen's frustration at his lack of involvement boiled over.

"I really wanted more out of this move but when you are not playing it is difficult to remain enthusiastic," he told the press. "If I look at the last two seasons I have to admit that it has not made me a happy person. Liverpool might have a problem keeping everyone happy at the club if they are not playing regularly. I would really like to play a bigger part in our championship race. It is purely the manager's choice and he does not explain why I'm not getting in. All I hear is that 'we have a big squad and everybody will play some games'. I know that Michael Owen and Emile Heskey are first-choice players, but if one of them was not playing last season it was either Robbie Fowler or Nicolas Anelka who would play. Houllier is the boss and at Liverpool nobody argues with him. I will not either. I just have to accept my situation, even if it makes me miserable at times."

His comments did not go down well with the manager, who the following day issued a scathing response without actually naming Litmanen as to what his 'solution' to the Finn's perceived problem would be.

"The atmosphere is good here," the Frenchman insisted. "Provided a player's attitude is right then there is no problem. He will be given a chance. But if it's not right, then their performance will mirror their attitude. What I don't tolerate is people sulking and people chipping away. If that happens I can be extremely ruthless and nasty because I am the protector of the team and of the club. If there is a cancer, it has to be eradicated immediately."

It was no empty threat as just days later Litmanen was released on a free transfer and returned to Holland to join former club Ajax, having made only 43 appearances in a season-and-a-half at Anfield, 24 of them as substitute. He helped them reach the Champions League quarter-finals that season but injuries continued to take their toll as he approached his mid-30s and he returned to Finland in 2004 with Lahti. Further spells with Hansa Rostock in Germany and Malmo in Sweden followed before in 2008, at the age of the 37, he briefly returned to the Premier League with Fulham.

Litmanen soon returned to Finland with Lahti, who he helped qualify for Europe for the first time, before finishing his playing career back at HJK, winning a league and cup double before retiring at the age of 40 in 2011. He finished as one of the few footballers to play at professional level in four different decades and having become his country's oldest international goalscorer the year before when bagging the 32nd goal of his 137-cap Finland international days.

Litmanen's Liverpool career may never have hit the heights it promised to and left many wistful it didn't happen earlier. Jamie Carragher later admitted: "He was brilliant, I wish we'd have got him years before. When we got him, I thought, 'Wow what a player'."

And although his time at Anfield did not live up to his or anyone's expectations, just being able to pull on the red shirt of the club he loved and still does ensures Litmanen is still able to look back on his 18 months on Merseyside with fondness.

"I was there for one-and-a-half years and I was really happy to be at Liverpool because it was my favourite club. So to be part of Liverpool Football Club was something special, I just expected to play more and it didn't happen. Anfield is something so special to me.

"Liverpool is Anfield and when you go there to watch a game or go to the stadium to see the pitch, you really feel there is something special. The history of the place, this is Liverpool. If there is a game on TV and I can see it, it feels so nice to see a game at Anfield, especially the Kop, that's something special. I know the history of the Kop and I have a feeling as a fan of the club, of course, with the Kop.

"When I meet Liverpool fans, the first question is always, 'Why didn't you play more?' I don't know. I just saw it as a really good period, one-and-a-half years where I could play at the club I have loved."

BOB
PAISLEY

Liverpool's Meanest Manager

First published: February 2021

"I AM only a modest Geordie but get me cornered and I am a mean b*****."

Never words you would have heard uttered publicly by the quietly-spoken man, who became English football's most successful manager by winning 20 major trophies in just nine seasons in charge of Liverpool. But ones he was quite happy to utter within the confines of the Anfield dressing room he ruled with, at times, an almost imperceptible steel.

Bob Paisley, who passed away aged 77 in 1996, has long had the reputation of the gentle, cardigan-and-slippers wearing grandfather-like figure who reluctantly took over at Anfield after Bill Shankly's shock resignation in 1974 and established the Liverpool dynasty after his Scottish predecessor had dragged an under-achieving club toward being the 'bastion of invincibility' he always felt it could be.

Many anecdotes about Paisley amply demonstrate there's more than the odd grain of truth to that perception, but it also belies the utterly ruthless streak which ran through him and enabled him to continually keep the Reds ahead of the rest.

To hear some of the stories about Paisley, it is not hard to imagine him being something of a figure of fun among his players at times with his verbal communication skills being very much at the other end of the spectrum as the charismatic and verbose Shankly.

Phil Neal once recalled: "Terry McDermott got us hysterical in the dressing room one time, laughing at Bob Paisley's expense. The boss had a habit of saying the word 'doings' all the time. He'd refer to opposition players as 'doings' instead of naming them. So Bob comes into the dressing room and starts a talk. Terry stood behind him with a big grin on his face and every time Bob says 'doings' he holds a finger up. By the time he gets to six, Terry is starting to titter and we're trying not to laugh. Ray Kennedy is kicking me and when he gets to ten, Ray just turns and flees into the toilet, he's in absolute fits. We were like a bunch of schoolkids."

His seemingly gentle, avuncular nature was also very much evident to Mark Lawrenson when the young defender completed a club-record £900,000 move from Brighton in 1981. "I was nervous as a kitten," Lawrenson remembered.

"I had on my best suit, shirt and tie, my best bib and tucker. I went down to reception and the doorman spotted me and said, 'Mr Paisley is waiting for you in his car outside'. When I got in the car I saw that Bob was wearing slippers and a cardigan. I couldn't believe it.

"That was my first meeting with Bob Paisley and I knew I'd

come to the right place. They'd just won the European Cup and there was this fellow, who everyone in football thought was an absolute God, driving me to the ground in his slippers and cardigan! I thought, 'you'll do for me!'"

Paisley retained the ability to grab the respect, attention and affection of his players when it mattered, despite his often incoherent oratory, because of his complete understanding of the game of football and appreciation of the small details which could, and did, give Liverpool a competitive advantage.

Woven into that was the ability to make the hard decisions necessary at times for the good of the team and the club that, for all Bill Shankly's justifiably messianic status in the LFC pantheon, the Scot had, at times, been unable to take, such was his devotion and loyalty to the players he loved and had built his empire on.

Paisley's players knew there was a pragmatism within him that would see them jettisoned if he felt they were no longer of use, with his ability to replace key performers just before they started getting past their best being regarded as one of the key traits which kept Liverpool at the top for so long.

The north-easterner's no-nonsense approach to management can probably be explained quite simply by his journey towards it. The son of a County Durham miner, born into poverty in January 1919 and robbed of the best years of his playing career because of World War II, where he served abroad as one of the 'Desert Rats', Paisley made his name on Merseyside as a diminutive but hard-working right-half, who helped Liverpool become the first top-flight post-war champions in 1946/47 and scored one of the goals which beat Everton in a Maine Road semi-final to give the club a chance of winning their first FA Cup in 1950, only to be dropped for the Wembley final which was lost to Arsenal.

He retired in 1954, having worn the red shirt 277 times, and showed his loyalty in the wake of Liverpool's relegation to the Second Division by accepting the role of reserve team boss, later becoming physio and first-team coach before being promoted to assistant manager under Shankly.

His understated approach proved the perfect counter-balance to the fiery Scot's rambunctious style, with Nessie Shankly – Bill's wife – once saying: "Bill depended a lot on Bob. They were like the terrible twins when they got going. I think Bill needed Bob. I think he calmed him down a bit."

They restored Liverpool to the top flight and brought the league championship back to Anfield, ending the club's long-standing wait for an FA Cup in 1965 and coming close to being the first British team to win the European Cup the same year only to fall foul of Inter Milan and referee José María Ortiz de Mendíbil.

Further league titles and the club's first European trophy, the UEFA Cup in 1973, would follow before Shankly's shock retirement after his second FA Cup triumph against Newcastle the following year.

The departing Reds boss had no doubt who his successor should be but Paisley would take some persuading. "It was definitely a crisis time when Bill left," former club secretary Peter Robinson admitted.

"It was a bombshell and Bob was very reluctant to take the position as manager. When we approached him he said no. In the end the chairman, directors and I had to gang up on him."

Paisley admitted he reluctantly took the job as much to keep the rest of the backroom staff in jobs as much as anything else, with the late Ray Clemence revealing his honesty to the players over his feelings when he first faced them as manager.

"I think when he first succeeded Shanks, he was a bit

overawed," Clemence said. "I'll never forget him standing in the dressing room in the summer of 1974 on the first day of pre-season training and telling us: 'Shanks has gone and they're giving me the job even though I didn't really want it. But we must try to carry on what he's started'.

"He saw it as his duty to take the job. Yet he set an incredible record that will never be beaten. Things just snowballed for him after that first season. For me, he was a better coach than motivator of men, but a shrewd judge of a player and very strong tactically."

One of Paisley's few public utterances on taking over confirmed he realised he would have to be his own man in the job and that would become further evident within the early weeks of his reign.

Despite his modest public speaking skills, he did have sharp one-liners up his sleeve, as displayed when asked inevitably about Shankly following a 2-1 away win at Luton Town in his first match in charge, replying: "He's trying to get right away from football. I believe he went to Everton."

Shankly, who regretted his sudden retirement almost immediately, had indeed been at Goodison Park for the Blues' season opener and was initially unable to keep himself away from Melwood, where he had been told he would always be welcome, turning up virtually every day in the early weeks of retirement where his former players, still in thrall, could not help but call him 'boss'.

It was down purely to the Scot's love of the game and the club, but was unhelpful to Paisley and threatened to undermine the crucial early stages of his transition into management, forcing him to take tough but necessary action.

"Shankly started taking the training," recalled Tommy Smith. "Prior to that, as a manager, he didn't actually take the training, he'd walk around and talk to Reuben Bennett, Joe Fagan and Bob Paisley and tell them what to do. But he started taking the training!

"In the end, Bob Paisley, purely for his own sanity, had to say to him: 'Bill, you don't work here any more. This is my team here, I've got things I want to do'."

It was the first true indication of Paisley's 'mean' streak with club chairman John Smith eventually forced to step in and ask the former manager not to visit the training ground during sessions, and in some part explains the stand-out character- istic of that 1974/75 season – it was the only one of the nine Paisley would be in charge for in which Liverpool did not win a trophy.

They finished second, only two points behind champions Derby County, and the following campaign normal service was resumed as the Paisley era truly got underway with a repeat of the league championship and UEFA Cup double of three years earlier.

The following May, the quest started by Paisley and Shankly a dozen years earlier to make Liverpool the champions of Europe was completed as – with the domestic title already retained – Borussia Monchengladbach were beaten in Rome to bring the European Cup to Anfield for the first time with Paisley quipping afterwards: "This is the second time I've beaten the Germans here... the first time was in 1944. I drove into Rome on a tank when the city was liberated."

Undoubtedly the key moment en route to the Italian capital was the quarter-final victory over French champions Saint Etienne when, having lost the away leg 1-0, Liverpool found themselves needing two goals in the final half after Dominique Bathenay's long range strike had cancelled out Kevin Keegan's early opener to give the visitors a crucial away goal.

Ray Kennedy's effort from the edge of the penalty area brought the Reds within one goal of a semi-final place but, with time running out and the French defence holding firm, Paisley sent on young Scouse forward David Fairclough to try and find the goal needed to reach the semi-finals – and one of Anfield's most iconic moments played out as the striker did just that.

Having played a fairly significant role in the previous two seasons of success, Fairclough was understandably disappointed to be left out of the side to face Manchester United in the FA Cup final four days before Rome, but said he had been assured he would feature in the Italian capital. He didn't.

Fairclough said: "It was crushing. To miss out on all that glory and the great things that were going on was tough and behind that, my dad was also having an illness problem which he ultimately died from.

"And obviously my attitude towards Bob Paisley... at that point you realise football is a business. It's not just a case of loving Liverpool for whatever. I've got a personal connection on it and I thought Bob Paisley let me down around that time."

Fairclough would start and get a winners medal in the following season's European Cup final against Belgian champions FC Bruges at Wembley, although had a transfer request written and ready to hand in if not selected, and would remain at Anfield until 1983, but the fact he only made 154 appearances – scoring 55 goals – in a Reds career lasting eight years spoke volumes about how the 'supersub' tag clung to him.

"In my early days, it was given as a positive, but it wasn't very long before I was pigeon-holed, and it became all about being more effective in the last 15 minutes," he said.

In his autobiography Fairclough was critical of Paisley's man-management, while also being quick to point to his proven track record of success.

"People always ask me what Bob Paisley was like, and I couldn't tell them in a few minutes," he wrote. "He just fobbed you off. He was never great at man-management. He avoided confrontation. I didn't like the '77 period, that did taint things, and leading into the '78 European Cup final he was slow to give me a pat on the back and assure me that I was in the team, because that would have done me the world of good. His man-management skills weren't the best.

"I had to be honest and give Bob Paisley some criticism because it's what happened. I kept diaries at the time. I don't want to tarnish Paisley's name, just give my version of events.

"I still give Bob lots of credit as he was doing what was right for the club. That it didn't work out perfectly for me was my problem and not his. But being on the fringes was soul-destroying at times, I won't lie about that. He was a genius but his broken promises hurt me."

Fairclough would not be the only young striker to get mixed messages from Paisley as he sought to establish himself at Liverpool, although Ian Rush would go on to ultimately benefit from them.

Having arrived at Anfield from Chester City as a raw 19-year-old, the Welshman knew it was not uncommon for Liverpool to sign young players and put them in the reserves for a year or longer to learn the ropes.

"After a couple months of training I realised I was good enough for Liverpool but it was hard to get a chance in the first team," he said. "They insisted that you learn your trade in the reserves and that was difficult and frustrating. After my debut it was straight back into the reserves for another while."

He played the final seven matches of the 1980/81 season but without scoring a goal and by the start of the next season he was in the reserves again and, feeling increasingly frustrated, went in to see Paisley and told the manager he wanted to leave because he felt he deserved to be in the team.

"Have you actually scored yet?" Paisley replied. "Can't you take responsibility? When I was your age I was in charge of a tank in the war."

After a second meeting went a similar way, Rush was told he was on the transfer list but it proved to be the making of a career which would leave him as Liverpool's all-time leading goalscorer.

"I was playing to leave Liverpool after that," Rush admitted. "It was, 'f*** you'. I didn't pass to anyone. All the weight went off my shoulders. I scored my first goal for Liverpool in a European Cup tie seven days later. I scored something like ten in five days.

"Bob called me in and said, 'now I'll give you that rise'. I said, 'does that mean I'm off the transfer list?' He said, 'you were never on it'. They talk about the psychology of managers now. Bob Paisley was 20 years ahead of his time."

The trophies kept flowing with monotonous regularity as the 70s turned into the 80s, with even a rare drop to fifth place in the league in 1981 being mitigated by a third European Cup triumph against Real Madrid in Paris and a first League Cup win.

Paisley was in the process of introducing new blood into the side and his uncompromising vision of what was necessary to take Liverpool forward again came to the fore when he felt it was necessary.

Jimmy Case and Ray Kennedy had been key elements of the Reds midfield through the latter part of the 1970s and close friends also. But when Bob felt it was time to inject new blood, he had no hesitation in moving them on.

The 1981/82 season which saw Case and Kennedy's departure

would prove to be one of the most testing of Paisley's career, with poor form in the first half of the season, as he sought to introduce youngsters like Rush, Ronnie Whelan and new goalkeeper Bruce Grobbelaar, leading to a Boxing Day nadir which saw Manchester City win 3-1 at Anfield to leave Liverpool an unheard-of 12th in the First Division.

Paisley again shook things up by taking the captaincy off Kirkby-born defender Phil Thompson, a figurehead of the backline for much of the previous decade, and handing the armband to midfield general Graeme Souness.

It proved a masterstroke as the Reds embarked on a tremendous run in the second half of the season, regaining the league title they had lost the previous year to Aston Villa with victory over Tottenham on the final day of the campaign, having also retained their League Cup with a Wembley win over the same opposition.

The ends justified the means but losing the captaincy was devastating to Thompson, who had achieved a lifetime ambition by skippering his boyhood club.

Paisley had explained his decision in the club programme at the time, saying: "It was a difficult decision to take because Phil has been a first-class captain for the club.

"My reason for the decision was that I felt Phil had been going through a rough patch playing-wise and I thought the extra responsibility of leading the team was having an effect.

"Phil told me he didn't believe his job as a captain had bothered him but I believe it has. Phil accepted the decision like the true professional he is saying, 'if it's for the best for me and for the club, that is all that matters'."

Thompson admitted time had helped him appreciate the merits of Paisley's decision.

"When I lost the captaincy we were 12th in the league and 18 points behind the leaders. We went on from there and won the title," he said. "My performance level went from five out of ten back to nearer ten. Losing the captaincy did make me respond.

"I improved my game overnight to show Bob Paisley he'd made a mistake giving Souness the captaincy. In fact this was leadership at its best. Making tough decisions for the best of the collective and the club. And you know what, when I had time to think about it, I realised he was right."

Souness as captain oversaw Paisley's final season at the helm, with the boss confirming at its outset it would be his last, and cajoled the now 63-year-old to lead the team up the steps at Wembley after the League Cup was won for the third year running following an extra-time victory over Manchester United, with yet another league title already a foregone conclusion.

Souness confirmed Paisley's modest demeanour was something he used to his advantage publicly to lull opponents and even some of his players into a false sense of security, and that within the velvet glove there very much existed an iron fist.

"I was to learn that praise from Bob Paisley was rather like a snowstorm in the Sahara," Souness said. "He may have been regarded as a fatherly figure by the supporters but, let me tell you, he ruled at Anfield with a rod of iron.

"You could tell when he was about by the changed atmosphere in the dressing room and training ground. He was a commanding man and there were few who dared mess around with him.

"If we looked as though we were becoming a little complacent or if we were not performing up to the standard Bob would say, 'if you have all had enough of winning, come and see me and I will sell the lot of you and buy 11 new players."

Paisley's final tally of six league championships, three

European Cups, a UEFA Cup, a European Super Cup, three League Cups and six Charity Shields may have been surpassed by other managers since but none of them did it within a timescale of only nine years.

While he never truly received the recognition outside Anfield many at Liverpool felt he deserved, his modest outward persona merged perfectly with a confident inner steel and proved a perfect fit for the city in which he became an adopted son, another of his one-liners wryly summing up his contribution after an association with the club which spanned close to half a century.

"Mind you, I've been here during the bad times too. One year we finished second!"

GRAEME SOUNESS

A Tarnished Legacy

First published: January 2022

THERE are some legendary figures who have worn the captain's armband over the years at Anfield.

From Bill Shankly's 'Colossus' Ron Yeats to local heroes like the 'Anfield Iron' Tommy Smith, the first Scouser to lift the European Cup Phil Thompson, the 'Huyton Hammer' Steven Gerrard and on-and-off the pitch leader Jordan Henderson, Liverpool have been blessed with a series of skippers who understood the club's values and became the living embodiment of them.

When all-time Liverpool XIs are discussed, however, there is one name which regularly features when thoughts turn to who might captain such a star-studded side: Graeme Souness.

The Scot's playing career was one of the most decorated and

impressive of anyone to have worn the famous red shirt, yet his time as manager is generally acknowledged as being a key factor in the sharp decline suffered following the all-conquering 1970s and 80s.

So how did such an iconic figure in Liverpool history manage to blot his copybook so badly and damage his reputation in the eyes of supporters who had previously held so much respect for him?

He arrived at Anfield little more than four months short of his 25th birthday in January 1978, having already had the best part of a decade's grounding in English football but it had initially been far from straightforward.

Having signed schoolboy forms with Tottenham at the age of 15 in 1968 after being recommended to Spurs' double-winning manager Bill Nicholson by legendary Scottish midfielder Dave Mackay, he struggled to settle in London and failed to make an impression in the first team.

"I went to Spurs at 15 and thought I was going to be a superstar," he told Simon Hughes for his book 'Men In White Suits'.

"I was headstrong and pretty soon I was knocking on Bill Nic's door asking why I wasn't in the first team."

After making only one first team appearance in four years in a UEFA Cup tie as a substitute, Souness was sold to Middlesbrough in 1972 where he gradually began to find his feet primarily under the tutelage of Boro manager and England World Cup winner Jack Charlton who was impressed by the young midfielder's physicality and combative nature as well as innate footballing instincts.

Having helped the Teesside club get promoted to the First Division as champions in 1974, Souness's raw ability and presence in midfield began to attract interest from the country's top clubs and, in January 1978, Liverpool manager Bob Paisley swooped, paying a record fee at the time between two English clubs of £352,000.

Despite the Reds being reigning domestic and European champions, Paisley – now in his fourth season as manager – was in the process of revamping his team with Souness becoming the third Scottish player the canny north-easterner had signed in barely six months following the acquisitions of Alan Hansen and Kenny Dalglish.

Over the next half-dozen years, the trio would form the spine of the team during arguably Liverpool's most successful period and Paisley's comments in the wake of signing Souness demonstrated his confidence that his latest new boy would be able to fulfil the tricky task of making a great side even better.

"There are not many players who come up to our standard," the Reds boss explained. "Graeme can pass a ball, he's got vision and he's got strength. He'll play in central midfield, which is his position, and we'll sort out the rest from there."

Talking years later to Sky Sports, Souness himself revealed how he was not intimidated by the expectation levels given his big-money move.

"I've always had a lot of confidence in my own ability," he said. "I was the youngest of three sons and I had great parents. I came from a very strong, stable background and that stood me in good stead.

"When I got to Liverpool, I was walking into a dressing room which contained some absolute legends, guys who were serial winners with big personalities.

"I felt I fitted in almost immediately. Without wanting to sound big-headed, I actually thought I should have been there before I was. I felt ready for a bigger challenge about a year earlier."

He would soon fit seamlessly into a Liverpool system which he arguably helped take to a new level but not without some acclimatisation which began on his very first day of training at Melwood.

"That first day at Anfield, 10 January 1978, was a revelation," he recalled. "It seems a long time ago now but I remember how normal and ordinary it all was, no prima donnas, no super-stars.

"I made only one error on that first morning, I asked Tommy Smith if I could borrow his hairdryer (I know it's hard to imagine tough guy Smithy with a hairdryer but it's absolutely true) and he turned to Phil Neal and said pointedly: 'Everyone is allowed one mistake'. I took my own in the future."

After two successive seasons in which Liverpool had been crowned champions and won a European trophy, 1977/78 was proving more difficult at Anfield – newly-promoted Notting-ham Forest would take their domestic crown the following May – and the Saturday before Souness' first training session, Paisley's men were dumped out of the FA Cup at the third round stage after a 4-2 defeat at Chelsea.

In line for a debut the following weekend in the First Division fixture at West Brom having impressed in training, Souness tried to have a quiet word with Joe Fagan ahead of the trip to the Hawthorns about what might be expected of him ahead of his first-team bow only to be told in no uncertain terms he would need to figure it out himself.

"Joe, I've been here a week and no-one has said anything to me. How does the manager want me to play?" he remembered asking Paisley's sagacious Scouse assistant.

"So Fagan raised his voice to ensure the whole dressing room could hear and replied: 'F*** off! We spent all this money on you and now you're asking me how to play football!'"

Souness quickly worked out what his new side required from him as the Reds won 1-0 at West Brom but his fourth match for the club saw him really make his mark and show a packed Anfield just what he was capable of.

With Manchester United in town and Liverpool having just reinvigorated their season by reaching the club's first League Cup final after a two-legged semi-final victory over Arsenal, Souness notched his first goal for his new club with a strike of majestic quality later voted BBC's Goal of the Season.

Having already gone close to opening the scoring with a venomous left-foot volley, the Scot broke the deadlock six minutes before half-time in what would be a 3-1 Liverpool win. Having played Terry McDermott into space down the right flank with a delicately chipped pass, he hared into the box with arm raised for the return pass and met the midfielder's cross with another thumping left-foot volley which left United keeper Paddy Roche rooted to the spot.

Souness quickly became firmly established in the midfield and, while Brian Clough's Forest would beat Paisley's men to that season's League Cup as well as the championship, his first campaign at Anfield would still end in glory with the Scot himself playing a major role.

Victories over Dynamo Dresden, Benfica and Borussia Moenchengladbach put the European Cup holders through to a second successive final and in sight of becoming the first English side to retain the trophy.

With the showdown against FC Bruges being held at Wembley, an estimated 90,000 Liverpudlians packed into the national stadium but had to endure the frustration of the Belgians' tactics stifling their heroes until the 65th minute when Souness received a defensive clearance on the edge of the box by controlling the ball on his chest, swiftly transferring the ball from left foot to right as two defenders converged and threading a sublime through-ball into the path of Dalglish who chipped home what proved to be the winning goal.

"The Liverpool team of the time gave off a feeling of invincibility and there was just no way we were going to lose that game," said Souness.

"Afterwards we went back to a hotel with the wives and girlfriends and we spent a few hours there, celebrating with lots of champagne. Then I took my medal to my mum and dad and my landlady who I lived with when I was at Middlesbrough. I went to see the three of them and woke them up at some ridiculous hour, ordered champagne and made them drink it with me. Very, very special times, and I'm so lucky to have experienced it."

Champagne wasn't solely confined to special occasions for Souness at that time and recollections of his first year at Liverpool would include a routine where drinking and socialising were regular features.

The penny soon dropped that some discipline would be needed to fulfil his undoubted vast potential and Souness soon knuckled down to become a permanent fixture at the heart of what many regard as Liverpool's finest ever midfield – Case, Souness, McDermott, Kennedy.

His first full season at Anfield, 1978/79, saw one of the club's most dominant title wins with a record points tally of 68 (which would equate to 98 in the three-points-for-a-win era), conceding a mere 16 goals in their 42 league matches with only four being shipped all campaign at Anfield.

Another championship medal would follow the next May as Souness's unique style, once described as 'a bear of a man with the touch of a violinist', proved perfectly suited to Paisley's side.

The next necessary evolution of Paisley's Liverpool meant something of a transitional season in 1980/81 and a fifth-place finish behind surprise champions Aston Villa but Souness's playing career at Anfield saw at least one trophy won every year and, just before the Reds took on West Ham at Wembley looking to win the League Cup for the first time (which they would eventually do after a replay at Villa Park), Souness made a major contribution to what would become the club's third European Cup triumph in five seasons.

After despatching Finnish minnows Oulu Palloseura and Alex Ferguson's Scottish champions Aberdeen in the opening rounds, Paisley's men took on CSKA Sofia of Bulgaria in the first leg of the quarter-finals at Anfield and all but booked their last-four spot with a 5-1 hammering embroidered with a savagely beautiful hat-trick from their Scottish midfield general.

Souness was part of the injury-hit side in the second leg of the semi-final against Bayern Munich which defied the odds after a goalless draw at Anfield to gain the score draw needed, and his street-smarts proved invaluable in the dour final against Real Madrid in Paris as Alan Kennedy's 82nd-minute strike proved decisive.

"They were cynical with a capital C", he told Planet Football.

"Their mission was to kick you off the park and they would pull your shirt, stamp on your toes, spit at you, pull your hair, do anything to knock you out of your stride. Getting around that was as big a challenge against Real Madrid in the 1981 final as overcoming them in a sporting contest in Paris.

"Like with Bruges, they made sure it wasn't a good game, but Alan Kennedy scored our winning goal near the end and a team that loved winning had another trophy."

Souness by this stage was clearly one of the chief lieutenants

Paisley was determined to rebuild his side around but, with the introduction of young future stars like Ronnie Whelan, Ian Rush, Bruce Grobbelaar, Sammy Lee and Mark Lawrenson inevitably having an impact on results, the first half of the 1981/82 campaign saw similar struggles to the previous season with a 3-1 Boxing Day defeat at home to Manchester City leaving the Reds 12th in the First Division.

It led to Paisley replacing Phil Thompson as captain with Souness and ultimately had the desired effect with Liverpool winning 19 of their next 20 league games to become champions again while also retaining the League Cup.

He claimed he was surprised to be offered the job ahead of more senior players, telling Sky Sports years later, "When the manager asked me to become captain in '81, my initial reaction was that I would love to but that there were two people in front of me. There was Kenny, who was a couple of years older than me and had been there longer than me, and Phil Neal, who was also older than me and more experienced. I didn't want to upset the others, but Bob said it wasn't a problem. He wanted me to be his captain and that was that.

"I didn't do anything differently when I was captain. It wasn't a case of becoming more verbal, because I already was.

"The message from Bob, Joe and Ronnie was to do my job first and foremost, and if it wasn't going well for my mate, then help him. I can remember Joe saying that to me more than once. Help your mate.

"I don't think it made me a different player being captain, but it was a terrific honour. I look at some of the players who have captained that football club and I know I was lucky to do that. Equally important was that Bob had seen me around the place and seen the way I was on the pitch and then come to the decision to give it to me. I'm extremely proud of that."

His first full season with the armband saw the league retained at a canter and the League Cup won for a third successive year with Souness touchingly sending Paisley – in his final season as manager – up the Wembley steps to receive the trophy following extra-time victory over Manchester United. Then in 1983/84, with Joe Fagan now having stepped up from the Boot Room to take over as manager, the Scot led Liverpool to the club's first treble.

After falling short in 1978 and 1981, the Reds won a hat-trick of league championships with the League Cup being retained for a fourth consecutive year, Souness himself scoring the only goal in the replayed final against Merseyside rivals Everton at Maine Road.

But the crowning glory came in Rome in what would prove to be Souness's final match playing for Liverpool as the European Cup returned to Anfield for the fourth time in eight seasons.

The Reds' run to the final had been built on a series of sterling performances away from home with away legs at Odense of Denmark, Spanish champions Athletic Bilbao, Portuguese giants Benfica and Romanians Dinamo Bucharest all having been won, the semi-final second leg in Bucharest providing one of the most iconic of Souness tales.

During the Anfield first leg in which Sammy Lee's first-half header gave Liverpool a slender advantage, Souness had been involved in an incident with the visitors' captain Lica Movila that left the Romanian with a broken jaw in two places. Souness said they were, "the nastiest, most physical team I have played against. Movila was the worst of the lot.

"He kicked everything that moved and three times caught me with punches off the ball. I went completely crazy when he came in late and high yet again and as he half turned I let loose with the best punch I have delivered in my life.

"I felt nothing at all for him as he was helped off but later when I was told of the extent of the injuries, I was full of remorse. I meant no real harm other than to warn him he had picked the wrong person to intimidate."

It was clear the Romanians would be seeking revenge even before they left Anfield that night with Ronnie Moran having to step in to prevent members of their entourage making their views known over what had happened on the pitch with the Liverpool skipper.

"At the end of the game at Anfield, I went off the pitch and started climbing the stairs. As I'm going up the stairs I can see the guy," Souness said.

"He's broken his jaw, he's got ice packed into a towel and he's got it tied around his head. And I'm obviously chuckling at him. These two big guys in long leather coats appear from nowhere and start making their way towards me, up the stairs.

"From nowhere, Ronnie appears. He was a great, big powerful man, Ronnie, with a massive chest. He said to them 'Okay then, what are you going to do about it?' with some blue language thrown at them and they thought twice about confronting me.

"I was forever grateful for Ronnie preventing me from getting a back-hander that night."

There was still the second leg in Bucharest to negotiate in front of a hostile 80,000 crowd and on arrival Souness was left under no illusions about the reception awaiting him, with local police reportedly gesturing to him at the airport he might expect to have his eyes gouged out and there was no let-up in the rain-soaked 23 August Stadium when he led the Reds out to warm up.

"I was greeted by a chorus of boos every time I touched the ball in the warm-up," he said.

Enjoying the boos, Souness proceeding to wind them up

further by dummying the next few passes played to him before doing real damage to the hosts' hopes when the action got underway by creating the opening goal inside 12 minutes with a cute pass for star striker Rush to clip home the crucial away goal which meant Bucharest now needed to score three times to reach the final.

Costel Orac got one of them with a free-kick shortly before half-time but Liverpool's experience and desire to put right the previous two season's surprise quarter-final exits to CSKA Sofia and Poles Widzew Lodz comfortably kept the hosts at bay and when Rush capitalised on a defensive error with six minutes left to restore the Reds' two-goal aggregate advantage, Souness knew he would be leading his side out in Rome.

He said: "The tackles became progressively worse, going from shin to knee to thigh. My socks were in shreds and one shin pad was split from top to bottom."

It was in some ways ideal preparation for the task still awaiting Souness and Liverpool – a European Cup final against AS Roma on their own Stadio Olimpico ground in Rome, the very same venue where the Reds had first been crowned kings of Europe seven years earlier.

"There were banners outside welcoming the English infidels," said Souness' team-mate Michael Robinson. "But it never crossed my mind that we'd lose. We were brainwashed into believing we'd win. Graeme was a Trojan that night. Every player on the pitch was in awe of him. He was brave and magnificent, and led the team like a warrior. Roma had Falcao and Cerezo – two fantastic Brazilian players in midfield. But I forgot they were playing because of Graeme's performance."

Souness's indomitable presence was evident from the moment he led his side out onto the pitch with tracksuit top open and, although Roberto Pruzzo's 44th-minute header cancelled out Phil Neal's 14th-minute opener, the captain's commanding performance in the middle of the park ensured Liverpool more than held their own in a hostile environment to take the match to extra-time and penalties, the first time Europe's showpiece occasion would be decided by a shoot-out.

Souness's final strike of a ball for Liverpool was a spot-kick arrogantly driven with the outside of his boot into the top corner and, after Grobbelaar's famous 'wobbly legs' helped induce Italian World Cup winners Bruno Conti and Francesco Graziani to blaze over the crossbar, Alan Kennedy stepped up to seal the Reds' fourth European Cup victory.

Souness later acknowledged he had given his greatest performance in his 359th and final game in the red shirt, saying, "It felt like we'd gone to the Colosseum and sacked the place.

"Nobody gave us a chance. But we had the most ridiculous inner belief. Had it been Barcelona in the Nou Camp or Real Madrid in the Bernabéu, we'd have done what we had to do to win the game and done a number on them."

At 31 he decided the time was right to play abroad, moving to Italy and the northern port of Genoa to join Sampdoria for £650,000.

"When I left Liverpool for Sampdoria in '84, Serie A was like the Premier League is now," he reasoned years later.

"I can't say I regret going to Italy because it was a wonderful experience. But, as you can imagine, leaving Liverpool after seven years of non-stop success was difficult."

The parting of ways arguably proved more difficult initially for Liverpool than Souness as the near-impossible task of replacing him in midfield coupled with Everton's rise to power under Howard Kendall saw a first trophyless season at Anfield since 1975.

Sampdoria were on the rise and would win their first Coppa

Italia in 1984/85 after a fourth-place league finish, Souness scoring the only goal of the San Siro first leg against AC Milan before a 2-1 win at home. They would drop to 11th the following campaign, by which time Souness had already accepted an offer to become player-manager of the team he supported as a boy, Rangers, in April 1986.

The Glasgow giants had not won the league in nine seasons but Souness's arrival ushered in a new era of success at Ibrox and, despite him being sent off 36 minutes into his debut away to Hibs, the new manager delivered the title and a League Cup in his first campaign in charge.

Three league titles and four league cups firmly established him as one of Britain's top young managers by the time Liverpool found themselves looking for a replacement for Kenny Dalglish after the Scot's shock resignation in February 1991. Club secretary Peter Robinson made initial contact with Souness, who two years earlier had reportedly agreed to become Manchester United manager if Michael Knighton's doomed takeover at Old Trafford had gone through, to see if he would be interested in returning to Anfield but, having heard the Liverpool board's preference was to appoint from within, the Scot hesitated and Ronnie Moran continued in caretaker charge.

Souness called Robinson back towards the end of March and, despite Rangers chairman David Murray making a last-ditch attempt to persuade him to stay by offering a blank contract he could fill in himself and warning returning to Liverpool would be a huge mistake, he was unveiled at Anfield as Dalglish's successor on 16 April 1991.

"I took the only job that I would have considered leaving Rangers for, which was the Liverpool one," Souness explained years later.

"I should have realised that I would have been offered that job further down the line. I believe it was the right job, but the wrong time for me to take it.

"Remember, I was still only 38. I should have sat back and enjoyed the success at Rangers for a little while, but I didn't do that and I regret it."

Although Liverpool's form had dipped following Dalglish's departure and put Arsenal in pole position in the title race, victories in Souness's first two matches in charge at home to Norwich and Crystal Palace briefly raised hopes the Gunners could yet be caught but in the end the championship trophy went to Highbury.

Peter Robinson and long-time youth development officer Tom Saunders had warned Souness of the scale of the challenge facing him at Anfield, with an ageing squad in need of rebuilding.

The Liverpool board immediately gave the new manager major backing in the market, breaking the British transfer record in the summer of 1991 by bringing in Welsh striker Dean Saunders for £2.9m from Derby, as well as the Rams' England centre-back Mark Wright for £2.2m, along with Rangers winger Mark Walters who came south to join his former boss at Anfield.

What would prove arguably as significant to Souness's era was his decision to take charge of negotiating players' contracts.

Since the Shankly years, an effective system had been in place where Robinson would enter discussions with a lower offer than the player expected. The manager would then take over and promise to talk Robinson into upping his offer to what Liverpool would expect to be paying anyway, and the player would feel his boss had got him a better deal thus strengthening their relationship.

But with Robinson increasingly uncomfortable with the skyrocketing sums of money involved, he offered the task to Souness who was used to having such an overarching influence at Rangers and he accepted the role.

With many of the senior players in the squad like Rush, Whelan, Grobbelaar and Nicol having been former team-mates of the new manager during his playing days at Anfield and keen to secure potentially their last big contracts while eyeing the huge amounts of cash about to flood into the game, it added an extra strain to the dressing room dynamic.

"Initially, I thought it was Peter's way of paying me a compliment but it was my first big mistake, agreeing to it," Souness later accepted.

"I couldn't understand why anyone would grumble with being paid what I thought was a decent sum to play for Liverpool. Whatever I offered, they always wanted more. Liverpool was the only team I wanted to play for and I would have stayed forever had the club not accepted a really good offer from Sampdoria for me. There was no place I'd rather have been."

His first full season in charge started brightly enough with three wins in the first five league games including a 3-1 Anfield derby victory over Everton putting the Reds second, record-buy Saunders recovering from an initially slow start to bang in four as Liverpool marked their return to Europe after the six-year Heysel ban with a 6-1 victory over Finnish minnows Kuusysi Lahti in the first round of the UEFA Cup.

The following round saw the Reds pull back a two-goal first-leg European deficit for the first time in the club's history with a memorable triumph over French side Auxerre, but inconsistent league form had already seen them drop to mid-table and an embarrassing League Cup exit at Third Division Peterborough United highlighted the side's fragility.

A ten-game unbeaten run over Christmas and New Year put Liverpool back into the fringes of the title race by the end of January but only two more league wins by the start of April left the Reds well adrift of pace-setters Manchester United and Leeds United and, following a UEFA Cup quarter-final defeat to Italians Genoa, the season rested on progress in the FA Cup. After needing replays to get past Second Division Bristol Rovers and Ipswich, Souness's side beat Aston Villa at home in the quarter-finals to set up a semi-final with another second tier side, Portsmouth, at Highbury.

Liverpool would reach Wembley after winning a replayed semi-final against Portsmouth on penalties, but by then Souness was recovering in hospital after it was announced he required an immediate triple heart bypass, a situation which led to the gross misjudgement that in the eyes of some should have seen him sacked immediately and will forever cast a shadow over his many other achievements for the club.

In the aftermath of the semi-final replay victory over Portsmouth, Souness had allowed himself to be pictured kissing his then-girlfriend Karen Levy on the front page of the S*n newspaper, a publication still boycotted on Merseyside and far beyond after the repugnant and unfounded lies it printed about Liverpool supporters after Hillsborough.

Under the banner headline 'Lover-pool', the picture was taken before the Villa Park tie on the condition it would only be printed if Liverpool reached Wembley but, with the match having gone to extra-time and penalties, fell too late for print deadlines and was published the following day, 15 April 1992, the third anniversary of the disaster.

Souness had a working relationship with the S*n's Merseyside reporter Mike Ellis, who eventually wrote his second autobiography in 1999.

The initial story of his hospital ordeal was published in the S*n the week after the initial semi-final without much reaction, Souness later pointing out the likes of Ian Rush and Tommy Smith had public dealings with the newspaper before him and after Hillsborough without any public fall-out.

But Ellis being on holiday the week beginning Monday, 13 April was significant, Souness said, as had the paper's local correspondent been at work his understanding of the situation would have prevented the second story being printed on the anniversary of the disaster.

"There were a series of circumstances that led to it being printed that day and he was the one person who could have said to the newspaper's office, you just can't do that," Souness claimed.

"I accept I made one almighty rick by doing an exclusive with them. The thing that really killed me, and makes me sad today is that the last thing I want to do is upset any Liverpool supporter – especially the people damaged by Hillsborough – in whatever shape or form."

Souness said he gave all the proceeds of his fee for the story to Alder Hey children's hospital and claimed, having been up in Scotland at the time of the disaster, he did not appreciate the strength of feeling which still existed against the S*n, although it later emerged he had written to a Liverpool shareholder the previous year giving assurances his players would be instructed not to deal with the reviled tabloid.

Some Liverpool supporters vowed not to attend matches again until he was replaced as manager and, while the club took no action, Souness later admitted he should have resigned.

"I have nobody to blame but myself. I knew I'd got it wrong. Ignorance is no excuse. I will regret the decision forever. I don't have a defence.

"What I really should have done is resigned. It looked terrible, me smiling and confident of a recovery on the same day a lot of people were still mourning.

"There is no-one who hurts more than me whenever the Hillsborough thing is mentioned.

"It hurts me because I had a great time as a player at Liverpool and I'd like to think I had a great relationship with the supporters at the time, and it hurts me.

"So I hold my hands up. I'm still a Liverpool supporter. They are still my team. I can only apologise and it's something I have to live with."

He returned to the bench at Wembley, pale and gaunt and with a doctor by his side, to watch his team beat Second Division Sunderland 2-0 in the FA Cup final with Liverpool having finished sixth – their lowest league placing since 1965 – in the final First Division table.

In his absence, Souness's side had played a significant role in the destination of the title after beating Manchester United 2-0 in late April to ensure Howard Wilkinson's Leeds United would finish on top, an afternoon which would have further consequences behind the scenes at Anfield.

After finishing his playing career at Sheffield United, Phil Thompson had returned to Liverpool in 1986 to join Kenny Dalglish's backroom staff initially as reserve team manager. The return of his old nemesis as manager in 1991 was initially handled smoothly, Souness assuring the former European Cup winning captain he saw him fulfilling a Ronnie Moran-type role in his new regime.

But it proved an uneasy truce, staff contract negotiations falling back under Souness's remit causing friction along with further issues.

Thompson was mooted as a potential replacement for

Souness as speculation whirled over his health and future as he recovered from his heart operation with claims reaching the recuperating manager that the Kirkby-born coach was attempting to 'promote' himself in the sudden power vacuum and dominating team talks before games.

When allegations Thompson had bad-mouthed him to Manchester United assistant coach Brian Kidd in the Anfield boardroom following the late April match got back to Souness, he told Peter Robinson he wanted to sack his former team-mate, a decision which was ratified by the club's board of directors the week after the FA Cup final.

Thompson took the club to an industrial tribunal following his dismissal before reaching an out-of-court settlement, later expanding on what happened from his perspective in his 1999 autobiography 'Stand Up Pinocchio'.

"The chairman was sitting at the head of the table with Graeme Souness next to him. He said: 'Phil, we have had a discussion and chatted about the situation. We are all in full agreement that we have to back the manager's decision over this.'

"I said: 'Fair enough, but what is the reason for my dismissal?'

"They said: 'We will give it to you in writing.' I said that the reason the manager had given me for my sacking was that I was shouting too much at the younger lads.

"I added that I was not accepting that as the real reason. I said: 'You know and I know that this is personal. It is wider than this and you are not going to tell me.'"

Thompson said he only learned 12 months later from former team-mates Alan Kennedy and David Johnson that his alleged comments to Manchester United assistant boss Kidd about Souness after United's April 1992 defeat at Anfield were the supposed real reason for his departure.

Thompson said: "Whether I had said those words about

Graeme, I don't know. I was always behind him and supportive of him while I was a coach. Even if I did say those words,
surely a rollicking would have been enough. Why did he have
to give me the sack?

"It caused me tremendous personal grief and affected all
of my family, not least my sons. I always think back to the
Monday after being told by Graeme that he wanted me out
and having to tell the boys."

With the advent of the new Premier League now at hand,
Souness still faced a big task to restore a club whose income
was still recovering after six years without European football
and facing further redevelopment of Anfield following the
completion of the new Centenary Stand.

Souness's task was not made easier by the limited success
of his initial acquisitions as Liverpool manager and recent
UEFA rules limiting only four overseas players to be named in
squads for European ties, which had a significant impact on his
attempts to revamp an ageing squad.

Having sold Peter Beardsley, Gary Gillespie, Steve Staunton
and Steve McMahon during his first season in charge, 30-year-
old Ray Houghton was transferred to Aston Villa in the
summer of 1992 and was soon joined by record buy Dean
Saunders, sold at a loss despite scoring 23 goals in his one full
season at Anfield.

New buys like midfielder Paul Stewart from Tottenham,
Danish European Championship-winning defender Torben
Piechnik and Hungarian winger Istvan Kozma were not of the
same quality as the seasoned campaigners they replaced and
Souness's failure to follow-up potential leads to sign players
like Peter Schmeichel, Eric Cantona and Alan Shearer proved
fatal in his attempts to build a new squad capable of challenging for the title.

The 1992/93 saw another sixth-place finish, the scale of the club's on-pitch decline being highlighted by a home FA Cup third-round replay defeat to third-tier Bolton Wanderers which essentially finished the Reds' season in mid-January.

With resentment still festering after his S*n dealings, Souness's absence from Liverpool's final fixture of a dismal campaign at home to Tottenham led to rumours around a jubilant Anfield that he was about to be replaced as manager as the Reds beat Spurs 6-2. A press conference the following day confirmed he had merely been on a scouting mission, confirming the Scot, still with three years remaining on his contract, would be continuing in charge with Roy Evans now promoted from within as his new assistant.

"The past few days at Anfield have probably been the most difficult in the club's history," chairman David Moores said.

"It has created a furore and we fully understand why. We have always tried to have excellent relations with the media and to be as open and helpful as possible. But this time we had to keep our mouths and doors shut until it was sorted out.

"Now it is sorted out and I am pleased to announce that Graeme will be remaining as manager of Liverpool for the three years of his contract – and I hope for much longer."

Souness expressed his relief at the speculation over his future being brought to a close and his belief that he could still be successful as Liverpool manager.

"At no time have I wanted to leave. I would like to serve out my contract and be awarded another," Souness said.

"I came here two years ago because of the feeling I have for this club and the pull of this place. I know how successful this club has been and I knew that before I took the job. It was always going to be difficult to follow in the footsteps of my predecessors.

"I'm hurt that we didn't win something this year. It hurts me far more than anyone else. This has not been an experience I've enjoyed, but you are stronger for it. I can't wait for the new season. I know we've just finished, but I wish next season was starting tomorrow."

By the time the new campaign did begin in August, Souness had again been backed in the transfer market with the £2.5m arrival of Spurs defender Neil Ruddock and £2.25m signing of Nottingham Forest's Nigel Clough, the Reds going top after winning their opening three matches against Sheffield Wednesday, Queens Park Rangers and newly-promoted Swindon Town.

But five defeats in the next six, including an abject 2-0 defeat at Goodison Park to an Everton side who would only survive relegation by the skin of their teeth on the final day of the season, brought back the dark clouds with supporters further perplexed and concerned at manager's eye for a player following his decision to allow promising youngster Mike Marsh and full-back David Burrows to join West Ham in exchange for full-back Julian Dicks the day before the Reds' derby collapse.

The emergence of Toxteth-born 18-year-old scoring sensation Robbie Fowler, alongside fellow youngsters like Steve McManaman, Jamie Redknapp, Rob Jones and Don Hutchison offered a glimmer of hope at times.

Liverpudlians weaned on decades of success, however, were under no illusions how far their team had fallen behind the leading pack.

When Manchester United visited Anfield in the opening week of 1994 they were stunned when, having raced into a three-goal lead inside 23 minutes, Liverpool – roared on by an indignant Spion Kop – fought back to snatch an unlikely draw.

It proved little more than a fleeting show of defiance and when second-tier Bristol City won an FA Cup third round replay at Anfield three weeks later to end Liverpool's season in January for the second year running it was the final straw, Souness himself realised his time was up.

Souness tendered his resignation to David Moores and Peter Robinson, with Moores calling it a "very sad day for everyone at Anfield" as the club released a statement on the departing manager's behalf which read, "After a great deal of soul searching I have reached the conclusion that the best thing for the club and I is that we should part company."

Roy Evans, promoted to assistant manager the previous summer, took over as manager as Liverpool looked to go back to basics with a man David Moores labelled the 'last of the Boot Room boys'.

Souness took some time out of football to lick his wounds and admitted with hindsight he would have done things differently.

"I lost the dressing room and that hurt me, because it started with some of the players I'd worked with and looked after as young boys," he said.

"I'm not blaming anybody but myself, because if I did it again now, I'd do a lot differently. I would hate to think this is coming across as me not holding my hands up."

He returned to football as manager with Turkish club Galatasaray in June 1995 where he showed his appetite for confrontation had not waned by nearly sparking a riot after placing a large Galatasaray flag into the centre circle of the pitch of arch rivals Fenerbahce after beating them in the Turkish cup final.

After a spell in charge of Southampton, Souness managed abroad again, taking charge of Torino in Italy and Benfica in Portugal before returning to the Premier League with four years in charge of Blackburn Rovers, where he won the League Cup in 2002, and 18 months as Bobby Robson's successor at Newcastle before embarking on a career as a television pundit.

His place in the Liverpool pantheon remains an ambiguous one and open to debate depending on the perspective.

There are some who believe the circumstances surrounding his dalliances with the S*n are unforgivable and will forever tarnish everything else he did at Liverpool while others, some of whom still hold strident views over that incident and that newspaper, cannot forget the commanding leadership and imperious football he treated them to during arguably the club's most dominant period.

Speaking about his time at Liverpool in a candid interview with Sky Sports' Monday Night Football in 2018, an emotional Souness opened up about his biggest regrets and why certain perceptions still hurt him badly.

He reflected: "I made many mistakes and my biggest crime was trying to make the changes too quickly.

"Liverpool will always be the place I look back in terms of the place where I enjoyed playing, it was just unique. If you are winning every week it's very easy to have a great dressing room but we went through hiccups and had a real bond. Liverpool will always be a very special place to me.

"There are things that happened there when I was manager which I deeply regret but I can't turn back the clock, and that hurts me badly, that I am perceived by some people to be something I'm not."

MARIO BALOTELLI

The Terrible Transfer

First published: February 2021

"I think we have done a really smart piece of business here. This transfer represents outstanding value for the club."

On the face it, £16m for a 24-year-old striker whose goals had already helped win domestic titles in Italy and England while bagging 13 international goals in 33 appearances appeared to tally precisely with Liverpool manager Brendan Rodgers' assessment of his new buy.

Sure, Mario Balotelli had 'baggage' but so had the last young foreign frontman Liverpool had brought in, the man Balotelli had been bought to replace. Luis Suarez had already made headlines for biting an opponent and turning a whole continent against him with his antics at a World Cup when he arrived at Anfield in January 2011, also aged 24.

While no-one could pretend some of the more unsavoury aspects of the Uruguayan's character did not play out during his eventful three-and-a-half years at Anfield, in a footballing sense it's hard to see how he could be regarded as anything other than "a really smart piece of business", wowing the Kop – and at times begrudgingly the rest of the league – with his trickery, goals and sheer single-minded will to win.

Eighty-two goals in 133 Liverpool games told only a fraction of the story as Suarez's world-class talent helped drag the Reds to the brink of ending the now quarter-of-a-century league title drought before his sale to Barcelona for £75million.

Devastating though the 2014 title near-miss had been, Liver-pudlians still hoped the basis of the side which had produced one of the most scintillating seasons in living memory could – with the right additions – build on the momentum of the previous campaign and mount credible challenges for trophies again.

Replacing Suarez was always going to be the biggest challenge and there was some sense of logic in gambling on replacing one maverick talent with another but, as all at Anfield would painfully discover, there would prove to be seismic differences between him and the man who would take his place.

Balotelli had broken through as a youngster at Inter Milan, being given his debut by the manager who he would enjoy his most successful spell in England under, Roberto Mancini.

Aged only 17, a double-strike against Juventus in a Coppa Italia quarter-final brought him national attention and played a part in helping the Nerazzuri win a Serie A and cup double in 2008. The following season saw him become the youngest player in the club's history to score in the Champions League and he managed eight goals in 22 Serie A appearances as the title was retained.

There were issues though. Unhappy with his application in training, Inter coach Jose Mourinho would repeatedly call him out publicly for not learning from the example of the experienced pros. In just his second Serie A campaign, Balotelli also found himself the target of persistent racist abuse from the stands, notably from Juventus fans who would sing about him even in matches not involving Inter.

It would have been all too familiar to a young man born in the south of the country in Palermo and abandoned by his Ghanaian parents at the age of two, before being adopted by loving foster parents in Concesio, Brescia, in the north where he found himself the only black boy in a white neighbourhood.

Speaking in 2015, Sergio Aguero said of his one-time teammate, "A lot of his behaviour, I feel, came from a feeling that he was somehow different and maybe a little insecure. Everybody loved him, though he drove us nuts at times."

The following season would be arguably the greatest in Inter's history with the club completing an unprecedented Serie A, Coppa Italia and Champions League triumph but while Balotelli managed to contribute 11 goals in 40 appearances in all competitions, his jarring relationship with Mourinho meant his days at the club looked numbered.

The Portuguese said his young striker, still not yet 20, had come 'close to a zero rating' in a November 2009 1-1 draw with Roma and a spat in the build-up to the Champions League knock-out clash with Chelsea saw Balotelli left out and heavily criticised by senior players Javier Zanetti and Marco Materazzi, as well as his own agent.

The final straw for the club hierarchy may well have been when he wore the shirt of city rivals AC Milan on Italian TV show Striscia la Notizia. And his actions in throwing his Inter shirt on the ground after being jeered following his performance in the first leg Champions League semi-final against Barcelona finished him off in the eyes of the fans.

He never got off the bench in the second leg or the final in Madrid where Inter beat Bayern Munich to seal the club's first European Cup since 1965 and he was sold to Manchester City.

It was felt the presence of Roberto Mancini could be the key to helping the young Italian – who turned 20 as his debut season in English football began – unlock his undoubted potential.

His Premier League career had a mixed beginning with his first goals in a win over West Brom at the Hawthorns being followed by a red card for violent conduct but his undoubted pedigree was highlighted that December when he was awarded the Golden Boy award, given to Europe's best young player.

Stories of wild antics around Manchester had begun to circulate but he ended the campaign having helped City win the FA Cup, their first trophy since 1974.

He incurred Mancini's wrath the following pre-season during a friendly against LA Galaxy when having been put through on goal, he turned full circle and flicked the ball behind his legs before trying to score with a backheel and missing, being immediately substituted in disgrace.

He scored 13 goals in just 23 Premier League appearances as City made their first serious modern bid for the title but was sent off four times, one of them at Anfield in a 1-1 November 2011 draw with the final dismissal being in an Easter Sunday defeat at Arsenal which seemed to have ended their title hopes.

A furious Mancini suggested after the game he wouldn't play Balotelli again that season but, with City having got themselves back in pole position ahead of the final round of matches yet trailing at home to Queens Park Rangers where victory would guarantee a first top-flight title since 1968, it was the Italian who produced an assist while falling to the ground to set up Aguero's last-gasp winner in one of the most dramatic finishes ever seen to an English season.

It cemented his place in Manchester City legend, having already given City fans a day to remember earlier in the campaign by sidefooting home the opener in a 6-1 win away to reigning champions Manchester United and unveiling a T-shirt which read 'Why Always Me?' having that Sunday morning been splashed all over the tabloids for an indoor fireworks show that had reportedly almost burned down his house.

James Milner, a key part of that City side before his move to Anfield in the summer of 2015 just as Balotelli was about to leave Anfield, wrote of his former team-mate: "The easiest way to describe him is to say that he was like a 12-year-old.

"That might sound like I'm digging him out but I'm just trying to explain what he was like. He had this fantastic skillset and a great physique but in other ways he was like a big kid who hadn't grown up.

"If a few of us were having a conversation and he was on the opposite side of the dressing room, he would make a loud noise or something daft so that he would get attention.

"A lot of the things he did – throwing darts, wearing that glove-style hat and even the car he drove with the camouflage wrap – seemed to be about trying to get attention. Whether that was out of insecurity, or whether he had found it hard to grow up because he had such a difficult upbringing, that was what he was like.

"I wasn't laughing the time he drove his car into mine in the car park. It's not easy trying to get camouflage paint off your car. But you couldn't ever stay frustrated with him for long."

Balotelli returned to Italy, joining AC Milan for £19 million plus bonuses and add-ons, after managing only one goal in the first half of City's title defence. He started well with the Rossoneri, equalling Oliver Bierhoff's record of four goals in his first three matches for the club and by the end of the following campaign had a more than respectable tally of 30 goals in 54 games but the scrutiny – and racial abuse – he continued to receive on home soil was unrelenting.

Meanwhile at Anfield, the task of replacing Luis Suarez was proving even more difficult than had been anticipated.

Brendan Rodgers had signed Southampton's Scouse forward and lifelong Liverpool fan Rickie Lambert along with young Belgian talent Divock Origi early in the summer of 2014 to bolster an attacking armoury which still included Daniel Sturridge and Raheem Sterling but hopes of bringing in Barcelona's Alexis Sanchez never got off the ground.

An £8.5m deal to sign QPR's French striker Loic Remy fell through on medical grounds so Balotelli's potential availability was put to Rodgers while on Liverpool's pre-season tour of the United States.

"I can categorically tell you Mario Balotelli will not be at Liverpool," Rodgers said on 3 August ahead of a friendly against Manchester United in Miami.

Yet a little over three weeks later with the Reds about to visit the Italian's former club, Manchester City, following a narrow opening weekend victory over Southampton at Anfield, Balotelli was at Liverpool with Rodgers now saying: "There is no doubting Mario's ability. He is a world-class talent and someone who, for such a young age, has vast experience of playing at the very highest level.

"I believe we have the infrastructure, culture and environment to get the best out of him and help him achieve his true potential."

Rodgers insisted the club had done their due diligence over Balotelli and had received the assurances they wanted over his behaviour and commitment to the cause, with his agent Mino Raiola stressing the player himself knew he was in something of a 'last chance saloon'.

"It's either make or break now," Raiola admitted. "If it goes wrong? Mario is 24 years old. He no longer has the alibi of his age."

The initial portents seemed good. Liverpool had been well beaten in the game at City the night Balotelli's transfer had been confirmed but he was handed a full debut away at Tottenham the following weekend and, although he didn't get on the scoresheet, played an encouraging part in an impressive 3-0 away win.

"For the first time in his life he marked at a corner," Rodgers said. "Seriously. An international player who has won three titles in Italy, cups, the Champions League. We were doing corners and I said to him 'I'm putting you on a man at defensive corners.' He said 'I don't mark at corners.' 'Ah, well you do now.' He went in and he had a great header today from a corner. Treat him like an adult and that's what happens."

He scored his first goal for the club, a smart 82nd-minute finish at the Kop end to open the scoring in the Champions League group match against Bulgarian side Ludogorets which led to a 2-1 win.

Defeat at West Ham followed days later, the Reds' third league defeat already in only five matches, and the following weekend saw a Merseyside derby which in some ways would go on to symbolise the kind of the season Rodgers and Balotelli were doomed to endure.

Having scraped past Championship side Middlesbrough in a marathon 14-13 penalty shoot-out win after extra-time days before, Steven Gerrard's free-kick put the Reds in front against Everton early in the second half but after Balotelli missed a presentable chance to double the advantage when hitting the bar from close range, Phil Jagielka's stoppage-time long-ranger grabbed a point for the visitors to deepen the gloom around Anfield.

By the following midweek's Champions League trip to face FC Basel, the old habits which Liverpool had been warned against ahead of signing Balotelli were resurfacing.

With some of his friends have driven across to Switzerland to see him, the Italian striker was seen staying up late with them and nipping out for smokes the night before the game in which he started and Liverpool lost abjectly 1-0.

Within weeks, Balotelli's team-mates were fast losing patience with him, with one anecdote from Liverpool's Premier League trip to Queens Park Rangers in mid-October illustrating how the situation was unravelling.

Although the Reds would return home from the capital with a fortuitous three points after Steven Caulker's 94th-minute own goal sealed a 3-2 away win following a madcap period of stoppage time, Balotelli – who had blazed over an open goal from three yards with the game goalless – and his attitude were now causing serious issues within the dressing room.

"He barely moved," one player told The Athletic.

"A lot of the lads caned him but there was very little comeback other than a few scowls and 'f*** you'."

A second Liverpool goal followed later that month in a League Cup win over Swansea but stories of the damage his behaviour was doing to the already-fragile team spirit at Anfield were becoming far more prolific.

After receiving criticism for swapping shirts with Real Madrid's Sergio Ramos as he was being substituted at half-time in a 3-0 Champions League hammering at Anfield, Rodgers began to regularly leave him out of the side as Balotelli gradually withdrew into his own world.

His hankering for home cooking reportedly saw him regularly have Italian food delivered to his Formby mansion rather than eat with his team-mates. One of his close friends became an increasingly irritating presence at Melwood, regularly being seen sleeping in Balotelli's red Ferrari as he waited for his pal to finish training and occasionally wandering into meetings and places he had no right to be.

Stories of their antics around Formby became legion, and with Balotelli now firmly on the fringes, he didn't start a game between the home defeat to Chelsea on 8 November and the Europa League last 32 defeat on penalties to Besiktas in Istanbul's Ataturk Stadium on 26 February.

The third and fourth (and ultimately final) goals of Balotelli's Anfield spell came as the side began to gain some real momentum in February, the Italian coming off the bench to score the late winner with his only Premier League goal for the club in a 3-2 Anfield win over Tottenham on 10 February, and the following week scoring a late penalty to gain a 1-0 first-leg advantage in the Besiktas Europa League tie.

Even the latter came with a caveat, Balotelli being publicly criticised by his captain Steven Gerrard for grabbing the ball off Henderson having not long come off the bench, which led to awkward scenes before the 85th-minute kick was taken.

"Jordan should have taken the penalty. Rules are rules," Gerrard said. "Credit to Mario, he's scored. But it's not nice to see when footballers are arguing. I think Jordan has handled the situation very well. He can see that Mario really wanted to score."

An incident before the Reds' match at Arsenal in April demonstrated just how Balotelli had become a complete law unto himself. With the Italian playing in a practice match ahead of the trip to the Emirates and frustrated at being on the weaker team made up of those likely to be substitutes, he turned on the halfway line and fired a shot into the back of the net of his own goal, laughing his head off as the the ball flew past a bemused Brad Jones.

He was unsurprisingly left out of the squad for the trip to London, a 4-1 defeat which saw Liverpool's season – and ultimately Rodgers' time at the helm – truly start to fall apart.

Though he started the late season goalless draw at West Brom and defeat at Hull, it was clear as day the Balotelli experiment had failed and his time at Liverpool was up.

Rodgers received a stay of execution despite a humiliating 6-1 defeat at Stoke City on the last weekend and was still entrusted with the club cheque book to bring in new frontmen Christian Benteke for £32.5m and Roberto Firmino for £29m, with Balotelli being loaned back to AC Milan before the 2015/16 campaign got underway.

He managed just one league goal in 20 appearances and, with Milan having no desire to make the move permanent, he had to return to Liverpool for pre-season training in the summer of 2016, where Jurgen Klopp had now taken over as manager.

The German made it clear he saw no future for Balotelli at Anfield, leaving him out of the club's American pre-season tour, and shortly after the Italian left the club on a free transfer to join French club Nice.

Anfield icon Gerrard, whose 17th and final season at Liverpool coincided with Balotelli's, spoke in his autobiography about how even from the start he had his doubts over whether his presence at Anfield could ever work out.

"In my last season, Brendan Rodgers came to me at Melwood one day in mid-August," Gerrard recalled.

"We had a chat on the training pitch. He said, 'You know we've missed out on a couple of signings. I'm basically left with no option but to have a bit of a gamble.'

"Brendan paused before he spoke again: 'The gamble is Mario Balotelli.' My instant reaction was, 'Uh-oh.'

"I'd never met Balotelli but I'd heard all the stories about the indoor fireworks and Jose Mourinho describing him as an 'unmanageable' player. I could see that, in the right mood, he was a quality footballer but the rest of his career seemed like a spectacular waste of talent. That was my opinion of Balotelli.

"I reminded myself that I had always allowed every new player to come into the club with a clean slate. Balotelli's reputation tested that resolve but I tried my best to be open-minded.

"After his promising debut against Tottenham he had lapsed in training and the subsequent games. His demeanour was very poor. I made up my mind pretty quickly after that about Balotelli.

"There was no friction between us. We got on fine. I still tried to help him and I kept looking for chances to praise him. But I could see Mourinho had been right when he said Balotelli is unmanageable.

"He is very talented with the potential to be world class, but he'll never get there because of his mentality and the people around him."

Rodgers, meanwhile, claimed a few months after his own departure in October 2015 that he never wanted to sign Balotelli but his arrival was at the insistence of FSG who believed the £16m gamble could become a £50m superstar.

"What we wanted and what we needed was a player who could really press at the top end of the field," Rodgers said.

"It wasn't just a goalscorer we were after. I felt Mario was someone who wouldn't work for us. But come the end of the summer, we were struggling to get someone who could do the role we wanted. I think the ownership group thought that this could be a player I could develop.

"They were thinking that maybe he is a £50m player that we can get for £16m. So, when the owners are wanting you to go down that route and there are no other options, then of course you give it a go."

The reality was any striker coming into Liverpool in the summer of 2014 would have faced an almost impossible task in trying to replace Suarez and galvanise a club still devastated by the loss of a long-overdue and yearned-for league title which seemed to have been written in the stars.

The sad truth was, even if those stars had been in perfect alignment, that striker was never likely to be Mario Balotelli.

PHIL THOMPSON

Phil Lives The Fantasy

First published: January 2022

IT'S every Liverpudlian's dream to pull on the famous red shirt and play for their heroes at Anfield.

For most of us, it remains a fantasy lived out vicariously through the terraces or five-a-side pitch, but every generation or so the stars align just right and enable one lucky soul to make it from the Kop onto the hallowed turf of L4.

Tommy Smith, Terry McDermott, John Aldridge, Steven Gerrard and latterly Trent Alexander-Arnold and Curtis Jones are all among those who have lived out boyhood desires by playing for Liverpool and written their names into the legendary fabric of the country's most successful club.

But few Scouse Reds have enjoyed the journey from Kopite to European Cup-winning skipper to training pitch and dugout leader as Phil Thompson. The Kirkby lad also went on to captain his country but his contribution over decades to the club he has always loved bears comparison to anyone who came before or after.

Although very much associated with Kirkby, Thompson was actually born in the Kensington area of Liverpool in 1954 before the family moved out to the overspill town which he credits with moulding him into the man he went on to be.

"It shaped me very much," he said years later in a wide-ranging interview looking back over his stellar career.

"It was a tough area, really tough area. You had to stand on your feet, have your own mind and stand up for yourself.

"It was a very young town and football was the only thing you had. There weren't any other sports. Everybody played football 24-7.

"It shaped you like that, you had to compete with some fantastic players. Being quite skinny, I had to have more drive and determination than the next fellow, so it shaped me very much in my early days.

"My dad was an Evertonian and once I started playing for Liverpool he turned but he was a merchant seaman so we didn't see him a lot of the time, he was away.

"So we followed my mum, she was a massive Red and as a youngster her and her twin sister used to stand right next to the dugout and they were there week in and week out. She was very passionate about her football and very much Liverpool, so we followed in her traditions."

It was thanks to his mum that Thompson's first taste of Anfield came on one of the old ground's most hallowed nights when, just three days after winning the FA Cup for the very first time against Leeds United at Wembley, reigning champions Internazionale of Milan were sent packing in the first leg of the

1965 European Cup semi-final with the Kop famously inviting the visitors to 'Go back to Italy' to the tune of the famous 'Santa Lucia'.

It made a big impression on the 11-year-old whose fanaticism for all things Liverpool was taken up a level after being part of what was, at the time, arguably Anfield's greatest ever night.

"That night was so special," he recalled.

"People had heard about the Kop and its reputation through the 50s and early 60s but I think that was the night it truly came of age. Despite it being such a tense game, the wit and humour still came shining through."

His schooling on playgrounds of Kirkby and terraces of the Kop, which he eventually graduated to, saw him sign apprentice forms with Liverpool at 15 years of age after a six-week trial and his anxiety over whether he would make the next step up was eased after an unforgettable exchange with the man who was already his hero and would go on to become one of the guiding influences of his career, Bill Shankly.

The legendary Reds boss once said about his young charge, "Aye, Phil Thompson. The boy tossed up with a sparrow for his legs and lost" but he clearly immediately had the young Scouser pegged as one of the new breed he could build his second great Liverpool side around.

"All the young lads wondered whether they would turn professional, it's always a very difficult time," Thompson recalled.

"They would always do it on your 17th birthday. My birthday is January 21st. This was December and I had been injured. You had heard all these stories about Shanks, if you were injured he didn't want to know. We didn't have people to give you rehab in those days and you were left to your own devices.

"I had a groin injury and was just walking around the B team pitch. Shanks came over to me and I thought 'He's going to give me a b******ing here.' He said: 'How are you, son? Are you sleeping well? Are you eating well?' 'Fine, boss', I said.

"Then he said: 'Your birthday is January 21st.' My eyes lit up that the great man wasn't just talking to me, he actually knew my birthday. I thought he was going to send me a birthday card.

"He said, 'I just want you to know not to worry. We have been more than pleased with how you have performed. Just to put your mind at ease, we will be signing you as a professional on your 17th birthday.'

"You can imagine that I couldn't wait to get home and tell my parents. It was a fantastic and a big, big day.

"Liverpool was my life. The team was your life and Bill Shankly was your life – those were the two things that you lived for. Shanks' words just made you feel special, made you feel proud to be a Liverpool fan.

"Every day your mum, your dad, your brothers and sisters would ask, 'What did Shanks say today? Did you see him?'

"Life is all about timing and he was sent for us. We believe that, as Merseysiders, we are special people anyway and this guy was here to help bring us out of the doldrums and make us a world super power."

Thompson's emergence in the early 1970s came at just the right time for Shankly with the Scot in the process of breaking up his first great Liverpool team – which had gone trophyless since 1966 – and he made his debut at 18 on Easter Monday 1972 away at Manchester United, coming on as substitute for John Toshack.

It was a baptism of fire but the smarts he'd learned on the streets of Kirkby served him well when he immediately came up against the great George Best, who years later would become a friend and punditry colleague on Sky Sports.

"He was moving towards me with the ball and I offered him to nutmeg me on the halfway line," Thompson told the Mail years later.

"He tried to slip the ball through but I closed my legs, the ball ricocheted off my skinny shins and off I went.

"I never got tired of talking about the nutmeg. The number of times he would say, 'Not that one again, Thommo! Not that one!'

"I must have bored him silly about it. But he was just fascinating. A fascinating man. A wonderful guy. He just loved being with other football people."

That would be Thompson's sole appearance of the 1971/72 campaign but the following year saw him just about reach the required figure of 14 league games required for a championship medal as Liverpool ended a seven-year trophy drought with a league and UEFA Cup double.

It would be the following campaign when Thompson, initially used as a midfielder, truly established himself at the heart of the Liverpool defence but his increasing involvement in the climax to that 1972/73 season saw him earn his place in one of the campaign's most decisive moments.

Don Revie's Leeds United arrived at Anfield on Easter Monday with Liverpool knowing a victory against one of their main rivals would all but seal the club's long-awaited eighth league title.

"It was such a memorable day for me," Thompson remembered.

"I was only 19 and Bill Shankly had picked me ahead of Brian Hall at the time when I was just an up-and-coming lad.

"We stayed in a hotel overnight and I remember coming to the game along Anfield Road with the nerves and butterflies really going.

"And I can remember starting to sing You'll Never Walk Alone to myself on the coach. It sounds daft and everything and I don't often relate it but the passion was burning so much inside me, I was nearly crying. I was looking out the window and thinking 'all those people, they're all looking at me here'.

"And as it has happened we played magnificently on the day, I was burning, burning with desire and pride and during the game, which we won 2-0, I remember going through a tackle with Allan Clarke and I really did… block tackle… just went right through him and carried on and I remember the Kop mid-game breaking out in song with my name.

"Usually a lot of the time during the game you don't always hear things from the crowd but I heard that and that was the first time I felt I belonged."

Further silverware would arrive a year later when Thompson, playing his 51st game of the season at just 20, helped keep a clean sheet in the FA Cup final against Newcastle at Wembley as the famous old trophy went to Anfield for only the second time.

Shankly's shock retirement that summer saw a brief transition period as Bob Paisley stepped up from the boot room to take charge and Liverpool finished as runners-up to surprise champions Derby County in 1975.

It would be the only full season Thompson played at Anfield which would finish without a trophy as the softly-spoken north-easterner built on the foundations his predecessor had laid to establish the Reds as the pre-eminent force at home and abroad.

Thompson was central to the Reds repeating the league and UEFA Cup double of three years earlier in 1975/76, missing only one league game and scoring the crucial semi-final aggregate winner against Barcelona which sealed the Reds' spot in the two-legged European showpiece final against Belgian side FC Bruges, capping a tremendous year of personal success by making his first full England appearance against Wales.

A third championship medal in five seasons followed in 1977, although a cartilage injury meant Thompson missed out on the club's maiden European Cup triumph against Borussia Moenchengladbach in Rome. He would not be denied a year later and played a crucial role in Paisley's side retaining the trophy against Bruges at Wembley by clearing off the line a late chance the Belgians had to equalise.

With skipper Emlyn Hughes coming towards the end of his Liverpool career at left-back, Thompson's consistency and authority made him a natural candidate to take over the captaincy, although Paisley initially handed the armband to Kenny Dalglish for a few games.

"All the players were absolutely astonished," Thompson revealed. "Alan Kennedy, Terry McDermott and everybody were saying to me 'We can't understand why he hasn't made you captain.' I was gobsmacked. Kenny was captain for about five or six games and then we were playing Arsenal at home and Bob said: 'I'm changing the captain. Phil is going to be captain.' I was so pleased and thrilled. I can always remember Phil Neal's words to me: 'Tommo, that shouldn't even have been an issue. There is only one person who has the divine right to be captain at this moment in time and that's you.'

"On that day we were playing Arsenal at Anfield. I went down the steps at Anfield, touched the sign. I came up the steps. I go out on the pitch, straight over to the edge of the penalty area. What I had in my mind was that my brother, Owen, was on the Kop. I was looking for my brother.

"I hear everybody laughing. Clapping first and then laughing. I am thinking: 'What's going on here?' I am waving to my brother and I turned round and the players were still in the tunnel. They allowed me to walk out on my own. They were killing themselves laughing."

One of Thompson's first jobs as club captain was to receive the 1979 league championship trophy after one of the Reds' most dominant title wins and he repeated the trick a year later after being ever-present. Then in 1981 he went down in history as the first Scouser to lift the European Cup as captain when Liverpool beat Real Madrid in Paris to secure a third continental crown in five seasons.

It was the pinnacle of an already outrageously decorated career and Thompson showed he had never lost touch with his roots by making sure the good people of Kirkby got to share in his success by taking the most prestigious trophy in club football back to his local pub, The Falcon.

"People always ask me 'what is your best memory in football?' and this was it for me," he admitted.

"I was fortunate enough to captain my country but nothing comes close to being skipper of Liverpool in '81.

"Being a Liverpool lad, leading my club up those steps was extra special. It was Roy of the Rovers stuff.

"Playing Madrid didn't worry us because we had so much confidence in our own ability. We were the top dogs at the time and we knew that if we played well then we would win.

"People always say to me 'is that stuff really true about you taking the European Cup back to the pub? It's become legendary and it certainly happened.

"When we won the League Cup earlier that season we had left the trophy on the coach and it had gone back to the depot. So when we got home from Paris, Peter Robinson (Liverpool secretary) told me as captain I had to make sure the European Cup was taken care of.

"I didn't need to be asked twice. After the parade I put it in the back of my Capri and went straight to The Falcon where I ran the Sunday league side.

"There was a big party going on and the trophy was perched behind the bar – we had a great night. There was a queue for the phone with everyone telling their mates to come down.

"The following morning Peter rang me about 9am and asked me where the cup was. I was still in bed and through bleary eyes I could see it sitting on the cabinet in my bedroom.

"I'd told everyone to come back to The Falcon for 11am and bring their kids so they could have their picture taken with the trophy.

"I couldn't let them down and stayed true to my word. I eventually got the cup back to Anfield about midday."

Barely six months later Thompson was left devastated when, after a poor run of form both for himself and the team, Paisley took the captaincy off him and gave the armband to Graeme Souness. It had an immediate impact with Liverpool winning 19 out of the last 20 league matches to secure the title yet again, also retaining the League Cup.

"The period when Bruce Grobbelaar had just come to the club was the most difficult time I'd had as a player. I'd had a great relationship with Ray Clemence," Thompson admitted.

"Bob thought the captaincy was part of it. In fairness he had a point. I took all the responsibility on my own shoulders. Every time there was a goal being conceded I wouldn't allow anybody else to take the blame. It was my fault.

"He said I was placing too much pressure on myself. I was disappointed because I felt Graeme Souness in the background was pushing for the captaincy himself."

With Liverpool struggling in 12th position, a 3-1 home defeat to Manchester City on Boxing Day 1981 marked by high profile errors by Thompson and Grobbelaar led many in the media to declare the Reds' unparalleled period of dominance over, with the Daily Mirror describing the Anfield empire as 'crumbling' and even the Liverpool Daily Post suggesting it might be time for Paisley to step down.

Souness claimed he was surprised to be offered the job ahead of Neal and Dalglish and believed Thompson had lost the job himself a few weeks earlier after giving Paisley 'a mouthful in front of the lads' after the manager had reacted to Liverpool's 3-0 defeat to Flamengo in the Intercontinental Cup final in Japan by asking his skipper whether the captaincy was proving too much for him.

With talk rife among the squad and audible to Thompson that he was about to lose the armband, he confronted Paisley and had his worst suspicions confirmed.

"I asked Bob, 'Who's going to be the new captain?' And he said: 'Well, I'm not...'

"I said: 'It's Graeme f***ing Souness isn't it, I know it anyways.'

"Bob choked on his words, which I was disappointed by.

"But it had the desired effect."

The pair's professionalism and desire for success enabled them to put their differences to one side with the league title and League Cup both being retained again in 1983 but their days as team-mates were numbered.

Souness would depart for Italian side Sampdoria after lifting Liverpool's fourth European Cup against AS Roma to complete a unique treble that season after the league title was retained for the third successive year and the League Cup for a fourth.

And that would prove to be Thompson's final full season as a Liverpool player, although injuries meant his only appearance was the Wembley Charity Shield defeat to Manchester United right at its outset. He moved on loan to Sheffield United and completed a permanent move to Bramall Lane in March 1985, retiring at the end of that season at the age of only 31.

His deep links to the club still saw him train at Melwood twice a week and within a year he was back on the staff, Kenny Dalglish – now installed as player-manager – offering him the chance in the summer of 1986 to manage the reserves.

It gave him the opportunity to channel what iconic Liverpool coach Ronnie Moran – still on the staff himself – had seen in him right from the start and eventually follow in his footsteps.

Moran had spotted Thompson's potential and character from the very first morning he arrived as a nervous teenage apprentice, saying: "Sometimes you can instantly spot players who are going to make it all the way to the top. You could see it in him right away.

"His attitude was right, he was positive and he wanted to win. He was the Liverpool prototype, who did the right things without being prodded along all the time. You don't make them, they make themselves."

With Moran in mind, Thompson carved out a similar 'sergeant major' role and reputation for himself among the young players over the next half-dozen or so years, with Robbie Fowler remembering just how much of a tough taskmaster he could be, saying, "He was a coach who would push youngsters to see how tough they were and a lot of the young lads coming through despised him for it. I'm amazed he never got properly sparked out there."

The return of Graeme Souness as manager in April 1991 initially saw the Scot be "quite content to let him (Thompson) get on with his job while I concentrated on mine".

But just over a year later, shortly after the 1992 FA Cup win, Thompson was dismissed, with the suggestion he had been fired for his supposedly harsh treatment of young players.

"I couldn't accept this," Thompson explained. "Yes, they got the verbals at times, but I had a great relationship with them. I felt they needed to know how to take criticism and still be positive. If they were ever to progress into the first team with Ronnie, they would know what a tongue-lashing was."

After a number of years as a television pundit with Sky Sports, Thompson was identified as the perfect man to assist Gerard Houllier – the club's first overseas manager – when he took sole charge at Liverpool in the early months of the 1998/99 season.

Coming back to Anfield was a dream come true for Thompson, who had only dared dream such an opportunity might come his way after the acrimony of his departure six years earlier.

"One morning I got a phone call just out of the blue from Peter Robinson. He said: 'I'd like you to come to a meeting.'

"'When?' I said, 'Right now. Do you know where the chairman lives?' he replied.

"When I got up to the chairman's house they were all sitting there. They said, 'We've spoken about what we need, and we need some discipline brought back into the club.

"We need somebody who can stand up to the players and be strong. Somebody who's got Liverpool's DNA in them.

"We would like you to be assistant manager.'

"I felt absolutely thrilled. Imagine, assistant manager of Liverpool? It was just a dream come true."

With Liverpool in need of modernising as the Premier League era took hold, the combination of Houllier's visionary approach to diet, fitness and tactics along with Thompson's passion and knowledge of the club proved very effective once their methods began to take hold with the Reds winning an unprecedented treble of cups in 2001 as well as qualifying for the Champions League for the first time.

The long-overdue return of major silverware to Anfield didn't lessen Thompson's desire for success and combustible nature which came to the surface before the following season had even begun.

He recalled: "Gerard and I had strict rules about bags of footballs and when and what they should be used for during training sessions.

"No-one was allowed to take any balls out until we had done our warm-up and were starting our session.

"This day, we've done the warm-up and all the balls are on the sideline. We were just waiting for Sammy Lee to say what we're going to be doing. As this is going on, I'm walking across the goalline and I'm about a foot away from the post.

"Next thing I know this ball flashes past my nose and misses by a couple of inches. I turned around and shouted, 'Who's just done that?' and everyone is looking the other way. I shouted again, 'Who's just done that? You know the rules, who was it?' and Robbie Fowler said, 'It was me'.

"So I said to him, 'You know the f**king rules' and added 'what if that had smashed a player's nose, then we'd have a problem wouldn't we?'

"Suddenly we are walking towards each other and we're squaring up and he said 'F**k off big nose' and I was furious.

"Gerard Houllier arrived on the scene then and asked, 'what the hell is going on here?'. I told him Robbie was out of order and that he knows the rules. So, Gerard separated us and after training he got the staff and players in to ask them what happened.

"Houllier then called a team meeting and told Robbie 'everyone knows the rules including you Robbie. You are not playing until you apologise to Phil'.

"That was part of the discipline. After about two weeks of it I asked Gerard if I could go to Robbie and square it, but he said, 'No, it's not about you now. It's not even about Robbie. It's about the football club now. If we back down now, we've lost all our credit in the bank. We're not doing that'."

Fowler eventually did apologise and by mid-October 2001, Thompson suddenly found himself really in the hot seat when Houllier suffered a life-threatening heart problem which required an 11-hour operation and months of recuperation away from football.

"Being caretaker manager was something new for me. It was also quite exhilarating," Thompson admitted to Coaches-Voice.

"I was in charge for six months. For three or four of those, Gerard was too ill. I would walk to his apartment after matches, and talk to him about the game. He'd either watched on TV or listened on the radio. He'd ask what the team was going to be that week. 'Gerard, forget it', I would say. 'Concentrate on getting yourself better'."

Thompson kept the Reds in contention for trophies both at home and abroad before Houllier returned to the dugout for a pivotal Champions League match against Roma which Liverpool won to qualify for the quarter-finals, where they lost out to Bayer Leverkusen.

Despite a promising start to the following campaign, the Frenchman seemed to have lost something after his illness and although there was another League Cup win in March 2003, he was sacked as manager the following May after only managing a fourth-place Premier League finish.

Thompson also departed but looks back with fondness and pride at how they helped take Liverpool into the 21st century while putting the club back on the European map.

"One of the greatest moments of my life was when we came

together in 1998," Thompson said after the Frenchman's passing in December 2020.

"Just to be in Gerard's company was an absolute treat. So loyal, so passionate and extremely fierce.

"So many wonderful times, bringing smiles back to people's faces. 2001 should never be forgotten."

Houllier offered Thompson the assistant's job when he returned to management with Aston Villa in 2010 but he turned it down meaning his involvement with the game since has been confined to regular television work for years with Sky Sports and LFC TV, where his passion, knowledge and sheer love for Liverpool and the game of football shines as brightly as ever.

Thompson put it best in the words he wrote in his testimonial brochure back in 1983: "It's difficult to explain what it means to a Liverpool supporter to come out of the Kop and enjoy so much success with his boyhood heroes. They don't write Roy of the Rovers stories like that."

RAHEEM STERLING

Sterling's Miserable Situation

First published: March 2021

FOR most football clubs, to make a 10,000% profit on a player would generally be seen as a pretty good bit of transfer business.

No-one ever wants to lose their best performers, particularly clubs of the stature of Liverpool, but in some circumstances receiving such a gargantuan financial boost would cushion the blow somewhat. That did not feel the case though when Raheem Sterling was sold to Manchester City for close to £50m in the summer of 2015.

Only a year before he had been at the forefront of a swash-buckling Reds side which defied expectations and thrilled Liverpudlians and neutrals alike when coming heartbreakingly close to ending the club's then quarter-of-a-century wait for a 19th league championship.

The devastation which ensued from Steven Gerrard's slip against Chelsea and the subsequent failure to gain the seven points required from the final nine available that would have confirmed the title cast an almighty shadow over Anfield for quite some time afterwards. The club found itself on a psychological downturn which even a manager as talented as Brendan Rodgers was unable to halt.

With the club's star player – Luis Suarez – departing Anfield in the wake of the 2013/14 title miss, it may be that little could have been done to stop an outstanding young talent wanting to go if he felt his ambitions to be successful would be better served elsewhere.

But it's also hard not to feel that Liverpool were very slow to react to Sterling's increasing influence on the team's attacking fortunes, and by the time they did look to reward him for his stellar progress, it was too late.

Sterling was just 15 years old when he joined Liverpool from Queens Park Rangers for £500,000 in the final days of February 2010. Having been born in Jamaica, his family had moved to the UK when he was seven and by the time the Reds swooped to bring him north, he had already been featuring regularly for QPR's under-18 team as well as the Hoops reserves.

A year after his arrival on Merseyside, a stunning performance in an FA Youth Cup tie when he scored five times in a 9-0 win against Southend United brought him to the attention of Reds fans who were in need of a ray of light after one of the most harrowing seasons in Anfield history.

By February 2011, the trauma of seeing Tom Hicks and George Gillett in the boardroom along with Roy Hodgson in the dugout had finally been ended but only fairly recently and any signs of hope for the future were seized upon with relish and even a touch of desperation.

Only the previous week, newly-installed caretaker manager Kenny Dalglish had said he would have no hesitation about using some of the club's brightest stars in the first team that season if needed and he handed squad numbers to the likes of Sterling, Suso and youth team captain Conor Coady.

The Anfield icon was in attendance for the cup tie against the Shrimpers and could not have failed to be impressed by Sterling's showing, with the Liverpool ECHO reporting afterwards, 'It was the dazzling efforts of the Jamaica-born Sterling, wearing the famous number seven jersey, that caught the eye of all those at Anfield. The England youth international only turned 16 in December, but he looks to have a bright future.

'His five goals as he cut in from the flanks before delivering superb finishes past Southend keeper Daniel Bentley were reminiscent of Liverpool's former wing wizard John Barnes. The Youth Cup has been the platform for many of the stars of the past, with Michael Owen bursting onto the scene during Liverpool's successful run to glory in 1996. Sterling has similar qualities to the young Owen, with pace, quick feet and cool finishing.'

The youngster's five-goal salvo won him a place in the first-team squad for the Europa League trip to Sparta Prague and, while he didn't make the bench, a little over 12 months later he was handed a debut as a late substitute in the Premier League clash against Wigan Athletic at Anfield in March 2012, before making two more appearances from the bench against Fulham and Chelsea before the end of that campaign.

That summer saw significant change at the club with Dalglish replaced as manager by 39-year-old Rodgers and the Northern Irishman proved as good as his introductory pledge to give young players a chance by handing Sterling his full league debut in only the second game of the season against newly-crowned champions Manchester City. Within weeks, his pace and directness from the right flank was bringing tangible reward with the 17-year-old creating a late equaliser for Luis Suarez at Sunderland.

"He is an exceptional talent, we want to make sure he is around for many years," Rodgers said. "I am sure it is difficult for him to take it all in as you get a lot of adulation for playing well. Part of me is trying to keep him level-headed and make sure the whole situation does not distort his reality. We want to nurture him and make sure he is around for many years, not just a few months."

A first senior goal, the winner in a 1-0 Premier League victory over Reading at Anfield, followed a month later and by November he had become the fifth youngest England player of all time when making his debut for the national side against Sweden in Stockholm.

Liverpool recognised Sterling's progress by signing him to a new, five-year contract in December 2012 to put the seal on a real breakthrough year just after his 18th birthday. However, 2013 would prove to be far more challenging for him.

It began with his second Liverpool goal on 2 January in a 3-0 win over Sunderland but, not helped by a niggling thigh injury, he struggled for fitness and form and made only four more starts before the end of the season, only two of them being in the Premier League.

The Reds' flying start to the 2013/14 campaign meant Sterling struggled to force his way into the team and by the start of December he had only made two starts, one of which was in the League Cup against Notts County. His return to the side didn't bode well as the Reds dipped 3-1 at Hull City but he kept his place for the midweek visit of Norwich City to Anfield and got on the scoresheet in a Luis Suarez-inspired 5-1 victory.

He never looked back. He put the seal on the 5-0 win away to Tottenham Hotspur and was rapidly becoming a permanent fixture in the side, starting both key away games against Manchester City and Chelsea just after Christmas and having a clearly onside goal chalked off in the defeat at the Etihad which would prove crucial come the end of the season.

As Liverpool began their new year charge, it was becoming clear Sterling was a key part of the Reds' attacking armoury with his lightning pace now being married to greater maturity and better decision-making. The month after he scored twice in the astonishing 5-1 rout of then league leaders Arsenal at Anfield which saw Rodgers' side blaze into a four-goal lead in the first 20 minutes and really started to get Liverpudlians dreaming.

"Raheem is a clever footballer," Rodgers said. "For a young boy, tactically he's very good. That's what we are trying to do, develop footballers, and it gives me more options. I think he could even play on the side of a diamond.

"When he starts in the centre he offers us penetration with his speed.

"Raheem is intricate in tight spaces. We encourage players to play under pressure with players tight on them, and he can play with bodies around him. He's maturing very well. We've seen we have options with him because of his tactical intelligence."

What had started as a pipe-dream was rapidly becoming reality as Liverpool racked up win after win before Manchester City arrived at an emotionally-charged Anfield two days before the 25th anniversary of Hillsborough in mid-April. All involved knew a home win would leave the Reds in charge of their own title destiny.

Sterling's rapidly increasing importance to the side was underlined again when he scored an opening goal of astounding composure, timing his run onto Suarez's through pass and sidestepping goalkeeper Joe Hart before calming slotting in front of a baying Kop to help set up a monumental 3-2 victory which seemed to bring the title dream ever closer.

He followed that up with two more goals the following week in the 3-2 win at Norwich which brought Rodgers' side to the brink of glory, now requiring only a maximum of seven points from the final nine to seal the championship, before cruel fate intervened.

It would be ridiculous to suggest that Liverpool's incredible run from virtually nowhere had not had an awful lot to do with the attacking brilliance of Luis Suarez and Daniel Sturridge.

The pair gelled superbly for much of the time and helped inspire many of their team-mates to greater heights, scoring 55 goals between them in all competitions with all but three of them being in the Premier League. But the harsh reality is that those goals dried up just at the point in the season when Liverpool needed them most.

After scoring his 29th goal of the campaign in the 4-0 win at home to Tottenham on 30 March, which put the Reds top with seven games to go, Suarez managed only two more before the end of the campaign – one in the 3-2 win at Norwich on April 20 and the other in the infamous 3-3 draw at Crystal Palace on 5 May.

Sturridge, meanwhile, having bagged his 23rd of the campaign with a curling strike against Sunderland on 26 March, did not score again until the final game of the season against Newcastle United at Anfield by which time the title hopes were all but gone.

It's impossible to be too critical of two outstanding talents who brought Liverpool supporters so much enjoyment that season but, as that crucial month of April wore on, it was

Sterling who was proving himself to be as important to the team's chances of glory as anyone.

His remarkable progress was acknowledged with a nomination for the PFA Young Player of the Year award, ultimately won by Chelsea's Eden Hazard, and by the England national team at the 2014 World Cup.

Yet by the time he scored Liverpool's first goal of the new season in a 2-1 home win over Southampton, the club had taken no steps to reward his startling progress over the last year with the player still on the reported £35,000-a-week contract he had signed in late 2012.

After notching as well in a 3-0 win at Spurs, Sterling scored his third league goal of the season in only the fifth game of the campaign away at West Ham United, but it was not enough to prevent a 3-1 defeat, already the Reds' third Premier League loss, and it was becoming clear a season of struggle and toil may well be on the cards. By the time Liverpool did look to open contract talks it was too late.

The team was clearly in decline, had been eliminated from the Champions League before the knock-out stages and had a battle on its hands to secure qualification for the following year's competition.

Rodgers had repeatedly answered questions about Sterling's future by saying he was confident he would put pen to paper on a new deal but in early April the player himself confirmed he had turned down a new £100,000-a-week contract with Liverpool and wanted to wait to the end of the season before making a decision on his future, while insisting he was not a 'money-grabbing 20-year-old'.

"It's not about the money at all," he said. "It's never been about money. I talk about winning trophies throughout my career. That's all I talk about.

"I don't talk about how many cars I'm going to drive, how many houses I've got. I just purely want to be the best I can be. I don't want to be perceived as a money-grabbing 20-year-old. I just want to be seen as a kid who loves to play football and to do the best for the team."

Interestingly Sterling also claimed he would have signed a deal for less than the £100,000-a-week now on the table had it been offered the previous year when Liverpool were pushing for the title.

"If, at that point in time, I was offered a contract, I most definitely would have signed straight away, probably for far less money than being said now," he said.

"I just think the timing was a bit off. I try to kill off speculation about other teams, but I don't think the public can see it that way.

"I think they just see it as this 20-year-old boy being greedy. I just want to take the time to think about what I've achieved in my career so far, where I need to go and what I need to do to get better as a player."

After a slight upturn in form in the new year, Liverpool's results tailed off woefully in the final two months of the campaign.

Comments attributed to Sterling's agent emerged that were critical of the club's approach to the contract talks, with Aidy Ward quoted as saying: "I don't care about the PR of the club. He is definitely not signing. He's not signing for £700,000, £800,000 or £900,000 a week."

Sterling completed his £49m move to Manchester City in mid-July with his agent a few months later launching a scathing attack on Brendan Rodgers and branding the now-former Liverpool boss 'sly' for his role in the England international's acrimonious exit from Anfield.

"Raheem could have stayed, he should be at Liverpool," Ward said. "I think for me it was like he was being told to be a good boy and sign a contract.

"In December I spoke to Liverpool and said we'll sign a contract if there is a buy-out clause – those clauses are now common practice. They said no to that.

"Then there was an underhandedness, there were sly remarks. In press conferences, Brendan told everyone Raheem would sign. Why do that?

"I knew, Brendan knew and Liverpool knew there was an issue. Right now he probably should be a Liverpool player, but he's not and he's in a great place at City."

The whole miserable situation stuck in the craw with many Liverpool supporters for a long time with Sterling booed when returning with City for years afterwards.

In March 2020, with Liverpool finally closing in on the 19th league title they'd threatened to win with Sterling, he was asked about his former club.

"Would I ever go back to Liverpool? To be honest with you, I love Liverpool," he said.

"Don't get it twisted, they are always in my heart. It's a team that has done a lot for me growing up so…"

This all indicates the picture painted at the time of his Anfield departure of Sterling being a greedy young footballer looking for as much money as he could get was an overly-simplistic interpretation of what really happened.

JAVIER MASCHERANO

Refusing The Reds

First published: November 2021

LIVERPOOL supporters have always loved flair players who get them out of their seats with the drop of the shoulder and a shimmy of the hips.

But many among the Anfield faithful always enjoy a midfield hard-case, a nark in the middle of the park who will get stuck in, rattle a few cages and make it clear liberties will not be allowed to be taken.

Tommy Smith, Graeme Souness, Jimmy Case, Steve McMahon, Steven Gerrard and Dietmar Hamann all became firm favourites in part due to their physical presence and ability to protect the defence.

Fabinho's arrival during the summer of 2018 is rightly seen as one of the significant moments in Jurgen Klopp's Anfield reign, becoming the 'lighthouse' and linchpin in front of the defence providing the platform to enable the flair players in front of him to shine.

Not since Javier Mascherano had the Reds been able to boast a truly top-drawer performer in that area of the pitch and the Argentine was the backbone to one of the club's most promising yet ultimately unfulfilled eras.

'El Jefecito', or the 'Little Chief' as he was known, was seemingly always destined for greatness, his ability even as a youngster ensuring he was in the unusual position of making his full international debut at 19 in July 2003 before playing his first game for River Plate in Argentina's Clausura league.

After moving to Brazilian club Corinthians during the summer of 2005 in a complex deal involving third-party ownership, he soon suffered the setback of a stress fracture in his foot but recovered in time to play every minute of Argentina's run to the 2006 World Cup quarter-finals, where they lost to hosts Germany on penalties.

The 22-year-old's abilities were beginning to attract the attention of some of Europe's top clubs so there was considerable surprise at the end of that summer's transfer window when Mascherano – who had already expressed interest in joining Real Madrid or Barcelona – and fellow young Argentine Carlos Tevez joined West Ham United together for an 'undisclosed fee'.

It was to become one of the most contentious deals in Premier League history as it soon emerged that the sellers were not Corinthians, but in fact four different investment funds.

The first was Media Sports Investments (MSI), headed by so-called 'super agent' Kia Joorabchian, who had been involved with Mascherano since his move from River Plate to Corinthians.

Mascherano was also part-owned by Just Sports Incorporated while Tevez was also part-owned by two clubs, Global Soccer Agencies and Mystere Services Limited (all represented by Joorabchian) making up the quartet.

It was English football's first real experience of third-party ownership of players, a more commonplace practice in South America but one which was not allowed in the Premier League at that time (it was banned worldwide in 2015).

The lack of transparency surrounding the arrival of the young Argentine pair in east London – the length of the players' contracts as well as the transfer fees remained undisclosed – aroused suspicion almost immediately and there would eventually be serious consequences for the Hammers.

The following March, the Premier League charged them with breaching rules over third-party ownership and acting in good faith, issuing them with a world-record £5.5m fine. That May, Tevez scored a winning goal on the final day of the season away at newly-crowned champions Manchester United (who he would then sign for that summer) which preserved West Ham's Premier League status at the expense of Sheffield United and the Blades went on to take legal action, the two clubs eventually settling on a £20m out-of-court settlement.

By the time Tevez notched his final West Ham goal at Old Trafford, Mascherano was already on loan at Anfield and, while the machinations around the midfielder's move were not quite as seismic as Tevez's, his eventual transfer to Liverpool proved laborious to complete.

In mid-January 2007, Liverpool requested special clearance from FIFA to take Mascherano on loan in light of the rules stating no player can play for more than two clubs between 1 July and 30 June the following year – he had already played for both Corinthians and West Ham during this time – and that was granted on the final day of the month. Although Liverpool submitted his registration details before the midnight transfer deadline, the Premier League did not immediately announce whether it would allow him to play for the Reds, saying it wanted to 'take time to satisfy itself with the proposed arrangements'.

Liverpool added him to their Champions League squad on 10 February while handing him the number 20 shirt and ten days later the Premier League formally approved the loan deal, meaning Mascherano could make his debut in the 4-0 home win against Sheffield United which saw Robbie Fowler score his final two Reds goals.

The Argentine quickly established himself as a key component in Benitez's side and was the perfect replacement for Dietmar Hamann who had left the previous summer, the Liverpool boss labelling him a 'monster of a player' after the 4-1 win over Arsenal at the end of March and Xabi Alonso marvelling at his remarkable tactical maturity, saying, "He has a cool mind on the pitch. He is analysing and thinking about the game in each moment."

Mascherano's tenacity in the tackle, efficient use of the ball and ability to inspire those around him rapidly ensured he became one of the first names of the team sheet and in only his 11th game he was arguably Liverpool's best player in the Champions League final defeat to AC Milan in Athens.

Despite the disappointment in the Greek capital, it was clear Mascherano was one of those players Benitez was planning the evolution of his side around alongside the incoming Fernando Torres, Yossi Benayoun and Ryan Babel, but it was not until the following February – a full year after his initial arrival on loan – that Mascherano's permanent transfer to Anfield for £18.6m was completed.

By this stage, Tevez had long completed his apparently straightforward move to Manchester United despite the issues over his initial move to West Ham and the knock-on effects of his Premier-League-status-saving goal for the Irons.

In an impassioned exclusive interview with the Liverpool ECHO at the time, Benitez said: "I would like to ask the Premier League a number of questions. How can a player with a signed agreement be treated like this? He has a document which is clear, but the Premier League prefers to believe the word of someone else who made a mistake.

"Then I would like to ask the Premier League why is it that Liverpool always plays the most fixtures away from home in an early kick-off, following an international break? We had more than the top clubs last season and we have four already to prepare for this season.

"Then I want to ask the Premier League why it was so difficult for Liverpool to sign Javier Mascherano, when we had to wait a long time for the paperwork, but it was so easy for Carlos Tevez to join Manchester United?

"It's going to be very difficult for us to win the Premier League because the other teams are so strong, but I want our supporters to know that despite the disadvantages we have, we will fight all the way."

That same kind of siege mentality was evident in Mascherano a month after he became a permanent Liverpool player when he was sent off at Manchester United.

Infuriated at the heavy and unpunished treatment being dished out by Rio Ferdinand and Nemanja Vidic to Fernando Torres, the Argentine's agitation boiled over in his persistent questioning of referee Steve Bennett who, evidently conscious of the media narrative regarding backchat to officials in the wake of a high-profile case involving Chelsea's Ashley Cole only days before, made an example of the Liverpool man and gave him his marching orders.

In 2008/09 the Reds racked up their highest points tally of the Premier League era so far – 86 – only losing two league games all campaign and again reaching the Champions League quarter-finals.

But despite beating Manchester United home and away, a series of home draws before Christmas proved costly and the Reds finished second.

Jamie Carragher explained to The Athletic that the balance Mascherano gave to that side's midfield was fundamental to their success and would surely have led to silverware had personnel in that area of the pitch been kept together longer.

"It was a midfield trio, really, and that balance was just about perfect. It had everything that you'd want," Carragher said.

"Someone to break it up, someone with a great range of passing and then someone chipping in with a lot of goals and assists. Javier was as good as anyone around in that holding role.

"It's just a shame they didn't play together for longer. That midfield should have won trophies together. As a team, we'd have been more successful if those three had been kept together but Xabi left in 2009 and, 12 months after that, Javier was gone too."

Like many who held Liverpool's fortunes close at heart however, it was no doubt becoming clear to Mascherano as 2009 wore on that civil war was gradually ripping the club apart as a result of the catastrophic ownership of Tom Hicks and George Gillett – and by the summer of 2010 the writing was on the wall after a dismal season which had seen the Reds miss out on Champions League qualification and Benitez sacked.

Liverpool had reportedly turned down an approach from

Barcelona for Mascherano the previous summer, understandably not being prepared to countenance his departure at the same time as Alonso's, but 12 months on, Mascherano had made up his mind he was going.

Believing he had an agreement with the club that he would be allowed to depart for Barcelona if an acceptable offer was received, the Argentine reportedly rejected calls from new Liverpool manager Roy Hodgson and returned to Melwood for pre-season training after the World Cup in South Africa hoping his future would soon be resolved to his satisfaction.

Although Benitez, now in charge at Inter Milan, wanted to take him to the San Siro, the Italian club would not match Barcelona's £22m offer and the situation remained unresolved as the Premier League season began in mid-August.

Mascherano started Liverpool's opener at home to Arsenal and created the opening goal of the campaign for David Ngog, but with the clock ticking on his dream move to Catalonia and frustrated at what he perceived to be broken promises, his anger boiled over and he refused to play in the Reds' away match at Manchester City.

"Liverpool fans weren't happy with me at all and I completely understood why," Mascherano reflected years later.

"On the other hand, the board at the time had promised me something and weren't keeping their word.

"In the pre-season after Rafa left, Roy Hodgson arrived. We had a meeting with the managing director, Christian Purslow, who told me I could go if a good offer came in. Then there was an offer on the table, but Liverpool were looking the other way.

"I was quite angry that they weren't keeping their word. Refusing to play at City was the way I found to show my annoyance. They'd promised me something for a whole year and they never fulfilled their promise."

It proved to be an enormously successful move for the Argentine, who despite his diminutive stature reinvented himself as a centre-back, and he won five La Liga titles along with two Champions Leagues, two FIFA Club World Cups, two UEFA Super Cups and five Copa del Reys during eight seasons in Catalonia which saw him play close to 350 games.

And it was after the first of those Champions League triumphs, against Manchester United at Wembley in May 2011, that Mascherano demonstrated his enduring affection for the Reds despite the deeply unsatisfactory end to his time on Merseyside.

Giving a rare interview in English on the Wembley pitch after the Catalans' 3-1 win over United, Mascherano said, "To win the Champions League for any footballer is the top title. I know that Liverpool supporters after my exit were a little bit sad with me so this is for them as well."

In an interview with FourFourTwo magazine earlier this year, he revealed his gratitude to Liverpool supporters and said no other set of fans during his career had made him feel as at home as he did in L4.

"Yes, I'm a Liverpool supporter. I really mean it," he said.

"Nobody has ever treated me as well as Liverpool fans did – never. Throughout the three-and-a-half years there, they made me feel like I was one of them; like I was at home.

"That's why I dedicated Barca's 2011 Champions League final win against Manchester United to them: it was the least I could do to pay them back somehow. I knew they weren't happy, and I wanted to share the moment with them."

MARKUS
BABBEL

The Brilliant Bosman

First published: August 2022

TO the modern generation of football supporters, free signings of out-of-contract players are a long-established aspect of the transfer landscape.

For over a quarter of a century now, a key element of many clubs' recruitment strategies has involved identifying players coming to the end of their current deals – often a year or two in advance – who can be enticed with an attractive signing-on fee and salary package in lieu of a fee to the selling club.

Liverpool's first experience of the 'Bosman' system – named after the Belgian footballer Jean-Marc Bosman, whose landmark legal case at the European Court of Justice in 1995 concerning freedom of movement for workers meant clubs could no longer retain the registration of players they no longer held under contract – was not a positive one, losing one of their most talented homegrown stars, Steve McManaman, to Real Madrid for nothing in 1999.

Like many, the Reds have learned to use the system to their advantage over the years with James Milner and Joel Matip being two examples of when the system has paid off at Anfield.

For years Gary McAllister held the unofficial title as Liverpool's 'best ever free transfer', arriving at Anfield at the age of 35 to add nous and experience to Gerard Houllier's treble-winning team at the turn of the century.

Markus Babbel had already established a reputation long before he appeared on the Anfield radar as one of the most decorated players in German history, making his name as a cultured yet sturdy defender who could play at both right-back and centre-half. Having signed schoolboy forms shortly before his ninth birthday, Babbel made his senior breakthrough with his hometown club Bayern Munich and, after a two-year spell with Hamburg, returned to the Olimpiastadion in 1994 and became a firm fixture as 'FC Hollywood' won the UEFA Cup in 1996, the same year he was part of the German side which won the European Championship in England.

By 2000 he was ready for a new challenge and Houllier was happy to bring in a player of proven quality without having to part with a transfer fee.

"I'm very, very happy because you do not normally get players of his calibre on free transfers," Houllier admitted. "When we were made aware he wouldn't sign a new contract for Bayern Munich obviously we showed some interest, who wouldn't? He is a player of quality and vast experience and one we have been interested in for the best part of two years. We tried to get him last summer but Bayern simply refused to sell him. We have beaten off competition from Real Madrid and from a number of leading Italian clubs. I think he'll do well in the Premier-ship; he is a winner and he has a very good character, which is important. I swear we haven't broken the wage structure to bring him here. He hasn't become the top earner at the club. I wouldn't do that. It is too dangerous for team spirit. He has always been a Liverpool fan and he has always followed this club's glory years."

Babbel himself was ready for a new challenge after 16 years with Bayern and, having grown up watching and enjoying English football from afar, could not wait to get started with a club he had long admired.

"As a kid, I was always watching Liverpool on television in the great times of the '80s," he said. "So I was very honoured when I got an offer from them and I didn't have to think much about it, I just signed. I'd been in touch with Liverpool from 1998 onwards. It was always a dream for me to play in England. I never thought about Spain or Italy. It was mainly the tremen-dous atmosphere I wanted to experience. I had a taste of it in Euro 96, and the German players who have played in England always came back and told us amazing stories about the crowds and the buzz you get in the stadiums.

"When Liverpool came in for me I thought, 'Oh my God, what a club, what a tradition'. I had an offer from Real Madrid to sign for them. I was on the way to the airport in Munich at 6am to fly to Liverpool to sign the contract when I heard on the radio that I was flying to Madrid to sign for Real. I had a smile on my face!"

It was another important summer of recruitment at Anfield as, despite a dismal end to the previous season which had seen Liverpool fade badly in the final five matches and miss out on the first qualification for the Champions League, Houllier was backed in the transfer market. Nick Barmby crossed

Stanley Park to join from Everton for £6m, Babbel's German team-mate Christian Ziege arriving from Middlesbrough for £5.5m and World Cup winner Bernard Diomede was signed for £3m from Auxerre. The aforementioned eyebrow-raising free signing of 35-year-old midfielder Gary McAllister, along with another Bosman deal for back-up goalkeeper Pegguy Arphexad, completed the influx of new blood.

A goal on the opening day by club record £11m signing Emile Heskey – who had only arrived from Leicester City the previous March – secured a win against Bradford City but defeat at Arsenal in a madcap game which saw McAllister (on debut) and Dietmar Hamann among three red cards shown by referee Graham Poll was followed by a late collapse and draw at Southampton.

Such inconsistency would be the tale of the tape for much of the first half of the campaign with decent league form at Anfield compromised with less effective performances and results away from home while Houllier's men made steady progress in the UEFA and League Cups, the latter seeing Babbel notch his first goal in Liverpool colours during an 8-0 quarter-final win at Stoke City which he followed up against Charlton Athletic three days later with a first Premier League strike.

Babbel's ability to slot straight into the back four had been a welcome feature of Liverpool's patchy opening to the campaign and he would start 60 of the 63 matches the Reds played in all competitions during 2000/01. His reliability and know-how was increasingly appreciated by his team-mates, as was his willingness to get involved in the dressing room with Robbie Fowler being among those who immediately took to the German.

He said: "The first moment Markus came into the dressing room, you could see he was a good lad. He wanted to mix straight away, he wanted to be part of the dressing room, which is highly important."

"The only problem I had with Robbie was I couldn't understand him because he speaks a really hard Scouser English," Babbel laughed. "But he was always trying to help.

"The biggest problem in English football at that time was they were not 100 per cent professional. On the pitch, they gave everything. Outside the pitch, they loved a drink. But Houllier changed this. He released all the players who loved to drink, and brought in many young players along with experienced guys like me, Didi Hamann, Jari Litmanen and Sami Hyypia. It was a good mix. In the beginning, the foreigners were a little bit outside of the English guys. With time, they saw that I was performing – not just coming in and taking the money. Every game I tried to give 100 per cent. In the end, I had their respect."

As the midpoint of the season approached, Houllier's Liverpool were beginning to win respect and it was Babbel who ensured the iconic year of 2001 began on a winning note.

Steven Gerrard had underlined his own startling development – which would see him named PFA Young Player of the Year months later – with a spectacular 25-yard thunderbolt against Southampton to help ease the Anfield crowd's New Year's Day hangovers, but Trond Egil Soltvedt equalised soon afterwards. With time ticking away, Babbel had to leave the field for treatment after a kick on the ankle but, with Liverpool having already used all three substitutes, courageously re-emerged to support his team-mates and proved to be the match-winner, heading home from close range after Sami Hyypia flicked on Gary McAllister's corner with just four minutes left.

By the end of the following month, the German had his first

Liverpool winner's medal when Houllier's men eventually saw off second-tier Birmingham City on penalties in the first final held at Cardiff's Millennium Stadium. It may not have been the most convincing of triumphs but the German was in no doubt about the crucial role that day in the Welsh capital played in what the Reds would go on to achieve in the following months.

"This was a very difficult game," he acknowledged. "We were the favourites against a Championship team and there was so much pressure on us. You saw the game, it was a 50-50 game and we didn't dominate them, they were fighting for everything. The most important final that year we won was Birmingham City in the League Cup, because if we didn't win this final I'm not sure we could have won the FA Cup or UEFA Cup."

Just days before ending the club's six-year trophy drought, Liverpool had recorded their most impressive European result of the season by seeing off Fabio Capello's AS Roma – who would go on to become Serie A champions that season – to reach the quarter-finals of the UEFA Cup where a comfortable victory over FC Porto set up a semi-final showdown with Spanish giants Barcelona. By this stage the Reds had already secured their second showpiece occasion of the season after beating Wycombe Wanderers at Villa Park to reach the FA Cup final.

A handsome home victory over Manchester United – Liverpool's first league double over the Red Devils since 1979 – ahead of a creditable goalless draw in the first leg against Barcelona at the Camp Nou had put the Reds in pole position to grab the necessary third Premier League spot but fixtures were inevitably beginning to pile up due to their cup exploits.

The Easter Monday programme sent the Reds to Goodison Park to take on Walter Smith's relegation-threatened Everton in what turned out to be one of the most spectacular Merseyside derbies in history. Duncan Ferguson had cancelled out Emile Heskey's early opener before Babbel put Liverpool back in front just before the hour mark with his fifth goal of the season, finishing off a classic counter-attack led by Hamann and Fowler by crashing the ball home from the edge of the penalty area. Although the Blues would equalise seven minutes from the end after Robbie Fowler had missed the chance to extend the lead from the penalty spot and Igor Biscan had been sent off, Gary McAllister's astonishing 44-yard free-kick four minutes into stoppage time breathed new life and belief into tired Liverpool legs and minds. Houllier's men rode the crest of the wave three nights later to beat Barcelona at Anfield and reach the club's first European final since 1985.

The new-found momentum continued with wins over Tottenham, Coventry, Bradford and Newcastle before a frustrating home draw with Chelsea in the penultimate Premier League fixture but Houllier's men knew their Champions League destiny was in their own hands if they could win on the final day of the season at Charlton. Before then though, history beckoned with two more finals and the chance of a never-before-achieved hat-trick of cup triumphs.

The Reds returned to south Wales to take on an Arsenal. Arsene Wenger's Gunners took an early stranglehold on proceedings in Cardiff's sun-kissed Millennium Stadium to such an extent that the only surprise when Freddie Ljungberg finally put them in front after 73 minutes was that it had taken so long. Liverpool's exertions during the 60 previous matches seemed to have taken their toll and only desperate defending prevented Arsenal finding the killer second goal before a sensational turnaround in the final seven minutes.

Babbel's stamina, determination and big-game temperament played a vital role in the equaliser, the German showing great upper body strength to hold off Gunners skipper Tony Adams as the ball dropped from McAllister's half-cleared free-kick to nod down for Michael Owen to swivel and volley Liverpool back on terms before the England striker – who would later that year be awarded the hallowed Ballon d'Or trophy as Europe's Footballer of the Year – scored a stunning solo winner two minutes from time to complete an unforgettable fightback.

There was precious little time for celebration as four days later the UEFA Cup final loomed with Spanish minnows CD Alavez standing in the way of Liverpool and a third cup success of the season. With the game being staged at Dortmund's Westfalenstadion, Babbel returned to his homeland with his team-mates and helped Houllier's men make the perfect start by nodding home the opener from a McAllister free-kick after only four minutes. When Steven Gerrard doubled the advantage soon afterwards, it seemed the Reds may spare their loyal followers any more unnecessary stress after the previous two nerve-jangling finals in Cardiff but they should have known better after the rollercoaster ride of the previous nine months and the Basques hit back to level at 3-3 early in the second half and then force extra-time after substitute Robbie Fowler had put Houllier's men back in front. Penalties seemed inevitable until Delfi Geli's 117th-minute 'Golden' own goal secured a remarkable 5-4 victory, an unprecedented cup treble and a place in Anfield folklore for the German and his relentless if exhausted team-mates.

"It was so special for me with my family and friends there in a stadium like Dortmund," he recalled. "The atmosphere was fantastic, even the fans from Alaves made a fantastic noise but they had no chance against our supporters. Sometimes it's not always about having the best players; the most important thing is to have the best team. It was one of the best finals ever. I feel proud to have been part of it."

There still remained one more hurdle to overcome with the final set of Premier League fixtures still to be played at the weekend and Liverpool knowing their one-point lead over Leeds United meant only a win at Charlton would guarantee a top-three finish and the Champions League qualification that had been the main objective when the season had begun. Their gruelling efforts seemed to have taken their toll in the first 45 minutes at The Valley with only a series of saves from goal-keeper Sander Westerveld preventing the hosts from going in front but it was a different story after the break, with Babbel again playing an important offensive role in addition to his defensive duties, flicking on McAllister's corner which was clawed out by Addicks' keeper Sasa Ilic only as far as Fowler whose clever improvised overhead kick broke the deadlock. Further goals from Danny Murphy, Fowler again and Owen secured the 4-0 victory which proved the icing on the cake of one of Anfield's most memorable and unlikely seasons.

"That drive home from London to Liverpool after beating Charlton was something special," recalls Babbel. "Finally, we could celebrate properly. The celebrations in the city were unbelievable, I'll never forget it. In this moment, I realised how big the club is. Liverpool is a big club, but on that Sunday when we were travelling on the bus, I saw how big the club is. I was so happy I could have that experience. It was one of the best times in my career. I never had this feeling before. I won titles with Bayern Munch and the German national team, but this was a different level for me. I'd never had this experience before: nearly one million people on the street, celebrating with you."

Having contributed six goals in 60 starts during his first

season of English football, Babbel was unquestionably one of the success stories of Liverpool's incredible campaign, his exploits on and off the pitch winning the admiration of the man increasingly garnering the majority of the headlines, Michael Owen, who said: "His command of English has come on in leaps and bounds since he joined us. He's quite a nifty mover off the field as well. At our victory party after the Worthington Cup final against Birmingham, he was the first on the dance floor and the last to leave it."

Babbel was in no doubt, however, who was the primary architect of bringing joy back to Anfield after the best part of a decade in decline.

"Gerard Houllier was very important for Liverpool," he said. "Many English players loved to go out partying and drinking. I always said he was like a lovely little Napoleon. Gerard was strict and focused on discipline. We had a good side, 13 or 14 players. We could beat anyone on our day but you needed better players from 14 to 20 in order to win a league. We didn't have that depth."

The respect and admiration was very much mutual at this stage with Houllier saying after Babbel's first season at the club: "Markus Babbel's contribution needs to be highlighted. He had a difficult time at first as all foreign players do, but that only lasted for two or three games and since then he's been very steady. The players all love him here. He has proved a tremendous asset and he is a tremendous winner."

It was hoped the strength in depth Babbel referred to would be added to the squad and enable them to take that next step and challenge for the league title Liverpudlians had already spent over a decade craving. But, before the following campaign had truly begun in earnest, the German – who was still only 28-years-old – began suffering symptoms of the mystery illness which would leave him in a wheelchair for months and ultimately hamper the rest of his playing career.

"After the Charity Shield against Manchester United I'd felt unusually tired but I thought it was something to do with the roof being closed and the air not being too good in the Millennium Stadium," he recalled. "But after the Super Cup against Bayern Munich in Monaco I felt dead. I looked at myself in the mirror and saw I was white like a wall. I knew the doctor from Bayern Munich was very good, so I went to see him, 'Ja, you look s***'. I went to Germany for some tests, and that's when it started. I had the Epstein-Barr virus. A few months later, things got worse. The virus led to Guillain-Barré syndrome. This is something that affects the nervous system and can attack muscles all over your body.

"I was paralysed from the knees down, numb in my hands and had no sensation down one side of my face, but I was lucky. There were people hooked up to respirators, helpless and unable to do anything for themselves. It never occurred to me to ask, 'F****** hell, why is this happening to me?' I still had hope. Being a professional footballer taught me how to fight in training and out on the pitch. Nobody could tell me how long it would take to get better though. If you have a broken leg, you know it's six months, plus or minus one or two. But the problem with this is that it changes. I was a different person to the next one – he was lying there for two years. I was only sitting in a wheelchair for five weeks. It was a very tough period, though. In this moment, you'd give everything away – all your money, all your success – just to come back healthy."

With Houllier also suffering serious health problems that same autumn and needing an 11-hour heart operation, it would be the following spring before Babbel was able to tentatively return to training and the next season before he was anywhere near strong enough to be considered for selection but he admitted the experience had changed him as a person.

"I wasn't the same person as before. I saw how quickly life can change, so I started to enjoy life. If you want to enjoy life and also want to be a professional footballer, this is not the best combination. I was going out a lot. Drinking a lot. Smoking a lot. I wasn't professional. Also, at this time I got divorced from my first wife, so I had many private problems as well. If you want to come back at the highest level, you need discipline. But, for one or two years, I couldn't show this because I was living. I was really living. It took probably two-and-a-half years for me to get back to being a bit more normal, but for me it was clear – if I want to come back to 100 per cent professional, then I had to leave the country. Because, as a single man, England is a paradise city. If you go out, it's very easy to do stupid things."

Although he came off the bench in the 2002 Charity Shield against Arsenal in Cardiff to make his first Liverpool appearance in almost a year, it was November before Houllier entrusted him with a start against Southampton in the League Cup and, while four consecutive starts followed later that month, the German was a shadow of his former self and an appearance in a League Cup quarter-final at Aston Villa the following month would be the 73rd and last of his senior Liverpool career.

Confined to the reserves, Babbel's frustration boiled over with two red cards for the Reds' second string. Houllier, who in truth had never been the same since his illness either, told the German to find another club.

"He is no longer in my plans," said Houllier. "When you have talent there is no question you are capable of doing well for your club, but the motivation has to be there too. The attitude has to be right, but in this case it has not been right. I think the club has been very fair to Markus. We stood by him when he was ill and handed him a new contract. I am very disappointed with him."

The German departed on loan to Blackburn Rovers, where he played 25 matches, ahead of a return to Germany and three years with VfB Stuttgart, helping them win the Bundesliga in his final campaign, even if he admitted he never felt back to 100 per cent and never fully regained feeling in his toes. He stayed with Stuttgart after retiring as a player, initially becoming assistant manager and then head coach, leading them into the Champions League in 2009. Further spells in charge of German clubs Hertha Berlin and Hoffenheim followed before he moved to FC Luzern in Switzerland and Western Sydney Wanderers in Australia.

Like with Houllier, it is impossible not to wonder how those early years of the 21st century would have panned out at Anfield had illness not intervened. He bore no grudges with his former manager though and paid an emotional tribute following the Frenchman's death in December 2021: "He built something big in Liverpool. Without him, Liverpool would not be the club it is today if Gerard hadn't pushed it back then.

"If I could have had a few more years of football in my legs at such a beautiful club as Liverpool it would have been easier for me to accept. My first season at Anfield was amazing. It was just such a shame I got ill soon after. I was lucky to come back but I couldn't perform to the same level as before. I had some problems with the manager because my lifestyle wasn't right. It wasn't his fault, it was my fault."

STEVE FINNAN

Searching For Steve

First published: July 2022

IT is inevitable that a club with a long and glittering record of success like Liverpool will have almost as many unsung heroes to treasure as sparkling superstars.

Those understated characters who quietly went about their business with the minimum of fuss and provided the platform for their more-heralded colleagues to grab the headlines, glory and adulation.

Each era has thrown up footballers whose work and consistency went largely unnoticed by many and was often only truly appreciated by their fellow team-mates who were able to see at first hand just what they brought to the side.

From the club's leading appearance holder Ian Callaghan, whose tally of 857 matches in a red shirt is unlikely to ever be beaten, to the likes of Ronnie Whelan, Sami Hyypia and Dirk Kuyt, unlikely candidates time and again have stepped up and written their names into Anfield folklore.

There is one such example, however, who inadvertently rose to the kind of prominence that no-one could ever have expected given his steady and unspectacular performances and persona.

Steve Finnan arrived on Merseyside in the same low-key fashion which marked his rise from non-league to international level and caused one of the most talismanic figures of Liverpool's recent history to fear for his future before playing a key, if unfortunate, role in one of the club's most iconic victories and ended his career with a unique record.

Such a feat would have been all the sweeter for the Republic of Ireland international because of the struggles he, like so many younger players, faced trying to get his first break in the professional game.

Although born in Limerick, by the time of his teenage years, Steve Finnan's family were living in the south of England and he suffered rejections from both Wimbledon and Crystal Palace after trials with both south London clubs.

He was playing for non-league Welling United before he finally got his big break at the age of 18 when signing for Birmingham City in 1995.

A loan spell and permanent move to Notts County followed where he made 80 league appearances over two seasons before catching the eye of Kevin Keegan.

The former Liverpool and England legend, bolstered by the funds of Harrods owner Mohamed Al-Fayed, had returned to management with Fulham after his memorable spell with Newcastle United in the mid-90s and identified the young full-back as someone who could aid his mission to take the third-tier Londoners back into the top flight for the first time since 1968.

It proved a good move for all parties with Finnan helping his new side win promotion to the First Division the following May and, even though Keegan left his post that summer to take charge of the England national side, Finnan and Fulham's progress continued with the Cottagers winning promotion to the Premier League as champions in May 2001, with Finnan figuring in all but one of that season's league fixtures.

He was already an established international for the Republic of Ireland by this stage after graduating from the under-21s to win his first senior cap against Greece in April 2000 while still playing for Fulham, and having provided the cross from which Jason McAteer scored the winner against Holland to take Mick McCarthy's men to the 2002 World Cup finals in Japan and South Korea.

Jean Tigana's departure meant life at Fulham became more difficult with the London side narrowly avoiding relegation the following season but Finnan's dogged defending, crossing ability and overall consistency meant his name was increasingly being linked to the country's top clubs and Gerard Houllier made his move in the summer of 2003, paying £3.5m to bring the 27-year-old to Anfield.

"All I wanted to be was a footballer," said Finnan. "So having to go for trials at non-league clubs and then coming all the way through the divisions and eventually coming to Liverpool and making international appearances was a different career. But it meant I did well and I wouldn't have had it any other way.

"As much as I was really enjoying my time at Fulham, Liverpool is such a big club and it was an opportunity that I could never turn down.

"They were professional in everything. I could see they really wanted me and I just felt it was the right move. I couldn't wait for it to happen."

The summer of 2003 when Finnan arrived was an uneasy one at Anfield. Twelve months earlier, Liverpool stood on the cusp of making a serious assault on the league title trophy.

Despite a decent start to the domestic campaign – and a League Cup win in Cardiff – the wheels came off following a late defeat at Middlesbrough which sparked an abject run of 11 league matches without a win from which the season never recovered.

As Liverpool aimed to recover lost ground on the top clubs, Finnan was joined by £5m Harry Kewell and young French pair Anthony Le Tallec and Florent Sinama-Pongolle as the new recruits.

Jamie Carragher realised the arrival of another international defender meant he was again facing a battle to stay in the side. Addressing the issue in typically forthright fashion at the time, he said: "There's no point in sulking about it. There's not a lot you can do, except impress the manager in training and in games. Or find out Finnan's address and send the boys round!"

Carragher got the nod at right-back for the opening game of the new season against Chelsea at Anfield with Finnan left on the bench and the Irishman would have to wait for the third game of the campaign against Tottenham for his first start, with Carragher reverting to left-back before suffering a broken leg at Blackburn a fortnight later. It gave Finnan the chance to cement his place in the side which he was initially able to do. Champions League qualification was achieved, but disappointing cup exits meant the writing was on the wall for Houllier long before his mutually agreed departure in May.

Both Finnan and Carragher may have wondered whether they too were on borrowed time when the Frenchman's

replacement, Spanish coach Rafa Benitez, made a right-back –
his compatriot Josemi – one of his first buys in the summer of
2004. Speaking years later about whether a signing had ever left
him feeling like Liverpool wanted him out, Carragher admitted
it was a regular occurrence for pretty much the first half of his
16-year career with the Reds.

"It happened to me most seasons," he said, "and it was
not until I got the age of 25 or 26 that it stopped happening.
Initially, John Arne Riise came in after I played left-back for a
season where we won three trophies. A couple of seasons later,
it was Steve Finnan. I was playing right-back then. It was funny
that Rafa Benitez came into the club [in 2004] and his first
signing was a right-back [Josemi]. It was almost this constant
fight of trying to prove myself better than x,y or z who came
in. It should be like that at a top club but it just felt like I had
it a little bit more."

In the opening match of the 2004/05 season away to
Tottenham the new manager started with Josemi at right-
back, Carragher alongside Sami Hyypia at centre-back in the
position he would go on to make his own over and Finnan
installed on the right side of midfield with Benitez seeking
to utilise the Irishman's crossing ability in conjunction with
his defensive nous to shore up the flank on that side. It paid
immediate dividends at White Hart Lane with Finnan's cross
being flicked on by Carragher to enable Djibril Cisse to score
Liverpool's first goal of what would be an unforgettable season.

With Josemi's inadequacies gradually revealing themselves
in a topsy-turvy campaign, by the turn of the year Finnan was
playing regularly in his accustomed right-back slot and he
began to develop a formidable understanding with Carragher
at the back.

Years later, Finnan even joked his move to Anfield actually

benefited Carragher in the long run, saying: "When I came to Liverpool he was playing in a number of different positions. But most of the time I was there, he was playing centre-back and he would probably say that was his most favoured position and enjoyed it there most. So I probably helped him."

The pairing indisputably helped Benitez navigate his way through a tumultuous first year on Merseyside where inconsistent Premier League form was offset by startling progress in that season's Champions League which saw the Reds reach their first European Cup final in 20 years.

Ahead of the showdown against AC Milan in Istanbul, Finnan reflected on the journey which had taken him from non-league to the biggest game in club football and what it meant to him.

"When I went to Welling I had to think about the possibility of getting another job outside of football. If that hadn't worked out then I would probably have joined the family building firm, working as a brickie or something like that. It is a big leap to be playing in the Champions League final – the biggest game of my career – but after what I've been through to get here, it holds no fears for me."

Finnan would later joke he "changed the game" in Istanbul and his involvement in the chaotic half-time scene in Liverpool's dressing room at the Ataturk Olympic Stadium remains one of the more surreal stories of that jaw-dropping night on the Europe-Asia border.

With the Reds staring down the barrel of global humiliation after the Italians raced into a three-goal lead after the first 45 minutes, Benitez initially told left-back Djimi Traore he was being replaced by Dietmar Hamann, only for the Irishman to reveal he was struggling with a thigh strain. Having already been forced to use one of his substitutes early due to Harry

Kewell's injury, Benitez had to revise his plans and substituted the reluctant but accepting Finnan.

"I wanted to stay on and it was disappointing, but I felt a bit of an injury in the first half and it was the right decision because I wouldn't have lasted long," Finnan later admitted after Liverpool's sensational three-goal fightback and eventual penalty shoot-out triumph. "I was actually inside the dressing room when I heard the sound of the first goal. You could tell the difference between the fans, so you knew it was us who scored. The comeback wasn't something you'd expect with the way the first half went, but it was surreal. That's why I moved to Liverpool."

Finnan's dependability had become increasingly valued by Benitez and even though the likes of Jan Kromkamp and Alvaro Arbeloa were brought in over the coming seasons to potentially play in his position, the Irishman's record of 99 Premier League appearances between August 2004 and May 2007 under a manager notorious for regularly rotating his teams spoke volumes for the esteem he was held in by the manager.

"Finnan is a player who will always play at a consistent level," Benitez said in January 2006 shortly after his side began an FA Cup run that would again see silverware lifted after another dramatic cup final fightback and penalty shoot-out success. "He will be seven, eight, nine or even ten out of ten every week."

"That's what people saw in me, I think, my consistency," Finnan himself later admitted. "I think I preferred it that way, rather than score three or four goals a season and be a little up and down form-wise."

Finnan's consistent excellence helped Liverpool keep a club record 22 Premier League clean sheets in 2005/06 and the Irishman was unperturbed by the arrival of Arbeloa midway through the following campaign, playing 47 times in 2006/07 and again winning a starting place in the Champions League final against AC Milan, this time in Athens.

"I guess I was a bit fortunate getting to two finals in my first three seasons in the Champions League," he later admitted. "And that's why I have to give Benitez credit for what he could get out of a team. He was suited to that type of football and knockout competition. I guess I was one of the fortunate ones. He did like to change the side around a bit. But overall he gave me a lot of game time. Working under him was enjoyable because the team had success. That was the main thing. Sometimes it was hard. He was a totally different manager to ones that I'd had in the past."

Finnan's involvement did tail off during his fourth and final season at Anfield with his overall appearance tally of 35 just beating the 31 of his tough first season and in the summer of 2008 he was sold to Espanyol in Spain.

"It was a strange ending at Liverpool," he recalled. "It was pre-season at the time and I wasn't really playing in those games, and you're not sure whether the manager is going to want you for that season. It was just a shame. The manager mentioned to me, very late in pre-season, that I could move. We're talking a couple of days before the transfer window closes, so it didn't give me much time. With Albert Riera coming in from Espanyol, I was put into that deal. It didn't go too well there. In hindsight I probably shouldn't have jumped at a move with a day or two to think about it."

Finnan returned to England a year later with Portsmouth and, although unable to prevent the administration-stricken club avoid relegation from the Premier League, he did help them reach the FA Cup final where they lost narrowly to dou-ble-winners Chelsea. It proved to be the final match of his professional career and after retirement he went into the property business with his brother, disappearing off the radar to such an extent than when a reunion was planned in 2015 to mark a decade since the Miracle of Istanbul, organisers were unable to find him and a #FindSteveFinnan hashtag trended on Twitter until the Liverpool ECHO tracked him down!

"I can confirm that I'm safe and well," he said. "Someone forwarded the ECHO article on to me yesterday. I thought it was funny as I normally think I'm pretty easy to get hold of. I think one of the reasons why people think I've disappeared is because I'm not involved in football any more. I loved training and playing, and I was privileged to play for a great club like Liverpool and win some big trophies, but I never wanted to stay in football once I had retired. Being a coach or a pundit never interested me. When you don't stay involved, people forget about you. They go from seeing you most weeks to never seeing you.

"I've never been one to crave attention and I like my life the way it is now. I'm also not on social media. I don't feel the need to tell someone what I've just had for my breakfast. Unfortunately I'll be away for the Istanbul reunion which is a shame. If I'd known a few months ago I'd have been there as I would have loved to meet up with all my team-mates and see the fans again. I hope they all have an amazing night. Being part of what happened in Istanbul was the greatest achievement of my career."

It was a career which had more to it than just that hallowed night in Turkey with comments from one of his predecessors in both Liverpool and Republic of Ireland colours Ronnie Whelan illustrating why Finnan was held in such esteem by his team-mates.

"His consistency has been first class and you can't ask for

anything more. He proved to be a very shrewd signing. His attacking play came on in leaps and bounds and it is no surprise that he got himself so many assists. On top of that, he defends really well. He knows when to pass, when to stay on his feet. In many ways, he's like Phil Neal. He is always steady and gives you 100 per cent every game. He's the type of player every successful side needs."

STEVEN GERRARD

The Transfer That Never Was

First published: July 2021

FOR as long as there is a Liverpool Football Club, tales will be told about the exploits of Steven George Gerrard.

The greatest player in the club's history? It's a timeless and endless debate that will probably never reach a truly definitive consensus.

What is without doubt to surely anyone privileged enough to watch him in a Red shirt over a stellar professional career at Anfield which spanned close on 17 years is that during that period the boy who grew up on a council estate in Huyton was a force of nature who carried the club during its darkest moments and inspired some of its most meteoric highs.

Gerard Houllier's treble, the miracle of Istanbul, the 'Gerrard' FA Cup final… the times when his strength of personality allied to innate football skill and physical prowess provided the blood, bone and sinew to the Reds' performances are too many to mention.

But as much as his performances on the football field elevate him to the very top echelon of the LFC universe, it is the fact he spent virtually the entirety of his playing career with his boyhood club – during a relatively undistinguished era, by Liverpool's standards anyway – that provides a strong basis on which his legend and legacy is founded on.

Despite a wealth of suitors from Europe's top clubs throughout his career, Gerrard stayed at Anfield throughout his peak years until semi-retiring to the United States and still managed to accumulate a haul of medals that would be the envy of most players.

That loyalty to the city of his birth and the club of his heart ensures tales of his passion and dedication to the Liverpool cause will be passed down from generation to generation.

But it could have been a very different story had events taken a different course when the unthinkable seemed to be on the verge of happening, with Gerrard publicly declaring his desire to leave Anfield just weeks after leading the Reds to an astonishing fifth European Cup triumph against all the odds in Istanbul.

By the summer of 2005, the 25-year-old Scouser had already established himself as Liverpool captain, a key cog in the international set-up for England and one of the most gifted central midfield players on the planet.

Having been noticed by Liverpool's scouts at the age of eight when playing for Whiston Juniors, he joined the club's academy the following year and, despite some initial concerns over his lack of height (he was the same size as Michael Owen at 15) and then injury problems caused by a growth spurt, made his first-team Reds debut at 18 coming off the bench against Blackburn Rovers at Anfield in 1998.

The following campaign he scored the first of 186 goals for the club, a memorable strike against Sheffield Wednesday at Anfield, and international recognition followed with a place in England's Euro 2000 squad – and his second full season saw him recognised by his peers as the PFA Young Footballer of the Year as the Reds won a brilliant cup treble.

It should have been the staging post for a serious assault on a 19th league championship but the manager's life-threatening heart problem in October 2001 ultimately plateaued the upward momentum.

By May 2004 there were few dissenting voices when Gerard Houllier bid au revoir to Anfield as Gerrard – who had been appointed Liverpool club captain at the age of 23 the previous October – headed off to Portugal with the England squad for that summer's European Championships.

Although the club had moved quickly to replace Houllier with highly-rated Spaniard Rafa Benitez, the Reds had finished a whopping 30 points behind champions Arsenal.

Chelsea, a year on from their takeover by Russian billionaire Roman Abramovich, had signalled their intent by capturing Portuguese coach Jose Mourinho from FC Porto within days of him matching Bob Paisley's feat of winning the UEFA Cup and European Cup in successive seasons and, having spent £110m on players the previous summer, it was clear the Londoners would go big again as they sought to financially bludgeon their way into the big time.

Benitez took a trip out to Portugal to meet with his new captain and some of his other new charges whose future was also up in the air – star striker Michael Owen only had one year left on his deal and would leave Anfield before the new Premier

League season – but his initial meeting with Gerrard, or to be more accurate Gerrard's mum, did little to ease the skipper's worries.

He revealed later on in his autobiography that Benitez happened to be on the same flight to Lisbon as his predecessor, Gerard Houllier, and Gerrard's mother, Julie Ann, with the Frenchman graciously introducing the pair to each other.

"Rafa shook her hand, said hello, and then immediately asked her a very blunt question: 'Does Steven like money?'" recalled Gerrard.

"Apart from a standard 'Hello, good to meet you' introduction, those were the first words Rafa said to my mum.

"My relationship with Mum is so close that I heard all about it even before my new Liverpool manager had climbed into a taxi to meet me."

It was an early insight into the checkered personal relationship Gerrard and Benitez would have, although the player would later admit that tactically the Spaniard was the best manager he worked under.

Mourinho had already got his new captain to try and persuade Gerrard to move south, with John Terry years later admitting he tested the water during the tournament to see if the fiercely-proud Scouser would be interested in moving to Stamford Bridge.

"Stevie was one of the best players in the world at the time and doing everything possible at Liverpool," his England team-mate said.

"Mourinho expressed his interest to the England players (at Chelsea) and asked if we could have a quiet word with Stevie, which we did. Stevie literally said from day one he didn't want to go but in the end, he kind of got turned."

Chelsea would have a £20m bid turned down later that

summer and Gerrard gave a press conference at the start of pre-season to confirm he would be staying at Anfield for now but admitted he had not been happy with the club's progress and had considered moving on for the first time in his career.

A seed had been sown and his comments later that year ahead of Liverpool's crucial final Champions League group match against Olympiacos showed he was still very much considering his future.

"If things aren't looking good, I'll have to see what happens in the summer," he said on the eve of the Greeks' visit to Anfield in a tie Liverpool had to win to reach the knockout stages, with Benitez's side already 15 points behind runaway Premier League leaders Chelsea in seventh place.

"I'm 25 at the end of the season and I've got six or seven years left in me at the top level to win things, so hopefully the turnaround can happen quite sharpish.

"I'm in a difficult situation because I'm a fan myself. I want to win things at this football club but I haven't got time on my side. I can't really wait three or four years for the club to be turned around and to be made into a title-winning side."

The fates would have it that Gerrard himself scored one of his most iconic Liverpool goals in the final minutes against Olympiacos to send the Reds through to the last 16 and a date with destiny with AC Milan in the Istanbul final.

Liverpool had finished the league season even further behind the champions – inevitably Chelsea – with the margin this time 37 points but in the Turkish capital Gerrard led the miraculous fightback from three goals down at half-time.

Having guided home the precise header which gave the Reds a glimmer of hope at 3-1, a typically-surging run into the box won the spot-kick which astonishingly led to the equaliser a handful of minutes later and he showed his vast talent and versatility by playing in three different positions over the course of the 120 minutes before Liverpool triumphed in the penalty shoot-out.

His own dreams and that of millions of Reds supporters around the world came true as he became only the second Scouser to lift the European Cup for Liverpool and in the ecstatic and emotional aftermath of victory Gerrard said the words all Reds wanted to hear.

"How can I think of leaving Liverpool after a night like this?"

He added: "I am really happy with the club. I will be having talks with the chairman and the manager shortly, but it is looking good."

All parties jetted off on holiday to enjoy the aftermath of victory and a well-earned rest in the full expectation that the skipper's signature on a new contract would be a formality but as the June weeks ticked by, the transfer rumour mill sparked up again.

Chelsea again – along with Real Madrid – were linked but on 16 June Liverpool chief executive Rick Parry said securing the captain on a new deal was still the top priority.

Benitez a few days later also made it clear Gerrard was central to his plans, saying: "We are preparing a special weightlifting plan for Gerrard's shoulders because we want him to lift a lot of trophies for us in the next few years.

"I am not in favour of selling him. We're building a great team around him as we want him to be the skipper who wins the most titles in our history."

Gerrard's own comments were more circumspect, however, the skipper hinting he was ready to talk but saying, "The ball is in Liverpool's court now. We haven't spoken about a new contract yet and I don't know how long those talks will go on for."

With holders Liverpool having to start Champions League qualifiers in mid-July, Gerrard and the rest of the squad returned to pre-season training only 33 days after Istanbul on 27 June with the situation still unresolved.

Two days later, Gerrard's agent Struan Marshall – who had been unavailable previously due to being on honeymoon – began talks with Rick Parry but the first signs of trouble became evident on 1 July when Spanish paper AS ran a story claiming Gerrard had told Benitez an offer from Real Madrid was "extremely tempting".

There were suggestions from the player's camp that conversation never happened but after a weekend of speculation Marshall revealed on 4 July that contract talks with Liverpool had broken down and were "unlikely to be re-opened".

Benitez held a press conference the same day to announce the signing of Netherlands international Bolo Zenden and insisted he wanted his captain to stay "forever", while Parry – reported to have held a meeting with Gerrard and Liverpool chairman David Moores where a club record contract offer of £100,000 a week had been tabled – declared himself "completely surprised", adding, "When we met on Wednesday, things were fine."

The following morning Parry declared Liverpool would turn down a £32m bid they had received from Chelsea but later that same day the bombshell happened – Gerrard told Liverpool, the club he had supported all his life and led to European glory just weeks before, that he now wanted to leave Anfield.

Releasing a statement, Gerrard said: "This has been the hardest decision I have ever had to make.

"I fully intended to sign a new contract after the Champions League final, but the events of the past five to six weeks have changed all that.

"I have too much respect for the club and people at it to get involved in a slagging match."

With reports suggesting Gerrard would not be allowed to leave until he had submitted a formal transfer request, the club also released a statement which said: "Steven has told us he will not accept our offer of an improved and extended contract because he wants to leave."

Rick Parry spoke about the situation publicly, saying: "The club has to be bigger than any individual. It's the ups and downs of football. Now we have to move on. We have done our best, but he has made it clear he wants to go and I think it looks pretty final."

The news sent shockwaves through the football world, nowhere more so than among the Liverpool fanbase where a couple of attention-seekers outside Anfield burned Gerrard shirts for the benefit of television cameras.

Virtually every Reds supporter was stunned and not a little distraught as they tried to figure out how such a situation had come to pass so soon after the jubilation of Istanbul.

They weren't the only ones in turmoil, however. The reality of leaving the team Gerrard had previously envisaged representing for his entire career was already beginning to hit home, with the Liverpool club doctor reportedly paying him a home visit to help ease an anxiety attack.

Once that eased, he was involved in lengthy discussions with his close family and friends to talk through what had occurred and what might happen next.

Dietmar Hamann and Igor Biscan had both swiftly been given new deals after Istanbul but in Gerrard's eyes the club had appeared in no hurry to sit down with their best and most valuable player, his unease being further added to by the changing football landscape.

Yes, Liverpool had somehow managed to overcome Abramovich's Chelsea en route to winning the Champions League but the club was still under the stewardship of David Moores who, while undoubtedly wealthy, was not in the same financial stratosphere as the London club's still relatively new owner.

The pull of working with the innovative and charismatic Mourinho was also a big draw given the already slightly uneasy working relationship he had with Benitez at Anfield.

"I was thinking, 'I'd love to play for Jose Mourinho'," he later admitted in his autobiography.

"I was certain that, under Jose, I would win all the trophies I craved.

"Jose Mourinho, rather than Chelsea, turned my head. He could have got more out of me as a player. And I know he would have brought me success.

"The decision boiled down to a simple choice: Do I want to win trophies with Chelsea – or do I stay loyal to Liverpool?"

And it was a heart-to-heart chat with his father and brother which underlined to Gerrard once and for all that, having already got his hands on some of the game's biggest prizes with the club he'd loved all his life, however many more he secured elsewhere would not be worth as much to him as those won with Liverpool.

"Dad was calm and, before he said much, he had me talk through my own feelings," Gerrard said in his book.

"I told Dad and Paul (his brother) that I didn't think the club had shown me the love I needed. I didn't feel that they had acted as quickly as they should have done.

"Chelsea were serious about me and the Mourinho factor dominated much of my thinking. Mourinho had turned my head. I wanted to play football for him. But as soon as I made everything sound so clear, I got lost – and I started talking

about Liverpool all over again. I spoke so much more about
Liverpool than Chelsea.

"I was so close to leaving but that hour with my dad and
Paul changed everything... 'What's best for you? What do
you want? Can you handle the Kop turning against you? Can
you accept the fact that you'll never play for Liverpool again?'.
These were the kind of questions that we picked apart inside
the four walls of my dad's front room.

"We all knew I would make millions more if I went to Chelsea
but the money was irrelevant. Would it mean more to me to
win two or three trophies with Liverpool than double or even
triple that number with Chelsea? I was far from convinced
about Chelsea. I was thinking only of Liverpool."

The most emotional day of Steven Gerrard's life – as he
himself labelled it in his autobiography – concluded around
11pm with him calling his agent and telling him to inform the
club he had changed his mind and wanted to stay at Anfield
after all, requesting an escape clause be removed from his new
deal as a further show of commitment.

Shortly after 8am the following morning, this second
bombshell emerged from Anfield to stun a football world now
entranced by this developing soap opera.

A relieved Rick Parry revealed the news of Gerrard's shock
U-turn, saying: "Stevie's decided to stay. It's a little bit like last
year, only even more dramatic.

"I think in the last 24 hours he has reflected on it, he's thought
it through and he wants to stay.

"There were lots of late-night phone calls and early morning
phone calls. I couldn't be more delighted. It is what we wanted
all along.

"I've apologised to Stevie if I have misread his emotions.
I guess after winning the Champions League in Istanbul I

thought I knew where we were going but he clearly thought for whatever reason that the club wasn't as enthusiastic about keeping him as we might have been.

"We've had some emotional moments together, cleared everything up and I don't think this will happen again."

One of the most tumultuous weeks in Liverpool's modern history ended happily on the Friday with Gerrard putting pen to paper on a new five-year contract with fellow Scouse heartbeat of the side, Jamie Carragher, agreeing a two-year extension to his deal on the same day.

"I just couldn't leave the club I love," Gerrard admitted at the time.

"After considering everything, I just couldn't go through with it. I never said I wanted to leave, but I felt I was being backed into a corner and had to push things on. I know it was going to look as though I wanted to go, but at one stage I thought I had no choice.

"When I thought about it more, I just wanted to stay. I admitted I've made mistakes and the club has acknowledged they've made some mistakes as well. But now we've sorted it out and I'm doing what I wanted to do all along, which is stay at Liverpool.

"I have learnt a hell of a lot from the past few days and more than anything, I have learnt that winning things here would mean more to me than winning them anywhere else."

Rafa Benitez was also delighted at the turn of events, the comments from a man Gerrard would later describe as being quite frosty to him on occasions illustrating the depth of his relief.

Benitez gushed: "I renew my deal with Liverpool in four or five years and when I do I would like Stevie to be my next coach, assistant manager and maybe even the next manager after me. He can even have the chief scout position if he wants it."

The value of keeping hold of their star midfielder was proven again to manager and club when the following season ended with another superhuman Gerrard cup final performance, this time against West Ham in Cardiff, an assist and two stunning goals, as well as a nerveless penalty in the ensuing shoot-out, bringing the FA Cup back to Anfield.

That was to prove the penultimate trophy win of Gerrard's career, even though he would play for Liverpool for another nine years.

Despite striking up a tremendous understanding with Spanish striker Fernando Torres and later on another world-class forward in Luis Suarez, the wrecking-ball ownership of Tom Hicks and George Gillett – who took over a little over 18 months after Gerrard's dramatic summer 2005 turnaround – proved fatal to Benitez's hopes of building on the two trophies won during his first two seasons in charge.

A solitary League Cup win in 2012 under Kenny Dalglish as the club began to stabilise under the new ownership of Fenway Sports Group proved to be the final trophy Gerrard lifted for Liverpool.

There can be little doubt that had he made a different decision back in 2005, he would have ended his playing career with far more medals.

But he would never have been loved and revered in Liverpool the way he is and will continue to be for the rest of his life, with the comments of his old nemesis and long-term admirer Jose Mourinho providing a fitting last word.

"He is a historical player for Liverpool, a historical player for the Premier League, and an opponent I have always admired and respected," Mourinho confessed.

"One of my favourite enemies. We did everything to try to sign him (with Chelsea) and it was almost there.

"But to me, personally, he never said he would come. Never. He was always a Red and I think the decision was right."

JOHN ALDRIDGE

Triumphy, Tragedy And A Brutal Exit

First published: January 2023

FOR a club as successful as Liverpool, goalscorers inevitably feature highly when the best-loved players to have pulled on the famous red shirt are considered.

Billy Liddell, Roger Hunt, Ian St John, Kevin Keegan, John Toshack, Kenny Dalglish, Ian Rush, Robbie Fowler, Michael Owen, Luis Suarez, Mohamed Salah... the names trip off the tongue and their achievements speak for themselves.

Yet in terms of pure goalscoring, few of the above can match the feats of one sharp-shooter who plied his trade at Anfield for a regrettably brief period but played a key role in one of Liverpool's greatest ever teams and finished his long career having scored more goals in post-war English league football than anyone else.

What's more, he did it having (eventually) graduated from Anfield's Boys Pen to the Kop and then to the hallowed turf of the pitch ensuring every strike meant that little bit more – not just to him but to many of the supporters watching.

John Aldridge's unerring ability to find the back of the net was perhaps written in the stars given his mother was told by a fortune teller when he was a baby that he would be gifted with his feet and, growing up as a Liverpool-mad youngster in Garston, he was soon following in the footsteps of his boyhood idol 'Sir' Roger Hunt by scoring prolifically in schools football.

"From an early age I knew I was a goalscorer but I wasn't sure how far that would take me in the game," he admitted in his book 'Alright Aldo - Sound as a Pound'.

"All top strikers say goalscoring comes naturally and for me it was the same. I was just able to find space in the box and had the knack of putting the ball in the net. It was never something I really had to think about, I was just born with it."

By the time he was 14, Aldridge's exploits had caught the eye of Garston gasman and part-time Liverpool scout John Bennison and, after being invited for trials, he found himself training with the club twice a week only to be left devastated when boot room sage Tom Saunders told him they were letting him go.

He got a second crack at the YTS contract every Liverpool-mad youngster on Merseyside dreamed of a year later when his dad pestered the club into taking another look at him and, after displaying his goalscoring talent over a six-week period, had reason for optimism when being told by Saunders after scoring for the 'B' team, "Great goal John. We'll definitely be giving you a ring."

The call from Liverpool never came though – at least not for another 14 years – but Aldridge's heartbreak at being snubbed by the club he loved couldn't thwart his passion for his team and he threw himself into following the Reds home and away as a fan.

"It was exciting times," he recalled to the Liverpool ECHO. "I was lucky in that at the top of the road the Woodcutters pub used to take a bus straight to Anfield and I didn't have to mess around with two buses to get there so I was really fortunate in being able to use that to get to all the home games and I travelled to the aways as well. Back then Liverpool and Everton were right up there with the best teams in the country and it was brilliant, having banter with your mates about who was top dog."

While following the Reds, Aldridge was still banging in the goals in local amateur football for Blue Union, Garston Woodcutters, Cheshire Lines and then one of Merseyside's best-known non-league sides, South Liverpool, before finally getting his big break into the professional game at the age of 20 in May 1979 when Fourth Division Newport County paid £3,500 for him.

He flourished in south Wales, scoring 87 goals in 198 games at Somerton Park, helping Newport win promotion to the Third Division as well as the Welsh Cup in his first season and then in his second embarking on a remarkable run to the European Cup Winners Cup quarter-finals.

In March 1984, Third Division promotion-chasers Oxford United moved for Aldridge in a £78,000 deal and, after immediately helping the U's achieve their initial objective of second tier football, in his first full campaign at the Manor Ground he broke the club's goalscoring record and became the first Second Division player in nearly two decades to score 30 league goals (bagging 34 in all competitions as Jim Smith's team knocked out Manchester United and gave Everton an almighty scare while reaching the League Cup quarter-finals), his new side winning back-to-back promotions and going up to the top flight for the first time in their history.

Within a month of his First Division debut Aldridge had his first goal against his beloved Liverpool, giving Oxford the lead in the Reds' first league visit to the Manor Ground and forcing Alan Kennedy into conceding a late own goal as the newly-promoted side gained a creditable 2-2 draw.

Under the ownership of infamous newspaper magnate Robert Maxwell, the mid-80s would be the greatest period in Oxford's history and they won the club's first major honour by going all the way to Wembley in the League Cup where they trounced Queens Park Rangers 3-0 in the 1986 final.

By 1987 Liverpool were in the process of figuring out how to replace star striker Ian Rush, whose £3.2m transfer to Italian giants Juventus had been announced the previous summer with the Welshman being loaned back to the Reds for one more season, and Aldridge's relentless goal-getting in a struggling side – he had bagged another 15 goals in 25 games by the turn of the year – along with his credentials as a die-hard Liverpudlian was making him impossible to ignore.

"It was obvious that Ian Rush was on his way to Serie A and would need to be replaced," said Aldridge. "Being the man to do that job naturally appealed, even if I never dared to think it would actually happen, it was a bit of a pipe dream. I was scoring goals and happy at Oxford which wasn't a big club but it was a great club. Thankfully Liverpool were the side who wanted to buy me.

"I had an agent called Eric Hall at the time and I was so anxious for the deal to go through, I told him he couldn't come and do the negotiations for me because Robert Maxwell had said the Daily Mirror, which he owned as well as Oxford, would be getting the exclusive story and he didn't want anyone to discover what was happening. So I just went up to Anfield on my own and when they put the contract in front of me I just signed, there was no haggling, it wasn't about money, it was about my dream."

The deal was done in January 1987 and Aldridge was finally able to realise his dream.

"Joan (his wife) had arranged a party in the Hunts Cross Snooker Club," Aldridge explained. "Touchingly, she had gone to great lengths to make sure all my family and friends were there to celebrate my move to Liverpool. The problem was we all ended up drunk and the night turned sour. I don't know how it started or how it finished, but somewhere in between I allowed my frustration to show by punching a window. If only I'd known there was a brick wall on the other side of the glass! Liverpool don't like new players turning up with broken hands, so I reckoned suffering the pain was preferable to telling Kenny Dalglish the truth.

"My first day at Anfield went well. I gave the obligatory interviews, posed for the cameras, and nervously sipped water from a bottle. Then Ron Yeats shows up – Big Ron Yeats, the captain of the Liverpool team when we won the FA Cup for the first time in 1965.

"'Hello John, how are you?' he said, grabbing my right hand and shaking it with enthusiasm. The pain shot through my body. On another day, a normal day, I might have fainted. But I had to keep up the facade so I grinned weakly at Big Ron, exchanging polite words with him. Screaming in agony could wait a little longer."

Aldridge's first Liverpool appearance would come a few weeks later at Aston Villa as a half-time substitute in a 2-2 draw and Dalglish gave him his full debut when Southampton came to Anfield the following weekend for a First Division fixture.

The Saints had ironically been the opposition for Aldridge's first game at Anfield as an eight-year-old fan alongside his dad in the Main Stand paddock just over 20 years previously in January 1967 and it would be a dream debut for the Scouser who scored the only goal of the game on the hour mark, planting a header past England goalkeeper Peter Shilton.

"I didn't want the moment to end," he admitted afterwards. "The roar from the crowd as the ball went in the net was immense. It was a magical moment and as good as all those thousands of times I'd imagined it."

Aldridge would not make another starting appearance until the final game of the season away to Chelsea – where he inevitably scored in a 3-3 draw – by which time Liverpool had lost their championship crown to Everton.

Although he always knew he had been brought in ultimately as Ian Rush's replacement, the lack of game time in those early months did cause Aldridge some concerns and he went in to see Kenny Dalglish about it.

"He just said to me 'Look John, you're going to have to be patient because we play through the middle at the moment with the likes of me and Jan Molby feeding Rushie. When you go up front next season we're getting wide people, lads who will get the ball into the box and play to your strengths so just trust me'."

The Liverpool manager was as good as his word, bringing in Watford winger John Barnes for £900,000 and paying a British record £1.9m for Newcastle forward Peter Beardsley during the summer, with Aldridge's good friend and former Oxford team-mate Ray Houghton arriving a few months later.

"We played Bayern Munich in a pre-season friendly," Aldridge recalled, "We'd only been back in training for about a week and it was the first game but I could just tell the link-up between Barnes, Beardsley and myself was going to be special, we just clicked right away."

A collapsed sewer inside the Kop meant Anfield would have to wait until mid-September for its first glimpse of this exciting new Liverpool side with the Reds' first three games all having to be played away from home but the new boys gelled with the old guard right from the off.

It was Aldridge who would open Liverpool's account for the campaign when he nodded home a Barnes cross nine minutes into a tricky-looking opening-day fixture away to Arsenal and he would remarkably score in each of the Reds' first nine league fixtures.

The last of those consecutive fixtures Aldridge scored in was against early-season pace-setters Queens Park Rangers in mid-October and saw Dalglish's men hit four goals for the fourth league match running to go top of the First Division, the position they would occupy when the season ended.

"We produced brilliant, breathtaking football," Aldridge admitted. "The goals were flying in and nobody could cope with us. It was what I'd hoped for as a kid. It was nearly perfect."

The plaudits kept flooding in, a 2-0 home win in mid-January over Arsenal which featured a typically predatory Aldridge strike at the end of a classic team goal, causing French legend Michel Platini to proclaim: "I never thought I'd see an English team playing like this. It was a continental performance. Liverpool played their football on the ground."

Platini was asked to rate Liverpool's current standing in European terms but replied it was difficult to answer until they had met some of the leading continental sides, an impossibility at the time given the ban on English clubs which had been in place since the 1985 Heysel disaster.

"I'm a realist, we couldn't do anything about it and could only watch from afar as AC Milan – who were a great side – dominated in that period, but I think we would have more than given them a game," Aldridge said.

With the league title virtually a foregone conclusion as the season moved into its final months, history beckoned as a 1-1 draw at Derby towards the end of March equalled Leeds United's record of 29 games unbeaten at the start of a season but, with Aldridge missing through injury, a 1-0 defeat at Goodison Park scotched the Reds' hopes of an 'invincible' campaign. A second defeat at Nottingham Forest followed in early April but the return league fixture at Anfield a few weeks later produced the stand-out performance of this most magnificent of campaigns.

Brian Clough's side had been arguably Liverpool's closest challengers for much of the season but were blown away 5-0, Aldridge scoring twice to take his season's tally to 26 as the Reds moved to within two points of sealing the title and England legend Tom Finney said afterwards: "That was the finest exhibition I've seen the whole time I've played and watched the game. The skills and the speed the game was played at was absolutely tremendous. You couldn't see it bettered anywhere, not even in Brazil. The moves they put together were fantastic."

Liverpool's 17th championship was duly confirmed with four games to spare ten days later following victory over Tottenham at Anfield and attention turned to the Reds' chances of achieving a second league and FA Cup double in three years where unfancied Wimbledon lay in wait in the final.

Aldridge had booked the Reds' passage to Wembley with both goals in the semi-final win over Forest at Hillsborough, the second of them winning the BBC's Goal of the Season competition (which was made up entirely of Liverpool efforts).

To the consternation of the tens of thousands of expectant Reds who travelled to the capital for the Wembley final, the so-called 'Crazy Gang' of Wimbledon caused one of the biggest upsets in FA Cup history, winning 1-0 through a Lawrie Sanchez header.

The fluency which had defined Liverpool's play for the previous nine months suddenly deserted them with Wimbledon's long-ball game and robust approach proving even more difficult to play against once they had something to hang on to, although the Reds were handed a chance to equalise on the hour mark when Aldridge went down under a challenge from Clive Goodyear and referee Hill generously pointed to the spot. The Scouse forward had converted all 11 penalties he had taken that season in his Golden Boot-winning tally of 29 in all competitions, but on this occasion Dave Beasant guessed correctly and parried the ball to safety, making him the first goalkeeper to save a penalty in the FA Cup final.

"I felt terrible and really took it to heart," he admitted. "Kenny said to me, 'Your two goals in the semi-final got us here so don't put it all on yourself' which was good of him but I did. I'm a big Liverpool fan and I just felt I'd let everyone down.

"People don't remember that I scored nearly 500 goals but what they do always recall without fail is the fact I missed that spot-kick against Wimbledon. Even decades later, somebody still mentions it to me almost every week."

A welcome distraction presented itself in the form of a trip to West Germany to take part in that summer's European Championships. Although proudly Liverpool born-and-bred, Aldridge's grandmother from Athlone qualified him to play for the Republic of Ireland and he had made his international debut two years before while still playing for Oxford.

Aldridge returned to Liverpool with some of his Wembley wounds eased only to find a little over a week before the start of his second full season at Anfield, another hurdle to overcome: the return of Ian Rush, At 29 – three years Rush's senior – he was under no illusions of the task at hand if he was going to hang on to the red shirt he'd had to graft through years in the lower leagues to get his hands on.

The question of whether they could play together would become an eternal debate, although the two strikers themselves were never in doubt and their record together when paired up front saw at least one of them score in all but a handful of games. Reflecting years later, Aldridge admitted there were mixed emotions at the time.

"I was gutted when I first heard he was coming back. I'd won the Golden Boot the year before with 29 goals and couldn't see why we needed another striker. Maybe Kenny didn't want him going to a different English club instead. The fans obviously wanted him back because he was a great player and rightly adored by everyone.

"I did think it was strange as Kenny had told me not long after I'd signed we'd be playing out wide once Rushie went and I'd come in but Ian was a friend of mine, so I welcomed him back. I just thought I'll lay down the gauntlet by scoring as many goals as I can and by helping the team win and that's what I tried to do."

Ever the realist, Aldridge knew goals were what mattered most and reacted in the only way he knew how, scoring twice as the Reds exacted a small modicum of revenge by recovering from a goal down to beat Wimbledon 2-1 in the Charity Shield at Wembley, and then bagging a hat-trick on the opening day of the season as Dalglish's side began their defence of the title with a 3-0 win at Charlton.

The Welsh striker would have to wait until his tenth appearance in mid-October away to Walsall in the League Cup to notch the first goal of his second Liverpool spell and would endure an illness and injury-hit first campaign back at Anfield.

Rush's travails mirrored that of Dalglish's side, certainly in the first half of the season, as with goalkeeper Bruce Grobbelaar laid low for four months with meningitis and skipper Alan Hansen missing until mid-April with a serious knee injury, Liverpool struggled to match their swaggering form of the year before.

Despite insecurities over his place in the side, Aldridge would ultimately score more goals and play more games – 31 in 47 appearances (42 of them from the start) – than the previous campaign.

That didn't seem the case in the first half of the season as his form suffered, along with his team's, and after being an unused substitute in December's games against Norwich and Derby, he found himself again on the bench when Liverpool travelled to Hillsborough on 14 January to take on relegation-threatened Sheffield Wednesday. Goals from Mark Proctor and Imre Varadi put the Reds two behind after only quarter of an hour but the Garston-born striker was thrown on for Steve McMahon early in the second half and, after Steve Nicol pulled a goal back with 15 minutes left, the substitute bulleted home a header two minutes later to grab a point and end his seven-game scoring drought.

It proved to be a big turning point in the season as a fantastic run of 11 wins and two draws propelled Liverpool right back into the title race, with Aldridge regaining his place in the side and his scoring touch with ten goals in just 13 games. A ninth successive win at Millwall on 11 April put the Reds top of the First Division for the first time all season, level on points with the Gunners but boasting a superior goal difference, with six matches each left to play.

"Kenny had chopped and changed a fair bit in the first half of the season and I think maybe one of the reasons was three of us – me, Rushie and Peter – fighting for two spots, so there was no continuity like there had been the season before when we hardly changed the side. I think that cost us and we lost our way a little bit but we got our belief back and just went on this run and it was brilliant."

From the gloom of mid-winter, Liverpool's season was now blooming into life with long-term injury absentees Hansen and Rush on the brink of returning to action and the possibility of another league and FA Cup double again on the cards. Victories over Carlisle United, Millwall, Hull City and Brentford had set up a repeat of the previous year's semi-final with Nottingham Forest at Hillsborough and thousands of Liverpudlians travelled over the Pennines to Sheffield on a beautiful spring morning full of excitement and belief that their team were on an unstoppable march to glory again. Alas, Saturday, 15 April 1989 would be a day that changed the lives of countless people, as well as the city of Liverpool and the game of football, forever.

After serious concerns raised after the draw by Liverpool over the arrangements following the previous year's encounter were ignored by the Football Association, catastrophic crowd mis-management before the kick-off by the South Yorkshire Police led to a lethal crush inside the caged pens of the Leppings Lane terrace. An inadequate emergency response that included dozens of ambulances being left outside and prevented from trying to save lives by police fixated with non-existent hooliganism, 97 innocent men, women and children were unlawfully killed in Europe's worst ever sporting disaster.

The city of Liverpool was plunged into grief with boyhood Kopite Aldridge deeply affected and for a time considering whether he would ever be able to play football again.

"If I hadn't become a footballer it is almost certain I would have been in the middle of the Leppings Lane terrace," he wrote in his autobiography.

"In the days when I was a fan I would never have considered missing an FA Cup semi-final involving Liverpool so I have to assume I would have travelled with everyone else to Sheffield. Fate decreed I was not on the Leppings Lane terrace but on the Hillsborough playing field instead, initially oblivious to what was going on. I was the Liverpool player furthest away from that end when the first fans came on to the pitch and I assumed it was some kind of pitch invasion. At six minutes past three, the players were ushered off the field and into the dressing rooms and on our way there we had the first inkling that, far from crowd trouble being the reason for the delay, there had in fact been a tragedy. I overheard people talking of serious injuries to Liverpool fans and, worse still, deaths. Deaths? At a football match? I could not comprehend it.

"In the dressing room, Kenny Dalglish told us to keep warm as the match was bound to restart. But he was walking around nervously, refusing to sit down. Most of us were seated, though some were standing, doing stretches and simple exercises. Some were reading the programme. I don't remember what I was doing but I do remember seeing fans walking past the dressing room door with tears in their eyes. The referee, Ray Lewis, came into our dressing room at around half-past three and told us to be ready to go back on as the match, he said, would restart as soon as possible.

"It was only when we heard screaming outside the dressing room that we finally understood something wasn't right. Kenny went out into a corridor and I heard a fan shouting at him, 'People are dying, Kenny' or words to that effect, and at four o'clock, Ray came back to say the match had been abandoned. The confirmation that Liverpool fans had died reached us while we were getting changed. I looked over to John Barnes and could see tears in his eyes. He was sitting there quietly, not wanting to be disturbed. A few of the other players looked stunned. I couldn't talk. Nobody could.

"I knew of people, fun-loving Liverpool supporters, who had tickets for the Leppings Lane terrace. My friends. Naturally, I had to find out whether or not they were safe. But how? My dad was in the stand above, he was in bits and later told me what he had seen, like a tide going out and leaving rubble behind. Kenny was determined to keep us all together in the dressing room, out of the way. When we were all dressed, the Liverpool manager told us to go quietly to the players' lounge upstairs. Minute by minute we could feel the situation getting worse. Even before we got into the lounge we could see the girls working there were sobbing. They obviously knew more than us. At the other side of the lounge there was a television screen showing live pictures. The reporter spoke of deaths, the figure rising minute by minute. It was only when I got home that night that it all began to sink in. I was watching television with Joan and, inevitably, it was the main story on the news. That was when we broke down, bursting into tears and hugging each other. We cried for most of the night and slept little.

"Kenny telephoned me the following morning. He said he wanted me to join the rest of the players at Anfield for a meeting. In the immediate aftermath of Hillsborough, Kenny showed tremendous leadership qualities a lot of people didn't think he possessed. He told us to be dignified and insisted we set an example. In the afternoon, I took my daughter, Joanne, to Anfield to lay some red roses by the Shankly Gates. There were already a lot of scarves tied to the railing and there was an overwhelming scent of flowers in the air. I didn't want to be seen but a group of reporters had spotted me. That spoiled what should have been a private moment. I was, after all, a Liverpool fan. I wanted the same anonymity as any other person.

"We had a special mass at the Catholic cathedral that night. Again, the enormity of what had happened hit me hard. We were beginning to see how it was affecting the city. People were breaking down, not really knowing what to do. All the players were at the cathedral that night to hear Bruce Grobbelaar read the lesson. Each player dealt with the tragedy in his own way. My first tangible response was to pull out of the Republic of Ireland's World Cup qualifying match against Spain in Dublin on 26 April. Playing football was the last thing I wanted to do, I had no motivation. I remember giving an interview to the ECHO in which I said I didn't care if I never played again. I meant every word. For the two weeks following the disaster I was in a state of shock, helpless to do anything. I feel no shame in admitting Hillsborough affected me mentally for a long time. I couldn't cope, it weakened me physically, emotionally and mentally.

"The thought of training never entered my head. I remember trying to go jogging but I couldn't run. There was a time when I wondered if I would ever muster the strength to play. I seriously considered retirement. I was learning about what was relevant in life. I didn't really see the point in football. Reading about the parents who lost sons or daughters at Hillsborough made me think of my own children. My son, Paul, was only seven at the time. I was only a little older when I went to my first football match in the 1960s. Paul and Joanne have never been less than the most important things in my life, yet after

Hillsborough they became more precious, if that was possible. We all became closer as a family.

"The Liverpool players spent much of their time talking to people affected by the tragedy. It meant going into hospitals to see the injured. In some cases, it meant trying to talk people out of comas. I was asked to try and do that for a young lad called Lee Nicol from Bootle. Lee was 14 but looked about ten and reminded me of my son, Paul; he looked a lovely kid. Lee was in the middle of the crush but still alive when he was pulled out. As he lay there in a coma, I whispered words into his ears. I asked the doctor about his chances of recovery. 'He's clinically dead, John', he replied. I hadn't realised how badly Lee was injured and that news ripped into me. My heart went out to Lee's family, decent people who didn't deserve to be victims of such a tragedy. He passed away on the Tuesday, shortly after being visited by Princess Diana and became the 95th person to die after the disaster.

"All the players went to as many funerals as we could. I had only ever been to one before Hillsborough when my grandmother died but I went to 11 in total. They were all so difficult to handle but one in particular killed me. In those days you had to drive yourself, I didn't know what day it was by that stage to be fair and my head was all over the place but I got there, paid my respects and was sitting in the church behind the family when the coffin came in, followed by a smaller one. I didn't know that it was a father and son, Thomas Howard and his 14-year-old lad Tommy junior. I hadn't been told and that broke me, just snapped me in two.

"I think people sometimes forget about how Hillsborough affected the players. Ray Houghton said the experience of visiting so many hospitals and attending so many funerals made him more upset than he'd ever been before. Alan

Hansen, the Liverpool captain, was said to be visibly shaking at times. Bruce Grobbelaar had, like myself, considered retirement. Steve McMahon claimed the Hillsborough tragedy was a watershed in his life and made him grow up almost overnight. Players openly wept in front of each other, which was incredible. There had never been such a display of emotion among the Liverpool players before. Usually we spent most of our time taking the mick out of each other, but Hillsborough pulled down the facade and showed us up for what we were: vulnerable human beings. What it was all doing to Kenny Dalglish would become apparent when he resigned as Liverpool manager in 1991, but at the time he did a remarkable job and was dignified throughout, working tirelessly to help however he could. I think he realised, for perhaps the first time, how much Liverpool Football Club meant to the ordinary person in the street. This, of course, carried with it certain responsibilities but Kenny was up to the challenge. He proved himself to be a good listener to those who had something to get off their chests.

"I was at rock bottom but my wife Joan was brilliant, she got me going and my dad helped as well along with even the bereaved families. I was getting lovely messages from them saying 'so-and-so wouldn't want you not to play, John' which helped focus me again, as did going to Celtic for a friendly game they arranged just over a fortnight later which was the first time we played as a team after the disaster.

"I've always been a Celtic fan since the Lisbon Lions so that day at Celtic Park was extraordinary, the way they opened their arms out to us that day. I'll never ever forget what they did, not just for the club and the fans but for the players that day, we were treated absolutely unbelievably. I came off the bench and we won 4-0 which was irrelevant but I scored two and that got me back into it. It wouldn't surprise me if Celtic allowed me to score those goals they were that good to us. I'd always liked Celtic and followed them from afar but since that day they've got a very special place in my heart."

After discussions with the families of those whose lives were lost and the football authorities, Liverpool returned to competitive action, fittingly with a Merseyside derby at Goodison Park against Everton who had stood shoulder-to-shoulder with their Merseyside neighbours in the aftermath of the disaster, having booked their place in the FA Cup final with victory over Norwich City at Villa Park in the other semi-final that fateful day only two-and-a-half weeks earlier.

"I was really p***ed off because I thought Kenny was going to leave me on the bench for the replayed FA Cup semi-final the following weekend. So I went and took out my frustrations in the dressing room. I lost the plot completely and started trashing the place. I think it was a combination of frustration and my grief coming out after all that had gone on. I'd been to so many funerals I think it took its toll."

To his relief, Aldridge kept his place in the team for the replayed semi-final at Old Trafford (and all of Liverpool's remaining games that season) and scored twice in Liverpool's 3-1 win. It set up the second all-Merseyside FA Cup final in four years and, given the emotion-filled circumstances, were the most important goals of Aldridge's career.

"Building up to the replayed semi-final, I have to say my stomach and my insides were in knots. The thought of us not winning that game was horrible. The pressure on us to win and reach the final against Everton was enormous because the thought of us not being there was unthinkable.

"We had to win it for the fans who died and the bereaved families and we were all very aware of that. It was more important than the final in many ways. They were without doubt the most important goals I ever scored."

Before the Wembley showpiece, however, Liverpool's attention had to turn back to the title race they had lost ground in after dropping two points to Everton on their return to league action. The Football Association's insistence that all outstanding fixtures be played before England's Rous Cup fixture with Scotland at Hampden Park on 27 May meant the Reds would be forced to play eight matches in 23 days, with the final one being Arsenal's postponed trip to Anfield which was due to have been played the weekend after Hillsborough. Three days after winning the replayed semi-final, the Reds faced their first match back at Anfield after the disaster with Nottingham Forest the opponents again and it took a nerveless 81st-minute Aldridge penalty to secure the three points.

The following weekend the Reds' hopes of staying in the race were hanging by a thread at Plough Lane when they trailed old foes Wimbledon at half-time following an Alan Hansen own goal but an Aldridge equaliser and John Barnes winner secured another victory which became even more valuable when Dalglish's men returned to the dressing room to learn a Dean Saunders double had given Derby County a shock 2-1 win over Arsenal at Highbury. It meant Liverpool's title destiny was now firmly in their own hands moving them only two points behind the Gunners having played a game less.

The two title contenders were in action the following midweek, Liverpool with a comfortable 2-0 win over Queens Park Rangers - Aldridge scoring again to make it five goals in his last four games – before the following night Arsenal were held 2-2 at home by Wimbledon.

Merseyside then decamped to London for the day as Liverpool and Everton met at Wembley for an FA Cup final very much played in tribute to those who had been killed, bereaved and injured in Sheffield five weeks earlier. Gerry Marsden led an emotional 'You'll Never Walk Alone' tribute on the pitch before kick-off and, when the action got underway, the two sides played out a classic with Aldridge gaining almost immediate redemption for his penalty heartache of 12 months previous.

Only four minutes had been played when Steve Nicol, who had just been voted Football Writers' Player of the Year, found McMahon's run which had split the Toffees' defence and the midfielder's square pass found Aldridge 12 yards out who, from virtually the same spot as where his last kick of the previous year's final had been saved by Dave Beasant, caressed a magnificent strike with his first touch of the match into the top corner of the net with Neville Southall rooted.

"To score that goal was lovely and meant the world to me," Aldridge later said. "I have to say I did feel really sorry for Everton Football Club that day because they wanted to win the cup, and the way they and the whole city had pulled together after what happened was magnificent. It was a shame we had to beat Everton but it was lovely that it was a Merseyside occasion and the Blues played their part in a great game."

In boiling May heat, Aldridge made way for Rush and the Welsh marksman repeated his brace from the 1986 final against the Blues as the Reds won 3-2 after extra-time.

The two sides embarked on an open-top bus tour the following day to thank the people of Merseyside for their support but Liverpool's celebrations had to be restrained with two more matches still to play in their quest to achieve the double.

First up was West Ham at Anfield, the Hammers needing to win their final game of the season to escape relegation and Aldridge continued his scoring run by putting Liverpool ahead after 20 minutes as the Reds went on to win 5-1. With Liverpool now three points clear, the Gunners – who had not managed a victory at Anfield since 1975 – would have to win by two goals to equal the Reds' goal difference, which would mean they would take the title by virtue of goals scored.

In front of a packed Anfield and global television audience of millions, Liverpool's marathon campaign concluded with a dramatic climax. Arsenal emerged from the tunnel with all 11 players carrying bouquets of flowers in memory of those lost at Hillsborough before the game inevitably settled into a tense affair.

The atmosphere changed seven minutes into the second half when full-back Nigel Winterburn's inswinging free-kick was glanced into the net by Alan Smith. The referee's watch was ticking into a second minute of stoppage time when in Arsenal's final attack Lee Dixon's punt forward found Smith who controlled instantly and hooked forward to the on-rushing Michael Thomas, who benefited from a fortunate ricochet which put him clean through on goal, and the London-born midfielder kept his nerve to prod the ball beyond Grobbelaar.

The final whistle sounded seconds later to confirm Arsenal as champions with Aldridge and his team-mates slumping to the turf in dejected exhaustion. The shell-shocked Anfield crowd stayed to applaud the Gunners as Tony Adams lifted the trophy and to also salute their own heroes who had given everything.

"We were very cautious and conservative on the night and didn't play our natural game," admitted Aldridge. "We didn't have to score or win and, while we never deliberately tried to sit back or anything, it had to have an impact on our mentality."

After a much-needed summer break, Aldridge returned for pre-season determined to help the Reds win their league title back but it soon became clear to him the concerns he felt over his future in the side would not go away.

"Even though we were good mates and had proved we could play together, Rushie's return was never going to be good news for me and I was always aware of that. I told Kenny I wouldn't go if he'd give me a chance but he made it clear that Ian and Peter were his preferred front two and so, with the World Cup coming up the following summer, I realised I couldn't just sit on the bench."

After being left on the bench for the first four matches of the 1989/90 season, matters came to a head when the Reds travelled to Spain to play an early-season friendly against Real Madrid in which the striker again found himself named as substitute.

Aldridge recalled: "After the game I spotted Peter Robinson and Liverpool chairman John Smith chatting with men who I had learned were from Real Sociedad. When I got back to Liverpool I asked Kenny about it and he told me talks between the clubs were ongoing. As it all slowly sank in that I was leaving I was devastated."

By the time Crystal Palace arrived at Anfield in early September, the finer points of Aldridge's £1.15m transfer to Spain had been all but ironed out with the 30-year-old striker aware this would most likely be his final chance to pull on the red shirt. He was again only named as substitute and had to watch from the bench as his soon-to-be former team-mates tore into the newly-promoted Londoners, going five goals up by the hour-mark. A few minutes later, Liverpool were awarded a penalty and – with Aldridge warming up and the Kop chanting his name – Dalglish immediately brought him on for Peter Beardsley.

"All I wanted was the chance to get one more goal. It was

a nice gesture from Kenny to send me on as a substitute and I got immense pleasure in putting the ball in the net from 12 yards. If I had to leave the club then this was the best way to do it, scoring a goal at the Kop end and having the crowd show their appreciation for what I had given the club over the years."

Speaking after Liverpool's 9-0 win that night, their biggest ever victory in the First Division, Dalglish acknowledged the bittersweet nature of the evening and Aldridge's situation, saying, "Obviously the evening is tinged with sadness as it looks as if he is on his way. He's our most popular player. He's achieved a lifetime's ambition by playing for the club and contributing so much to it. We're only selling him because we can't give him what he deserves."

Less than 48 hours later, Aldridge and his wife flew to Spain where he was unveiled as a Sociedad player.

"Suddenly I wasn't a Liverpool player any more. Something that I'd wanted so badly for so long had been taken away from me against my will. I'd lived my dream, had a stint at my club and it was now over."

As part of the proud Basque nation, Real Sociedad – like neighbouring Athletic Bilbao – usually employed only home-grown players and Aldridge's transfer made him the first non-Basque player to join the club in over 40 years. Protestors turned up outside the hotel where he met with club officials. 'No outsiders' was scrawled on the walls of the training ground in Spanish and someone in the street spat on the floor in front of him during those uncertain early weeks. But getting off the mark with a double against Barcelona in his fifth game helped begin to bring the barriers down and Aldridge's goals, along with his willingness to learn the language and adapt to life in his new country, soon made him as loved in San Sebastian as he was on Merseyside.

By the following March he had become the first player in the club's 86-year history to score in six straight games, receiving 40 bottles of wine and 20 kilos of Spanish sausages as a reward. His tally of 16 goals saw him finish fourth in the La Liga's top scorer 'Pichichi' standings as Sociedad qualified for the UEFA Cup. Though the team struggled more in his second season, Aldridge's 17 goals was just three short of Real Madrid legend Emilio Butragueno's 'Pichichi'-winning total.

One year remained on his contract but, with his family ready to come home, a move back to England was on the cards with Leeds United and Everton mooted as possible destinations for the 32-year-old, whose impressive tally of 40 goals in 63 games for Sociedad showed his predatory powers were still intact – but he shocked the football world by returning home to Merseyside and signing for Tranmere Rovers in a £250,000 deal.

A winning goal against Liverpool in the last pre-season friendly of the summer five days before his Rovers debut at Brighton – where he inevitably scored both in a 2-0 win – set the tone for the final goal-laden chapter of Aldridge's playing career. After scoring a club-record 40 goals in his first season, he spearheaded the greatest period in Tranmere's history and for three successive seasons Aldridge's goals took Rovers to the brink of top-flight football for the first time in their history only to fall just short each time.

Aldridge would take over from Johnny King as manager in April 1996, initially as player-manager before finishing with a brace against Wolves in his final game as a professional two years later at the age of 39 to leave his Tranmere tally at a more than respectable 174 goals in 287 appearance, which included nine hat-tricks. Although the club never again threatened promotion under his stewardship, Aldridge's time in the Prenton Park hot-seat elevated their reputation as cup giant-killers to a new level, taking them to their first major final in the League Cup in 1999/2000 when they lost narrowly to Leicester City.

After leaving Tranmere in 2001 he would never again return to management, despite twice applying for the Republic of Ireland job. His natural enthusiasm and love for football and Liverpool along with his vast knowledge and experience of the game made him a natural fit for a career in the media, with his passionate commentaries and vociferous celebrations when things have gone well providing the soundtrack for many Reds successes of modern times.

His goalscoring record bears comparison with anyone to have played the game. His overall tally of 476 goals in 889 matches puts him top of the list of all-time post-war goalscorers in British football.

For all the accolades, plaudits, matchballs and medals he picked up during a life in football, the greatest experience was simply being able to fulfil the dream he had when first taken to Anfield at the age of eight.

"Family and football is my life and wherever I've gone I've put my heart and soul into it, just like I did when I supported Liverpool as a kid home and away on the special trains," he said. "That's why I go crazy when I'm doing the commentaries; it's in my blood and I just can't help it, I'm still like a teenager at times because I'm so passionate. That's just the way I am and the way I've been brought up.

"But the biggest honour for me was just wearing that red shirt of Liverpool."

HEARTBREAK
AND HOPE

First published: July 2020

ANFIELD has played host to moments over the last 12 months which will live in the hearts and minds of Liverpudlians forever.

Some for the sheer brilliance, verve and authority of Jurgen Klopp's evolving team of champions like the systematic dismantling of soon-to-be deposed Manchester City in early November.

Others for the sense of history bending back Liverpool's way and the growing realisation this was not just another false dawn, such as Mohamed Salah's clincher against Manchester United in January and the moment the ground could hold back no longer from singing 'We're gonna win the league'.

Even the turbulent loosening of the grip on that hard-won sixth European Cup after an epic extra-time battle against Atletico Madrid in March with the dark clouds of the coronavirus crisis looming added to the sense of factors beyond football at play in a season rapidly proving itself to be like no other.

On the face of it, the 2-1 home victory over Brighton & Hove Albion on the final Saturday afternoon of November would not appear to be one of the more significant memories of a season which will be talked about for generations.

Virgil van Dijk's two headers from Trent Alexander-Arnold set-pieces in the first 24 minutes seemed to have set the league leaders up for a comfortable passage to their 13th league win in 14 matches.

Alisson Becker's uncharacteristic rush of blood and red card for handling outside the area on 77 minutes along with Lewis Dunk's strike from the ensuing free-kick led to a slightly nervy last ten minutes before the final whistle confirmed the Reds had stretched their lead at the top of the table to 11 points.

But the build-up to kick-off that day and early stages of the match itself were dominated by the issue which hung heavy over the club and the city for the previous 30 years: Hillsborough.

Almost exactly 48 hours before the Reds kicked off against the Seagulls, a jury in Preston had delivered a devastating verdict in the retrial of the match commander who had been in charge when 96 Liverpool supporters had been unlawfully killed at the 1989 FA Cup semi-final in Sheffield.

Despite David Duckenfield's previous admissions that he had a duty of care of those whose lives were lost, that his professional failings had been the direct cause of the fatalities and that he had initially lied over the opening of the exit gate which led to the lethal crush on the Leppings Lane terrace, he was found not guilty of gross negligence manslaughter after what many justifiably regard as a hugely flawed judicial process, final confirmation that no-one will ever be held criminally responsible for the deaths of close to a hundred innocent men, women and children in Britain's worst ever sporting disaster.

It was a shattering blow at the end of ten-and-a-half years of steady progress in the fight for truth and accountability, following the cries for justice at the 20th anniversary memorial service in 2009, the formation of the Hillsborough Independent Panel shortly afterwards and the watershed publication of its findings in 2012, the quashing of the original inquest verdicts of 'accidental death' and the launching of new criminal investigations later that same year, and the new inquest verdicts of unlawful killing in April 2016.

Within hours of Duckenfield's acquittal, supporters group Spion Kop 1906 confirmed Saturday's home game would see Hillsborough-related flags displayed on the Kop not just before the match but for the first six minutes of play, as a gesture of unity for the courageous and obstacle-laden battle the families, survivors and supporters had fought for over the past three decades.

The day after the verdict, Liverpool captain Jordan Henderson and West Derby-born defender Trent Alexander-Arnold laid 96 red roses at the Anfield memorial, accompanied by a simple note, which read: 'In memory of the 96 and solidarity with the families and survivors. With love. The Liverpool players'.

Later that same Friday in his pre-match press conference ahead of the Brighton game, Reds manager Klopp reiterated the support Liverpool will continue to provide the families, survivors and campaigners.

"The most important thing is our thoughts and love is with the families and we are there for them," Klopp said.

"It is a big disappointment, a big frustration and sadness, of course, that this looks like the final verdict.

"I understand and respect a lot how much they fought, how long they fought, and it shows how much it means to them.

"But we are there for them, 100%."

The following day, as promised, the Kop's array of flags pre-match centred on those concerned with the campaign which had gone on to define much of the club and city of Liverpool's identity since 1989, with fans singing a constant chorus of 'Justice for the 96' for the first six minutes of the match, just as they had almost 13 years earlier at the start of an FA Cup tie against Arsenal following comments from reviled former S*n editor, Kelvin McKenzie.

Further tributes were paid four days later before the Merseyside derby against Everton, with a mosaic on the Kop and Blues fans showing their solidarity in the Anfield Road end.

While there remains a further criminal trial related to Hillsborough, the prosecution of David Duckenfield felt symbolic to many.

His cowardly lie that Liverpool fans had forced an exit gate that he himself had given the order to open, allowing around 2,000 fans to enter the already-full central pens of the Leppings Lane terrace, was the founding myth of the disaster and set the tone for the decades of pain which followed for those who simply wanted the truth about why their loved ones were killed, as well as the traumatised survivors who found themselves blamed for their fellow supporters' deaths.

There was some anger and frustration when the Crown Prosecution Service's charging decisions were announced two months after the unlawful killing inquest verdict in June 2016 and numbered only six, later reduced to five when charges against former Merseyside Police chief constable Norman Bettison, a South Yorkshire Police chief inspector in 1989, were dropped. Those charges related to alleged lies about his role in the aftermath of the Hillsborough tragedy and the culpability of fans.

The vagaries of a legal system in which criminal responsibility does not follow the transfer of responsibilities from one company to a successor organisation meant the failings of the emergency response on the day and Sheffield Wednesday Football Club were able to evade criminal scrutiny, with many also feeling the likes of the Football Association and Sheffield City Council should have been made to answer for allowing such a high profile match to take place in a stadium without a valid safety certificate.

But Duckenfield – the match commander who had taken early retirement in 1991 on a full pension at the age of 46 thus avoiding internal disciplinary action, who had refused to give evidence in the private prosecutions held in Leeds in 2000 and had been able to walk away smiling when a jury was unable to reach a verdict on two specimen charges of manslaughter with the trial judge, Mr Justice Hooper, placing a 'stay' on him ruling out any retrial – in a criminal dock was a sight many families thought they would never live to see.

Sadly there were many who didn't live to see him charged, such was the passage of time taken for it to happen, and in fact Duckenfield never even had to sit in the dock during either of his criminal trials at Preston Crown Court, the judge allowing him to remain in the main courtroom due to 'post traumatic stress disorder and anxiety'.

But, given the scale of his admissions to the new inquests, there were real hopes beforehand of a successful prosecution even if, with hindsight, the establishment closing ranks came as no surprise to those who had seen it all before in the preceding three decades.

The fact that the heartbreaking blow of Duckenfield's acquittal should occur in the midst of one of Liverpool's most joyous footballing seasons, which saw the holy grail of a 19th league title finally attained, provides an inescapable parallel to the last time the Reds were champions with both campaigns being touched by the shadow of Hillsborough.

The 1989/90 season began for Liverpool with a Charity Shield win for the FA Cup winners over an Arsenal side which had stunned Anfield at the end of the previous elongated season, Michael Thomas' last-minute goal denying Kenny Dalglish's side a second double.

Peter Beardsley's goal at Wembley came just eight days after the publication of Lord Justice Taylor's interim report on the disaster, on 4 August 1989, which provided – at this very early stage – some hope that answers to the questions held by family members and survivors would now emerge.

Following the submission of 3,776 written statements of evidence, 1,550 letters, 71 hours of video footage and the oral evidence of 174 witnesses, Taylor found the main cause of the disaster to be the failure of police control, fully exonerating Liverpool supporters from the stream of accusations which had been hurled at them and praising them for their efforts in supporting the rescue operation.

The slow reaction of police to initiate the Disaster Plan, the Football Association, Sheffield City Council and Sheffield Wednesday Football Club were all criticised in the report as well but the most scathing verdict was reserved for David Duckenfield.

His decision to open Gate C and failure to guide fans away from the tunnel leading to the packed central plans were described as 'blunders of the first magnitude' while he was also condemned for his failure to take effective control.

Duckenfield was suspended from duty on the day Taylor's full report was released the following January and in July 1991, the Police Complaints Authority instructed South Yorkshire

Police to commence disciplinary proceedings against Duckenfield and his second-in-command Bernard Murray, Duckenfield facing four charges of neglect of duty and one of discreditable conduct.

However, Duckenfield's retirement the following year due to ill health meant the disciplinary action against him was dropped, with South Yorkshire Police deciding it was unfair to proceed against Murray alone.

Liverpool first returned to Hillsborough for a First Division fixture in November 1989, with the fixture coming during the shakiest period of the Reds' 18th title season, Dalian Atkinson's two second-half goals sealing the Reds' fourth defeat in seven league games.

An estimated 4,500 Liverpool supporters made the journey across the Pennines on a cold Wednesday night, with flowers and scarves being dropped onto the empty terraces of the Leppings Lane from fans situated in the West Stand above.

Before the match – which had kick-off delayed by 15 minutes to allow Hillsborough's biggest crowd of the season to gain entry – Alan Hansen and Owls goalkeeper Chris Turner laid wreaths at the Leppings Lane end, while at the home end banners read 'Hillsborough will always share your sorrow' and 'For all you Reds a new tomorrow'.

Liverpool's defeat, which lifted the home side off the foot of the First Division table, was to prove the penultimate one of the league season for Kenny Dalglish's side and by the time the first anniversary of the disaster came around they were closing in on the title.

The fates of the fixture computer decreed that Nottingham Forest, of all teams, should be scheduled to come to Anfield on Saturday, 14 April 1990 and 95 red balloons were released before kick-off, Hillsborough's 96th victim, Tony Bland, then still being on a life support machine at Airedale General Hospital near his home in Keighley which was not switched off until nearly three years later after a landmark legal ruling allowed doctors to withdraw his treatment at the request of his family.

Liverpool and Forest drew 2-2 the day before Anfield held its first annual memorial service, and three days later John Barnes' late equaliser at Arsenal, coupled with Aston Villa's defeat at Manchester United the night before, put Dalglish's side on the brink of the title, which was duly confirmed ten days later when Queens Park Rangers were beaten at Anfield.

Dalglish made his final playing appearance as a substitute in the final home game against Derby County after which the trophy was presented at Anfield and some of the narrative in the wake of Liverpool's tenth league title in 15 seasons centred on normal service being resumed and the club 'moving on' from the horror of the year before.

But in truth, the full impact of the disaster on the club – and the city – was only just beginning to reveal itself and it would become apparent as the following three decades wore on how the fortunes of the campaign for justice and the football team itself would dovetail at times.

Steve Nicol who, along with wife Eleanor, played a key role alongside Kenny Dalglish and his wife Marina in counselling the bereaved in the aftermath of the disaster, revealed years later in his autobiography that he was never the same player after Hillsborough and believed the impact on the club was the key factor in the post-1990 decline.

"After Hillsborough, and up until I finally left Liverpool in January 1995, I never had the same focus that I'd had before the tragedy," he said. "I should have left Liverpool Football Club long before I did. That sounds like a terrible thing to say, but it's true. I loved the club – still do, always will – but I simply could not rid my mind of Hillsborough. Consciously and sub-consciously, it was eating away at me.

"Eventually, I just couldn't take it anymore. God alone knows how the survivors and families have coped."

Kenny Dalglish's shock resignation as manager in February 1991, a month before the original inquests into the disaster delivered their verdict, was the first real indication of Hills-borough's legacy on the club, the Scot admitting years later it was the most important factor in his decision to leave his post as manager with his personal health suffering from the strain it had left him under and another anecdote from Nicol's auto-biography illustrates the change in Dalglish post-April 1989.

"Five months after Hillsborough in September 1989 we beat Derby County 3-0 at the Baseball Ground," Nicol said.

"The night before the game, I went to see Kenny in his hotel room. I knew I wasn't right, but I didn't know why and had no idea what to do. I was lost.

"I trusted him and wanted to share my thoughts and feelings. He asked what was wrong. I told him I was drinking too much. I told him I didn't feel myself. I told him I wasn't focused.

"I was half-expecting a response along the lines of, 'Right. Get a grip of yourself and don't be so stupid. If you know you're drinking too much then you just need to look after yourself better'. The real Kenny would have told me off. Told me to stop drinking. Told me to get my arse in gear. But this version of Kenny didn't say that.

"At the time I was shocked at his response. But now it makes sense – he was in the same boat as me. He just couldn't let it go either."

Five weeks after Dalglish's resignation, on 28 March 1991, after the (then) longest inquest in British history lasting 90 days, a verdict of accidental death on the victims of Hillsborough was returned by a majority verdict of 9-2 to the dismay and anger of families gathered in Sheffield Town Hall who felt much of the proceedings had focused on the unsubstantiated allegations of ticketless, drunken fans (the blood alcohol level of every single victim, including the children, was read out in court even when zero) that Lord Justice Taylor had refuted in his report.

Two days later, Liverpool were beaten 3-1 at home by Queens Park Rangers, precipitating a run of only four wins in the last nine league matches as the title was ceded back to Arsenal and began its long absence from Anfield.

Two years later, in March 1993, with Liverpool enduring one of their worst post-war seasons and lying only a handful of points above the relegation zone as spring approached, a flicker of hope emerged as six families won the right to have a judicial review into the accidental death inquest verdicts of their loved ones. But six months later, as Graeme Souness' ill-fated managerial reign was lurching towards its inevitable conclusion, the Royal Courts of Justice denied their application, backing Sheffield Coroner Dr Stefan Popper's verdict and stating he had made a 'full' inquiry, rejecting compelling medical evidence from the period after the 3.15pm cut-off point Popper had arbitrarily imposed which had prevented any meaningful inquiry into the emergency response.

The promise of a new investigation into Hillsborough which Labour campaigned on in the build-up to their election victory in the spring of 1997 coincided with an exciting new Liverpool team under Roy Evans which threatened to bring the glory days back to Anfield.

Evans' talented but brittle side ultimately flattered to deceive and though Labour once elected did set up a 'scrutiny of evidence' led by Lord Justice Stuart-Smith, it proved to be the same old story, his decision to reject a new inquiry into the disaster being confirmed in the same February 1998 week that Liverpool supporters were prevented from laying flowers before the Reds' Premier League match at Hillsborough, a game which was also sponsored by the S*n.

The new millennium saw new hope at Anfield under French manager Gerard Houllier and in the summer of 2000 a private prosecution led by the Hillsborough Family Support Group against David Duckenfield and Bernard Murray saw a six-week trial at Leeds Crown Court on charges of manslaughter and wilful malfeasance, with a further charge of perverting the course of justice filed against Duckenfield.

The jury found Murray not guilty of manslaughter and, after eight days of deliberation, were unable to reach a verdict on Duckenfield, indicating that if allowed more time they may have been able to reach a majority verdict but the judge, Mr Justice Hooper, who had already taken the unusual step of telling both defendants before the trial began they would not go to prison even if found guilty, decided against this and also refused a retrial.

The cycle began again not long into Rafa Benitez's Anfield reign, when a few months after the 2006 FA Cup win which followed the previous year's miracle of Istanbul, Anne Williams – who was one the 1993 judicial review families and had secured a parliamentary debate at the House of Commons into the circumstances of her 15-year-old son Kevin's death the following year – took her hard-won evidence and crusade for a new inquest to the European Court of Human Rights after the three unsuccessful appeals to the Attorney General.

But just weeks before the 20th anniversary of the disaster in April 2009, as Liverpool's most credible title bid since 1990 was about to hit the skids, the European court finally ruled her application should have been lodged within six months of the Stuart-Smith scrutiny in 1997 and said she was 'out of time', a phrase which was to prove sadly prophetic for the campaigning Formby mum.

The tide had slowly begun to turn after the cries for justice at the 20th anniversary service which led to the formation of the Hillsborough Independent Panel and on 12 September 2012, a month into Brendan Rodgers' first season as Liverpool manager, their landmark findings set in motion the quashing of the original accidental death inquest verdicts, the launch of new criminal investigations and new inquests which began in Warrington on 31 March 2014, the day after Liverpool had beaten Tottenham 4-0 at Anfield to go top of the Premier League with six matches to play and suddenly become favourites to win the title after a stunning run of wins.

Two weeks later – with the new inquests midway through hearing profoundly moving background statements of each of the 96 by their loved ones detailing their lives, passions, hopes and dreams – and two days before the 25th anniversary of the disaster, Liverpool beat title rivals Manchester City 3-2 to tighten their grip on the title race at an emotional Anfield.

Cruel fate decided a fortnight later that a slip by the Reds' talismanic skipper and best player over the last decade – Steven Gerrard – against Chelsea at Anfield would lead to defeat and the title race shifted back into Manchester City's favour.

Two years later, by the time the new inquests reached their conclusion – on 26 April 2016 – that the 96 had been unlawfully killed by the gross negligence manslaughter David Duckenfield was guilty of to a criminal standard of proof and that behaviour of Liverpool supporters did not contribute at all to the disaster, Jurgen Klopp had become Reds manager.

He had spoken at his unveiling of the need to turn 'doubters into believers' and 12 days before the jury in Warrington delivered their historic verdict, Liverpool delivered the most compelling evidence yet that the German's mission statement was achievable.

The new boss' former club, Borussia Dortmund, arrived at Anfield the night before the 27th Hillsborough anniversary for a beautifully poised Europa League quarter-final second leg after a 1-1 draw in Germany the week before and, after an emotional You'll Never Walk Alone sung by the whole ground and perfectly-observed minute's silence, scored two away goals without reply in the first nine minutes.

There followed a topsy-turvy match and with the clock ticking past 90 minutes, Dejan Lovren leapt at the far post to head James Milner's cross into the Kop end net to complete a 4-3 win and what was, at the time, Liverpool's greatest European fightback on home soil.

Just eight days earlier, the Hillsborough inquests jury had retired to consider their verdict after sitting for over 300 days of evidence and, with some family members and survivors in the Anfield crowd that night, Liverpool's against-the-odds victory felt symbolic, with many hoping it could perhaps be a positive omen.

By the time Duckenfield's criminal trial began on 14 January 2019 at Preston Crown Court for the gross negligence manslaughter of 95 Liverpool supporters – he was not charged over the death of the 96th fan to pass away, Tony Bland, because he died in 1993 and laws at the time prevented prosecution for the death of someone more than 366 days after they were injured – Klopp had taken Liverpool to a second European final in three seasons, this time in the Champions League where they had been beaten, somewhat unfortunately, by Real Madrid in Kiev the previous May.

Though Liverpool again harboured European ambitions the following season, having qualified for the Champions League knock-out stages, hopes were very much focused on another attempt to secure that elusive 19th title, with defeat away at reigning champions Manchester City 11 days before the trial began being the Reds' first of the league season and still leaving them four points ahead of their hosts and nearest challengers.

The jury in that initial Preston trial did deliver the first ever criminal conviction over Hillsborough when they found former Sheffield Wednesday club secretary Graham Mackrell guilty of a health and safety offence for which he was fined £6,500 and ordered to pay costs of £5,000, but they were unable to reach a verdict on Duckenfield and were discharged on their eighth day of deliberations on 3 April 2019, with a retrial scheduled for the autumn.

Six days later, with Manchester City having clawed Liverpool's lead back to now hold a slender one-point advantage themselves in the title race, the Reds beat Porto 2-0 at Anfield in the quarter-final first leg of a Champions League run which would lead to glory in Madrid and the first trophy of Klopp's Anfield reign, after City held on to win the league by that solitary point despite Liverpool gaining 97 points, the most recorded by a side not to win the title and the third highest in history.

During a summer which saw celebrations across Liverpool and the global fanbase, heated meetings took place between the Crown Prosecution Service and Hillsborough families who called on them to improve what some felt was a substandard performance in the initial Preston trial, with key evidence like Duckenfield's admitted 'terrible lie' barely mentioned and other aspects omitted altogether.

Some families also called on the CPS to apply to have the judge, Sir Peter Openshaw who was due to also handle the retrial, replaced after raising concerns about his impartiality, but they declined to do so.

Margaret Aspinall, chair of the Hillsborough Family Support Group, whose 18-year-old son, James, was one of the 96 people killed, said about the judge's 'one-sided' summing up: "I found it disgusting. Like the judge was saying my lovely innocent son and all our 96 were a different kind of people, hooligans, and their families.

"Even in death, after 30 years."

The retrial, which began on 7 October 2019 with Liverpool eight points clear at the top of the league having won their opening eight matches, again saw the established truths of Hillsborough, determined by a jury on comprehensive evidence given on oath in front of a senior judge, seemingly airbrushed from history.

Duckenfield's defence, led by Benjamin Myers QC, was allowed by Judge Openshaw – who at one point in front of the jury referred to a defendant facing charges relating to the deaths of nearly 100 people in front of some of their aghast families as a 'poor chap' because he had a chest infection – to indignantly deny any failings at all by his client, while reintroducing the victim-blaming tactics of three decades ago, alleging Liverpool fans arrived late, drunk, without tickets and tried to push their way into the ground.

Families were devastated but not surprised by the majority not-guilty verdict at the end of the seven-week trial, with Steve Kelly, whose 38-year-old brother Michael was among those killed, saying: "It's been a 30-year wait to hear that.

"It was like a dagger to the heart, it was just unbelievable.

"I believe the die was cast many years ago so today's decision is no surprise. Now, sadly, the decision means we will just have to try and get on with our lives, forever cheated.

"I am and will be forever grateful for others who have supported the campaign for truth, justice and accountability for the 96. God bless them."

Hillsborough, of course, is not the only tragedy which left its mark on 2019/20.

The coronavirus pandemic claimed the lives of so many in Merseyside and across the world, with questions remaining unanswered about the real impact of allowing Liverpool's Champions League tie with Atletico Madrid to go ahead at a packed Anfield just days before football was suspended.

With people unsure how lives would continue to be affected by the impact of the virus, the words of Jurgen Klopp in his programme notes for the final home match of the season against Chelsea were apt in the context of both disasters and illuminate football's ability to break and mend hearts.

"The times we live in in this moment test us all," Klopp wrote.

"For some, the test is unfair and too much to bear.

"I know we are living through a period where for many joy must feel like a horizon you cannot reach or see.

"But I hope for the Liverpool family, what we have collectively experienced this season brings some warmth and comfort."

The presence of Kenny Dalglish, Liverpool's manager in 1989, now a director and arguably the most loved figure in the club's history, on the podium as Jordan Henderson received the Premier League trophy was symbolic of the journey taken over the last 30 years as the club fought to free itself of being a prisoner of the past.

And the Liverpool captain summed it up perfectly less than 24 hours after lifting the trophy, writing on Twitter: 'To lift the Premier League trophy on the night we achieved 96 points shows that some things are just meant to be. Never forgotten. You'll Never Walk Alone.'

EPILOGUE

SINCE his tragic passing, much has been said and well-written about Dan. He was a beautiful human being who achieved so much. His legacy has touched us all to be a 'bit more Dan'.

While I could, and regularly do, talk all day about Dan's incredible attributes and character, one of the best insights into the person he was can be seen through his writing. Dan took a huge amount of pride in writing for his beloved Liverpool ECHO, and rightly so.

Dan's friends and family are enormously grateful that this book has been written so that there is a fitting memorial and record of Dan's finest work.

A huge thanks go out to Dan's friend and former ECHO colleague, Sam Carroll, whose concept this book was, and to Maria Breslin, editor of the ECHO. Sam and Maria were both responsible for putting the idea into print.

I would also like to thank Reach for agreeing to publish the book, and for a portion of the proceeds to be donated to The Dan Kay Foundation.

I, and many others, have been extremely fortunate to work with Sam and Maria who are fellow trustees at The Dan Kay

Foundation, which aims to continue Dan's legacy by spreading kindness while tackling stigma around mental health.

I would also like to send a massive thanks to the other trustees, volunteers and others, too numerous to name, who played an integral role in ensuring The Dan Kay Foundation became a registered charity in August 2024.

Our aim is to continue Dan's amazing work. It all started with some fundraising. There was so much love and goodwill for Dan, that setting up a charity in his name seemed the obvious option.

The fact that it is taking so many of us to continue his work is a testament to the man Dan was. We look forward to announcing several exciting events and projects and hope that we can count on your continued support.

Having read Inside Liverpool, I am sure you will agree that it showcases many of Dan's finest attributes. In particular, his analysis, attention to detail, loyalty, honesty and integrity, generosity, empathy, encyclopaedic knowledge and his storytelling.

I was very close to Dan from an early age. He was only two years older than me. He was essentially brought up by our grandpa Jack and grandma Edna. He cared for his parents, Larry and Vick, until they died. After they died, he looked after our grandparents. They would have been so proud of him and his achievements.

I always looked forward to his warm, smiley face, his chattiness and his humour. There was never a dull or quiet moment. From an early age we would get together at my grandparents' house in Wallasey several times per year for Jewish festivals and on Christmas Day.

Later on, I worked in Liverpool occasionally and would meet up with Dan. He always knew great places to eat, and we both loved our food. He knew so much about the city and loved it. It was his city.

When my grandpa Jack died, Dan cared for my grandma and would take her out. I went with them whenever I could. We treated my gran to her first taste of Indian street food at the age of 95 at Mowgli – she loved it!

Dan was such a family man. He was so selfless. He provided match tickets and was a brilliant tour guide for family members who wanted to attend a Liverpool match at Anfield.

Dan's passion and knowledge for Liverpool Football Club was astonishing. It impressed anyone who met him, but his intellect extended way beyond football.

If you needed someone to talk to, Dan was always there. He was so easy to talk to, so modest and humble. He never accepted or acknowledged the extent of his amazing achievements. If you spoke to him, he would make you feel like the most important person in the room.

In recent years, we rescheduled our Christmas Day get togethers. Dan would tell us that he spent Christmas Day helping homeless young people. It later transpired that he had been delivering food parcels, for weeks, not just on Christmas Day.

He often used the word 'Mensch' to describe others, a word my grandpa Jack used. It was the perfect way to describe Dan: a person of integrity, morality, dignity, with a sense of what is right and responsible. To be a mensch is to be supportive, to be a friend, to be calm in troubled times.

It is only right to acknowledge the campaigning and reporting Dan did around Hillsborough, which was outstanding and acclaimed. He hated social injustices. The dedicated and committed support that he gave to the affected families was incredible. After his passing, Dan was awarded a posthumous doctorate from Liverpool Hope University for his social justice campaigning.

Dan was so modest about the award-winning book and script he co-wrote with Sara Williams, another trustee of The Dan Kay Foundation, for the ITV drama about her mother Anne, With Hope in Her Heart. A brilliant book and a powerful and compelling drama, Dan's work was raised in Parliament by the MP for Wirral South, Alison McGovern.

For someone who devoted his life to others, it was tragic, as we heard at his inquest in November 2024, that he did not receive the support or mental health treatment he needed and deserved during his own time of need. He did, however, receive some justice for himself.

At the time of publication, we have raised over £20,000 since Dan's passing. Following the inquest into his death, mental health provision and suicide prevention is something The Dan Kay Foundation will continue to campaign for change in. By reading Inside Liverpool, you are helping to further the incredible and unrivalled legacy of Dan Kay.

Amos Waldman,
Founder and Chair of The Dan Kay Foundation